Ethics and Accountability on the U.S. Supreme Court

SUNY series in American Constitutionalism
—————
Robert J. Spitzer, editor

Ethics and Accountability on the U.S. Supreme Court

An Analysis of Recusal Practices

Robert J. Hume

Published by State University of New York Press, Albany

For information, contact State University of New York Press, Albany, NY
www.sunypress.edu

Production, Eileen Nizer
Marketing, Michael Campochiaro

Library of Congress Cataloging-in-Publication Data

Names: Hume, Robert J., author.
Title: Ethics and accountability on the Supreme Court : an analysis of recusal
  practices / Robert J. Hume.
Description: Albany : State University of New York Press, 2017. | Series:
  SUNY series in American constitutionalism | Includes bibliographical
  references and index.
Identifiers: LCCN 2016053168 (print) | LCCN 2016055190 (ebook) | ISBN
  9781438466972 (hardcover : alk. paper) | ISBN 9781438466989 (ebook) |
  ISBN 9781438466965 (pbk. : alk. paper)
Subjects: LCSH: United States. Supreme Court. | Judges—Recusal—United
  States. | Courts of last resort—Political aspects—United States.
Classification: LCC KF8748 .H86 2017 (print) | LCC KF8748 (ebook) | DDC
  174/.3—dc23
LC record available at https://lccn.loc.gov/2016053168

10 9 8 7 6 5 4 3 2 1

Contents

List of Illustrations

Figures

Tables

Preface

The U.S. Supreme Court is an institution that operates mostly in secret. Political scientists who study the Court do not expect the justices to sit down for interviews and speak candidly about their decision-making processes, so we infer what we can from the justices' voting behavior, their opinions, and their private papers. But even with such diminished expectations, it is striking how little we know about the recusal process. The justices rarely talk about it, and they make no records available to the public. The justices do not even communicate basic information, such as why they choose to withdraw from disputes or how often they have considered withdrawing from cases but did not. Perhaps it is for this reason that there has yet to be a full-length analysis of the causes and consequences of recusal behavior on the U.S. Supreme Court.

Yet the importance of the subject constantly reasserts itself. As I was preparing the final draft of this book for publication in the spring and summer of 2016, the Supreme Court was dealing with the aftermath of Justice Scalia's sudden passing and the delayed confirmation of his successor. The threat of dividing evenly often loomed. It occurred to me that the dynamics on the Court were probably similar to what happens behind the scenes whenever a justice withdraws from a case. The difference was a matter of degree, with the typical recusal affecting a case or two, not the Court's entire term. In both circumstances, the Court must figure out how to operate without its full membership. Are the justices capable of fulfilling their institutional responsibility to decide cases and controversies? When will the justices find compromise, and when will they divide four to four? We do not have clear answers to these questions.

Meanwhile, the subject of judicial ethics has gotten renewed attention, not just in the federal courts but in state judiciaries as well. Many of the state controversies are the result of problems that are unique to state tribunals:

the participation of judges in cases involving their campaign donors. U.S. Supreme Court justices are not elected, so they do not face this particular dilemma, but the broader concerns are the same. How ethical are judges? Can we really trust them to make decisions that are free of bias? Once again, we do not know the answers to these questions because the justices have given us few insights into their behavior. For all we know, the justices are regularly taking part in cases when they should not be.

It seems like a good moment, then, to take stock of the causes and consequences of recusals on the Supreme Court. What can we learn about the justices' practices using the tools of social science? If we are short on direct accounts from the justices, we can still observe how withdrawing from cases affects the justices' decisions on the merits, their opinion writing practices, and their docket. We can examine the justices' financial disclosure reports to determine whether the justices are participating in disputes that involve their listed assets. And we can see if the justices decline to recuse themselves when they have incentives to stay, such as when cases present important legal questions or have substantial public policy implications.

Such an undertaking would not have been possible without a great deal of help and support, first and foremost from my colleagues at Fordham University. I am very grateful to be in a department with such generous colleagues and with an administration that supports faculty research. The first phase of this project was completed as the result of a faculty fellowship during the spring of 2014, and production assistance was later provided by a grant from Fordham's Office of Research in July 2016. I would like to thank the chief research officer, Dr. Z. George Hong, as well as his predecessor, Dr. Nancy A. Busch, for providing this support. The original survey data in Chapter 5 were also made possible because of internal university funding in the form of a grant awarded in 2016 though Fordham's Faculty Research Expense Program. Jeffrey Cohen, from the political science department at Fordham, was a collaborator on that survey. He has also been a good mentor and friend. Additionally, I received advice on the survey from two of my colleagues, Monika McDermott and Ida Bastiaens.

Outside Fordham, I received valuable feedback on draft chapters at several academic conferences. Early versions of material appearing in Chapter 5 were presented at meetings of the Midwest Political Science Association in Chicago, Illinois, in 2013 and 2014. Jennifer Williams commented on a paper about dividing evenly ("Why Recusals Don't Matter: Strategic Voting and Split Decisions on the United States Supreme Court"), and Sara Benesh gave advice on a paper about Supreme Court legitimacy ("The Impact of

Recusals on Public Confidence in the Supreme Court: The Case of *Bush v. Gore*, 2014"). I presented a draft of Chapter 4 in 2015 at the annual meeting of the Southern Political Science Association in New Orleans, Louisiana, where I got feedback from Eve Ringsmuth ("The Policy Consequences of Recusals on the U.S. Supreme Court"). A version of Chapter 3 was published in the *Law & Society Review*,[1] and I thank the editors, Tim Johnson and Joachim Savelsberg, as well as the anonymous reviewers, for their comments.

Finally, I am forever grateful for the love and support of my wife, Shannon, and two children, Megan and Sean. I dedicate this book to my family and to all of those who contributed to the development of this project, in ways great and small.

1

The Conspiracy of Silence

It has become increasingly commonplace whenever an important issue is before the U.S. Supreme Court for there to be demands that justices recuse themselves. That is to say, justices are called upon to withdraw voluntarily from cases because of bias or the appearance of bias. For example, when President Barack Obama's health care law was before the Supreme Court, calls for recusals came from the right and the left.[1] Justice Elena Kagan was criticized for participating because she had served as the Solicitor General when the legal defenses for the Affordable Care Act, or "Obamacare," were first developed. Justice Kagan insisted that her recusal was unnecessary because she had not done any real work on the case. At her confirmation hearings, she testified, "I attended at least one meeting where the existence of litigation was briefly mentioned, but none where the substantive discussion of the litigation occurred."[2] However, commentators suggested that her involvement was more extensive than she was letting on. They even hinted that Kagan was deliberately shielding her work on the case so that she would be eligible to participate when she became a justice.[3]

Meanwhile, Justice Clarence Thomas's participation in the health care dispute was questioned because of the political activities of his spouse. Virginia Thomas, known as "Ginni," has had a long association with conservative causes, working for the Heritage Foundation and more recently for Liberty Central, a nonprofit lobbying group that she founded. These activities have occasionally prompted calls for her husband's recusal, most notably in *Bush v. Gore*, which decided the outcome of the 2000 presidential election.[4] The trouble with Obamacare derived from a 2010 speech at the Steamboat Institute in which Ginni Thomas stated, "I think we need to repeal Obamacare."[5] Had these comments been made by a sitting justice, there would have been a strong argument for a recusal. However, it was unclear whether Ginni Thomas's advocacy work implied any prejudgment of the case by her spouse.

Ultimately, both Justices Kagan and Thomas chose to participate in the health care dispute, and the Court voted narrowly to uphold the individual mandate, one of the core provisions of the Affordable Care Act. Consistent with the Court's customs, neither justice offered any explanation for his or her refusal to sit out of the case, but Chief Justice Roberts devoted his 2011 *Year-End Report on the Federal Judiciary* to the subject of recusals, no doubt in response to the controversy.[6] Without commenting directly on the merits of Kagan or Thomas's situation, Roberts offered general reassurances that he "had complete confidence in the capability of my colleagues to determine when recusal is warranted."[7]

The episode highlighted just how little we know about the recusal process. Despite the large amount of commentary on the subject,[8] recusals are among the poorest-understood features of judging, particularly on the U.S. Supreme Court.[9] Exacerbating the problem is the fact that the justices have consistently refused to comment on their behavior. Chief Justice Roberts's 2011 *Year-End Report* is notable primarily for how unrevealing it is about the justices' recusal practices. When the justices withdraw from disputes, the most that one can typically expect is a brief statement announcing that a justice "took no part in the consideration or decision of this case."[10] The justices rarely say more, declining even to make public the names of the cases in which they considered recusing themselves but did not. One commentator described the justices' reluctance to speak on the matter as a "conspiracy of silence."[11]

Yet understanding the recusal process is vitally important. At the most basic level, the participation of justices has the potential to affect who wins cases and who loses. Given the ideological consistency of the justices' voting records[12] and how closely divided they have become on important issues,[13] it is reasonable to expect that case dispositions will turn on the recusal of particular justices. In the context of the health care controversy, for example, Justice Kagan's recusal would have denied the majority the fifth vote that it needed to uphold the constitutionality of the individual mandate. Assuming that none of the other justices changed his or her vote, the Court would have found itself deadlocked, generating no majority opinion to guide the lower courts and leaving the future of the Affordable Care Act uncertain.

Recusals can also affect the Supreme Court's docket, decreasing the likelihood that the justices will agree to hear cases. By convention, the justices grant petitions for *certiorari*, accepting cases for review when at least four justices are supportive, a practice known as the Rule of Four.[14] The likelihood of a grant is generally low, but, as several commentators have noted, the likelihood becomes even lower when justices disqualify themselves because then there is a smaller pool of justices from which to find the necessary votes.[15] Indeed, the justices themselves observed in their 1993 *Statement of Recusal Policy* that recusals have "a distorting effect upon the *certiorari* process, requiring the petitioner to obtain (under our current practice) four votes out of eight instead of four out of nine."[16] Petitioners are at a particular disadvantage because, without at least four votes to grant review, lower court opinions are automatically affirmed, which invariably favors the respondents.

More generally, understanding the recusal process is important because it helps us to understand the extent to which the justices, and by extension the federal judicial system, are committed to principles of impartial justice. Federal law requires judges, including Supreme Court justices, to disqualify themselves when their "impartiality might reasonably be questioned."[17] The federal recusal statute also identifies several categories of behavior in which recusals are required, such as when justices have financial stakes in cases, when they have participated previously in proceedings as counsel, and when they have already expressed opinions on the merits.[18] These guidelines are intended to eliminate bias from judging, fostering a judicial decision-making process that is principled, and thereby building public confidence in courts.[19] However, there is considerable uncertainty about whether the justices actually follow the statutory guidelines. Neither federal law nor the Judicial Conference's Code of Conduct for United States Judges requires Supreme Court justices to report the reasons for their recusal decisions, nor is there a higher court to review their practices.[20] In fact, the federal recusal statute establishes no procedures whatsoever for Supreme Court recusals. For the most part, the justices recuse themselves *sua sponte*. Litigants rarely file recusal motions, perhaps in part because they do not want to offend the justices by suggesting that they are prejudiced;[21] and responses to these motions are practically nonexistent.[22] One commentator characterized the process as "a personal, independent, unreviewable decision by an individual Justice whether to participate in an individual case."[23]

In competition with the federal recusal guidelines are the justices' other institutional and policy goals. Research has well documented that Supreme Court justices are policy-motivated decision makers who are forward thinking about the consequences of their behavior.[24] We know that policy goals influence the justices' final votes on the merits,[25] opinion assignments,[26] contents of majority opinions,[27] *certiorari* grants,[28] and oral arguments,[29] so there is every reason to think that policy considerations also affect justices' decisions about whether to recuse themselves. Sitting out of cases denies justices the opportunity to influence the final votes on the merits and the contents of majority opinions. These policy costs might sometimes be too great for justices, even if they risk damaging the Court's legitimacy by participating.

Justices also have institutional incentives to participate in cases that they must balance against the statutory guidelines. Among these incentives is the need for the justices to decide the cases before them, an institutional responsibility that is compromised when recusals cause the Court to lack a quorum or divide evenly. Justices have stated that this "duty to sit" is meaningful to them and can be at odds with the statutory goal of reducing bias.[30] For example, Justice Ruth Bader Ginsburg has remarked that "on the Supreme Court, if one of us is out, that leaves eight, and the attendant risk that we will be unable to decide the case, that it will divide evenly. . . . Because there's no substitute for a Supreme Court justice, it is important that we not lightly recuse ourselves."[31] Chief Justice Roberts echoed these concerns in his 2011 *Year-End Report*, noting that, unlike lower federal court judges, who "can freely substitute for one another," when a Supreme Court justice withdraws, "the Court must sit without its full membership."[32] If the justices are unable to achieve consensus because their membership is down, important questions of federal law go unanswered. When faced with this possibility, the justices might determine that the benefits of recusals are not worth the costs.

Consider, for example, Justice Kagan's situation in the health care case. She certainly could have recused herself because of her work as Solicitor General. Even if there was no actual conflict of interest, the mere appearance of a conflict might have persuaded Justice Kagan to err on the side of caution and to sit the case out, thereby ensuring that the Court's legitimacy would not be threatened by her participation. But what would a recusal have cost her? The Court would have lacked the fifth vote needed to secure the constitutionality of the Affordable Care Act, and Justice Kagan would have missed the opportunity to shape the law in this important area. Surely these opportunities were too great for her, or any justice, to pass up.

Because the justices refuse to comment about their recusal practices, it is unclear whether the justices follow the statutory guidelines or some other criteria. It is also unclear what effects their recusal practices have on law and policy. The purpose of this book is to penetrate the myths surrounding recusals by studying their causes and consequences systematically.

If the justices themselves are unwilling to say much about recusals, then the techniques of empirical legal scholarship might reveal what the justices' words do not. By carefully analyzing their behavior, one can identify when the justices are more likely to sit out of disputes, how their absence changes the composition of the Court, and whether these changes affect case dispositions, opinion content, the Court's institutional efficiency, and the Court's agenda. The inquiry can help us to evaluate some of the common assumptions that people have about the recusal process, shedding light on this important but little-understood dimension of judging. It might also help us to understand why the justices maintain so much secrecy about their practices.

Recusals in American Politics

It may be surprising to learn that only recently has the subject of recusals entered into regular political discourse about the U.S. Supreme Court. Previously, recusals were only an occasional subject of popular or media interest. Figure 1.1 on page 6 traces commentary about recusals in the *New York Times* and the *Wall Street Journal* from 1915 to 2012 and shows that for most of the twentieth century there were hardly any editorials, letters to the editor, or opinion pieces on the subject.[33] The first piece, from 1916, was a letter to the editor of the *New York Times* about Justice James McReynolds's ineligibility to participate in several cases brought under the Sherman Antitrust Act because he had worked on the cases as President Woodrow Wilson's Attorney General. The letter stopped short of taking a position on McReynolds's recusal, but the author did point out that the cases would be heard by "an even numbered court" and that there was "some division among the members of the court" on antitrust issues.[34] Because there was a chance that the justices would divide evenly, the author urged the appointment of additional justices to the Court who "could be absolutely depended upon to vote for the prosecution."[35]

This type of commentary was uncommon prior to the 1970s, but when the subject did arise, it was almost never to demand the recusal of particular justices. Indeed, much behavior that today would be certain to provoke controversy brought little or no coverage. For example, Justice Robert Jackson went vacationing with President Franklin D. Roosevelt while the landmark commerce clause case *Wickard v. Filburn* was before the Court,[36] and Justice Byron White went skiing with Attorney General Robert Kennedy and his family while the Court was considering two cases

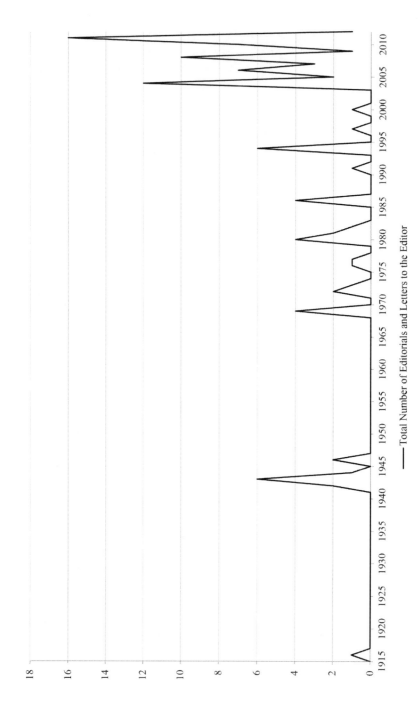

Figure 1.1. Commentary about U.S. Supreme Court Recusals in the *New York Times* and *Wall Street Journal*, 1915–2012.

in which Kennedy was a named party.[37] To be sure, these events predated the changes that would come in the early 1970s to the recusal statute and the American Bar Association's ethical guidelines. However, it is notable that these sorts of *ex parte* communications between justices and executive branch officials did not bring demands for reform at the time.

Instead, as in the McReynolds letter, commentators tended to oppose recusals because of the administrative problems that they caused. These tendencies are illustrated in Figure 1.2 on page 8, which traces the tone of media commentary about recusals in the *New York Times* and the *Wall Street Journal* from 1915 to 2012. The figure shows that prior to the 1970s, the subject of recusals received sustained attention only in the 1940s, and that the tone of this commentary was primarily opposed to recusals. A review of these articles reveals that the authors were concerned that recusals would reduce the Court's efficiency by causing the justices to divide evenly or lack a quorum, concerns that were not without some foundation.[38] In one important antitrust case, the Court lacked a quorum because four of the justices had recused themselves, postponing the matter indefinitely "until such time as there is a quorum of Justices qualified to sit in it."[39] Commentators criticized the Court for bringing about "certain unnecessary delays of justice."[40] After considering proposals to reduce the Court's quorum to five,[41] Congress finally authorized the Second Circuit to act as the court of last resort.[42]

The tone of the commentary began to change in the 1970s at the time of Judge Clement Haynsworth's unsuccessful bid for the Supreme Court. As a circuit court judge, Haynsworth had declined to recuse himself from several cases in which he had a financial interest, and the revelations brought a series of opinion pieces that were critical of his participation because of the potential damage to public confidence in the judiciary. "It is of utmost importance that litigants and the public maintain complete confidence in the impartiality of the judiciary," wrote a letter writer to the *New York Times*.[43] Another letter writer agreed: "If the judge is confirmed and takes his seat, the Court itself will function for years in an atmosphere of legitimate doubt."[44] Unlike previous commentary, which almost uniformly opposed recusals, the coverage of Haynsworth was mixed, with more commentary favoring his recusal than not.

During this same period, the recusal practices of the sitting justices also began to receive more regular media scrutiny, much of it negative. Perhaps most prominently, Justice William Rehnquist was criticized for failing to recuse himself from three cases that he had worked on, or commented

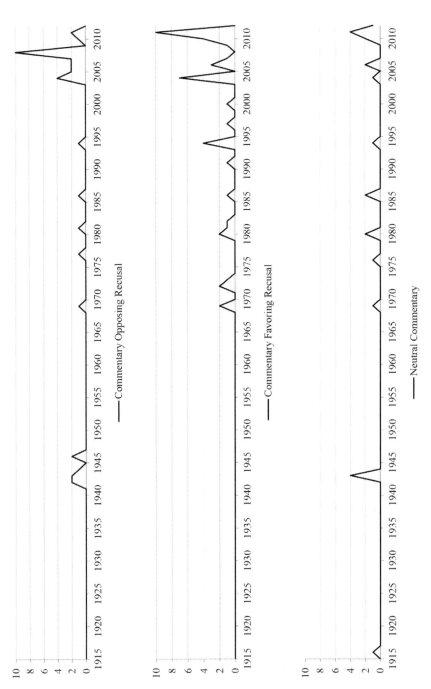

Figure 1.2. Tone of Commentary about Recusals in the *New York Times* and *Wall Street Journal*, 1915–2012.

about, as an Assistant Attorney General in the Nixon administration.[45] All three of the cases were decided by narrow 5-4 margins, with Rehnquist casting the deciding votes. Among them was *Laird v. Tatum*, which challenged the Army's surveillance of antiwar protesters.[46] Because Rehnquist had testified before Congress about the surveillance program as an Assistant Attorney General in the Nixon administration, the respondents challenged his participation in the case and filed a motion requesting that he recuse himself. In response, Rehnquist took the unprecedented step of defending his participation at length in a memorandum, insisting that he had not worked directly on the case and that "it is not a ground for disqualification that a judge has prior to his nomination expressed his then understanding of the meaning of some particular provision of the Constitution."[47] Yet commentators remained skeptical of Rehnquist's motives, especially because he had chosen to recuse himself from several other cases in which his votes had been less decisive. "The results may be coincidental," wrote one letter writer to the *New York Times*, "but they raise grave questions, not merely about his judgment, but about his integrity."[48]

Soon afterward, in 1972, the American Bar Association developed a new Judicial Code of Conduct, which required judges to disqualify themselves from cases in which their "impartiality might reasonably be questioned." The ABA Code was widely adopted in most states and the District of Columbia, and in 1973 the Judicial Conference of the United States applied it to most federal judges, excluding Supreme Court justices.[49] The Code also became the foundation for the 1974 revisions to the federal recusal statute, which more precisely defined the circumstances in which federal judges should recuse themselves.[50] Unlike the Judicial Code of Conduct, the newly revised federal recusal statute did apply to Supreme Court justices.

These reforms took place in the context of the deepening Watergate crisis, in which the subject of ethics in government was of growing national concern. Yet after 1974, media commentary about recusals remained episodic, if somewhat more frequent and negative in tone. The subject came up most commonly during confirmation hearings, such as when Rehnquist was nominated to be Chief Justice in 1986.[51] More recently, both Justices Stephen Breyer and Samuel Alito received criticism at their hearings for their failures as lower court judges to recuse themselves from cases in which they had financial interests. For Breyer, it was his investments in Lloyd's of London,[52] while for Alito scrutiny came from his ownership of Vanguard mutual funds.[53] Chief Justice Roberts also faced questions at the time of his confirmation hearings for meeting with President George W. Bush about his potential nomination to the Supreme Court while he was deciding *Hamdan v. Rumsfeld*,[54] a case that concerned the Bush administration's use of military commissions at Guantanamo Bay.[55]

The turning point for coverage about Supreme Court recusals was January 2004, when Justice Antonin Scalia went duck hunting with the sitting Vice President, Dick Cheney, shortly after the Supreme Court agreed to decide a case in which Cheney was a named party. According to Justice Scalia, he "never hunted in the same blind with the Vice President," and he and the Vice President were never in an "intimate setting."[56] But critics were not satisfied, and over the next few months more media attention was devoted to the subject of recusals than at any time previously.[57] "Justice Antonin Scalia has shown surprisingly poor judgment in going on a social trip with Vice President Cheney while Mr. Cheney is a party in a case before the Supreme Court," a letter writer commented to the *Washington Post*.[58] Scalia was failing his "obligation to the institution of the court" by creating doubt about the "propriety or neutrality of the justices' jurisprudence." The controversy became so great that Justice Scalia issued a memorandum explaining his decision to participate in the case, maintaining that no conflict of interest was created by his relationship with the Vice President. "A rule that required Members of this Court to remove themselves from cases in which the official actions of friends were at issue would be utterly disabling," he wrote.[59] Justice Scalia dismissed the possibility that his trip with the Vice President, which had included a ride on a government plane, had compromised his impartiality or established any sort of *quid pro quo* arrangement. "If it is reasonable to think that a Supreme Court Justice can be bought so cheap, the nation is in deeper trouble than I had imagined."[60]

After the Scalia debacle, popular attention to the subject of recusals skyrocketed. Figure 1.3 documents changes in the amount of commentary about recusals in six major newspapers from 1990 to 2012.[61] The trends show that prior to 2004, there were never more than a handful of opinion pieces about recusals per year, with most years seeing no commentary, but since 2004 media coverage has become more sustained. While no year has approached the 2004 levels, every year has seen at least some commentary about the subject, with the next-largest spike coming in 2011, shortly before the Supreme Court was to consider the constitutionality of the Affordable Care Act. It would be fair to say, then, that the past decade has witnessed a transformation in media coverage of recusals. Where once the commentary was relatively rare and tended to oppose recusals, today attention to recusals

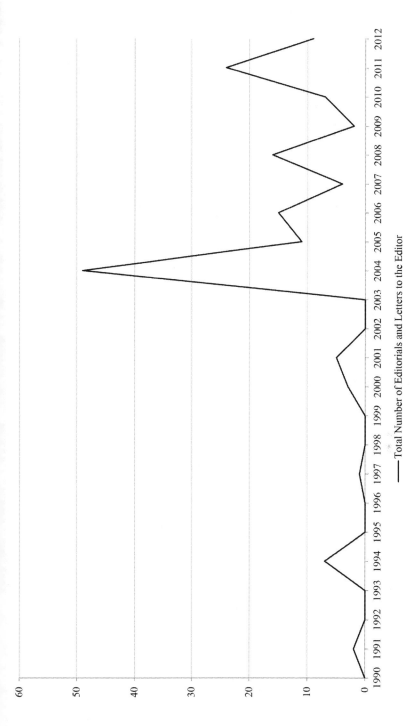

— Total Number of Editorials and Letters to the Editor

Note: The six newspapers were the *New York Times*, *Wall Street Journal*, *Washington Post*, *Los Angeles Times*, *Chicago Tribune*, and *St. Louis Post-Dispatch*. Commentary includes editorials, letters to the editor, and opinion pieces.

Figure 1.3. Commentary about U.S. Supreme Court Recusals in Six Major Newspapers, 1990–2012.

has become more sustained and politicized, with commentators about as likely to support recusals as they are to oppose them.

Yet despite all of the attention to the issue, we still understand very little about the justices' recusal practices. Indeed, the most notable aspect of Justice Scalia's memorandum was not his refusal to disqualify himself, but the fact that he wrote the memorandum at all. As discussed above, Supreme Court justices hardly ever explain their recusal decisions. Their "conspiracy of silence" stands in stark contrast to the lengths that the justices take to explain their decisions on the merits. Outside of the recusal context, the justices seem to understand that written opinions can help to enhance the Court's legitimacy by making their decision making appear principled.[62] Because the justices are unelected and not directly accountable to the public for their decisions, it benefits the institution for the justices to maintain this perception.[63] Even when their decisions are motivated by politics, the justices can build confidence in the institution by offering reasons for their decisions that will withstand public scrutiny.[64]

It is puzzling, then, that the justices refuse to defend their recusal practices. The silence has persisted, even after Scalia's duck hunting incident and despite the recent recusal controversies on the Roberts Court. It begs the question: Why *don't* the justices explain their recusal decisions? While it is not unusual for the justices to be silent about administrative matters—they also do not explain their *certiorari* decisions—a lack of transparency about recusals risks opening up the justices unnecessarily to charges of bias. Chief Justice Roberts was criticized for his 2011 *Year-End Report* because he refused to break the code of silence. "A chief justice looking out for the historical legacy of the court should encourage [an] associate justice to be publicly transparent about such an important ethical question," wrote Eric Segall for the *Los Angeles Times*. "He should not defend her silence, even by implication."[65] These comments echo concerns that have been around for decades.[66]

Candor would seem only to benefit the justices. By explaining their justifications in writing, the justices could preempt charges of bias by putting out in the open their potential conflicts of interest and describing the principles that they use to evaluate them. Creating a written record would enable the justices to codify their practices, making it easier for them to determine when recusals are warranted.[67] The justices might even find that they withdraw from cases less frequently by reaching consensus about when disqualification is necessary, thereby reducing the number of cases in which their membership is down. If the justices will not accept these benefits of transparency, then there must be a reason.

Plan for the Book

This book explores these questions through an intensive examination of recusal practices on the U.S. Supreme Court, evaluating both the consequences of recusals as well as the motivations of justices who are making recusal decisions. To preview the book's conclusions, I find that recusals advance certain judicial goals but frustrate others, giving the justices good reasons to be wary of recusing themselves from cases too easily. The primary benefits of recusals are to maintain the integrity of judicial proceedings and to preserve public confidence in the Supreme Court. Recusals function as a type of legitimacy-conferring behavior that contributes to the perception that the justices are principled decision makers, and justices have incentives to maintain this perception in order to preserve their legitimacy and the public's trust.

However, for the justices there is a tradeoff between adhering strictly to the ethics rules and achieving their other institutional and policy goals. There are times when the costs of disqualification are too great, even when recusals might technically be warranted. For example, the Court might be at risk of dividing evenly, or cases might be doctrinally important and would benefit from the participation of a full Court. There might also be cases in which the justices feel that their participation is necessary to advance their policy goals. In these circumstances, the justices have incentives to deemphasize the statutory recusal guidelines to advance these other objectives. They also have incentives to maintain silence about their recusal behavior so that they can engage in these tradeoffs more easily. It does not necessarily benefit the justices to have a written record that codifies their practices too rigidly, obligating them to withdraw from future cases regardless of the institutional and policy needs. Nor does it serve the justices for the public to be aware of the balancing act that is occurring behind the scenes. The Court prefers instead to keep quiet, defending ethical controversies only when public confidence in the Court appears to be in jeopardy. On these rare occasions, the justices break their silence and speak out.

By focusing on recusals, then, one can gain insights into broader questions about how the justices balance their concerns about institutional legitimacy against their roles as national policy makers. In fact, studying recusals might be among the best ways to understand the justices' use of legitimacy-conferring behaviors and symbols because, in most other circumstances, the justices do not have discretion about how and when to deploy them. Many of the other legitimacy-conferring symbols of the judiciary, such as the justices' robes and the other ceremonial trappings of the office, are passive institutional features. When the justices decide to withdraw from cases, they are making a deliberate choice to prioritize ethical rules—and the legitimacy of the institution—above other goals.[68]

In Chapter 2, I describe the competing statutory, institutional, and policy motivations that have an impact on the justices' recusal decisions, beginning with the requirements of the recusal statute, which establishes the presumption that the justices will recuse themselves whenever their "impartiality might reasonably be questioned."[69] To ignore the statute would be to put the Court in direct confrontation with Congress and perhaps threaten the Court's legitimacy by making the justices seem unprincipled, but to follow the statute too closely would make it harder for the justices to decide cases and controversies, which they are also obligated to do. The justices honor this institutional responsibility through their continued reliance on the "duty to sit" doctrine, which maintains that the justices should resolve any uncertainty about a recusal decision in favor of participation, particularly if the Court is at risk of dividing evenly or lacking a quorum. Additionally, the justices take into account the public policy consequences of withdrawing from cases. Justices have incentives to shape legal policy consistent with the expectations of their appointing presidents and their own judicial philosophies, and recusals can threaten these goals if the justices' absence will move legal policy in other directions.

Then, in Chapter 3, I develop a theoretical framework to explain how the justices are likely to balance these incentives, and I use an augmented version of the Supreme Court Database to test a number of hypotheses that are derived from the framework. Perhaps most notably, I find that the justices are more likely to participate in cases that advance their policy goals. Justices who are close to the center of the Court, and thus more likely to be swing votes, are more likely to participate, as are the justices at the ideological extremes of the Court, whose views might otherwise be unrepresented. Additionally, I find that the justices still apply the "duty to sit" doctrine because they tend to participate in divisive cases. Together, these findings indicate that the justices may not be fully compliant with the ethical guidelines. Yet my research also suggests that the justices do not simply ignore the recusal statute either. In cases in which one would expect the justices to have ethical conflicts, such as when business interests are before the Court, the justices are more likely to recuse themselves. The justices are also more likely to withdraw from cases when they own stock in the companies appearing before them. Consistent with my theory, then, it appears that the justices are selective in their conformance with ethical rules, balancing multiple goals when making recusal decisions.

In the second half of the book, I investigate the consequences of recusals for law and policy. In Chapter 4, I examine how recusals have influenced the ideological content of the legal policies that the Court produces, and I find that, ordinarily, recusals do not change case outcomes unless a justice who is usually a part of the majority coalition withdraws from a case. However, recusals do influence the ideology of opinion coalitions. The recusal of conservative justices shifts the median ideology of majority coalitions to the left, while the recusal of liberal justices shifts the median to the right. Substantively, this finding means that recusals affect the contents of majority opinions and thus the scope of the precedents that the Court establishes.

I find less evidence that recusal behavior has some of the other adverse consequences that commentators have put forward. In Chapter 5, I examine the impact of recusals on the justices' administrative efficiency, public attitudes about the Court, bargaining activity, and the Court's docket, and I find that in each of these areas the influence of recusals has been small. It is unusual for recusals to cause the Court to divide evenly, and the impact on bargaining activity is limited as well. While a 4-4 vote does sometimes occur, it is primarily when a member of the majority coalition withdraws, and only if a case is otherwise close. Additionally, I find little evidence that recent recusal controversies have caused public support for the Court to decline, not even when Justice Scalia brought so much negative publicity to the Court after his refusal to withdraw from the *Cheney* case.[70] Finally, after examining Justice Harry Blackmun's docket sheets, I conclude that recusals affect the outcomes of *certiorari* votes only in exceptional cases.

All of these findings complicate the evaluation of proposals for reforming the recusal process, which I take up in Chapter 6. On the one hand, my conclusions reinforce the concerns of those who see a conspiracy in the justices' silence about their recusal practices. My research suggests that, as some have feared, the justices are not withdrawing from cases as often as they could be. The justices' critics might well be justified in demanding procedural reforms to ensure that the justices are accountable to the ethical guidelines. These reforms might include establishing procedures for reviewing the recusal decisions of particular justices, either by the Court as a whole or by an external panel, or mandating that the justices defend their recusal decisions in writing.

Yet, on the other hand, my research suggests that reforms might not be needed because recusals do not routinely have substantial consequences for law and policy. Moreover, increasing the Court's accountability is not without costs. The same discretion that permits the justices to avoid disqualifying themselves for policy reasons also lets them participate in cases when necessary to serve the public's interest. For example, the justices might anticipate that they are at risk of dividing evenly or that the legal ramifications of a case are so important that it merits the consideration of the full Court. It is not unreasonable for the justices to take these types of institutional concerns into account, particularly when the arguments in favor of recusal are not clear. Reforms that are too aggressive could impair the justices' ability to fulfill their institutional responsibility to decide the cases before them.

2

Competing Explanations for
Supreme Court Recusals

Much of the controversy surrounding the Supreme Court's recusal practices focuses on the merits of particular recusal decisions. Why are the justices withdrawing from some cases but not others? Can we be sure that the justices are adhering to the federal guidelines when they are deciding whether to disqualify themselves? Proposals for reform point to the Court's lack of transparency and demand greater public reporting of the reasons for recusal decisions, with many legal commentators insisting that the justices follow the example of Justice Scalia in the *Cheney* case and issue written memoranda.[1] These proposals might seem at first to be unduly suspicious of the justices, but the truth is that we understand very little about their recusal practices, and the justices have sent mixed signals about their motives.

Consider, for example, the testimony that Justices Kennedy and Breyer gave in April 2011 to a House Appropriations subcommittee. The justices were before the committee to discuss the Court's budget for the next year, but, as has become customary, members of Congress used the occasion to ask the justices a wide variety of questions relating to the Court's operations.[2] Among the topics covered that year was the subject of judicial ethics. Representative José E. Serrano asked the justices to comment on "several proposals . . . to make recusal decisions by the Justices more transparent to the public."

Justice Kennedy responded that the justices take ethical rules very seriously. "Of course the Court has to follow rules of judicial ethics," he said. "That is part of our oath. That is part of our obligation of neutrality." He told the members that "if there is some question that we haven't complied with the letter or spirit of those rules, there can be comment about that," but he insisted that "I really think there is no problem at all."[3] Justice Breyer agreed, noting that "I personally have seven volumes of ethics rules, the same that every district judge has, right in my office." He said that when ethical problems arise, he consults these rules and tries to apply them faithfully, even consulting "ethics experts" when confronted with difficult problems. "I think all the justices do what I do," he continued, "which is we do follow the rules."[4]

Yet, almost immediately, Justice Breyer went on to explain why Supreme Court justices could *not* always follow the rules. "It is a different thing, which I discovered, being a Supreme Court justice in respect to ethics and disqualification than a district court or court of appeals." Justice Breyer said that as a lower court judge he saw little cost to disqualification because other judges were available to serve as substitutes. "But you can't do that on the Court. So you have to think about it in a different way, and you have to remember that you also have a duty to sit."[5] Justice Kennedy agreed, reinforcing Justice Breyer's testimony by describing the institutional hardships that recusals cause. He noted that "if we have one of us recuse from a case and we come out four to four, we have wasted everybody's time."[6]

In the span of just a few minutes, Justices Kennedy and Breyer summarized some of the competing motivations that influence recusal decisions and, in the process, deepened the uncertainty about what drives their behavior. The contradictions in the justices' testimony were readily apparent. On the one hand, the justices were assuring the subcommittee that they were following the ethical rules, but at the same time they were describing why they could not possibly follow the rules because the Supreme Court was different from other courts. Justice Breyer even suggested that policy considerations influenced his application of the ethics rules, observing that if he were to withdraw from a case, "that could sometimes change the result."[7] It is little wonder, then, that commentators have sought more transparency in the recusal process. From the justices' testimony, it is by no means clear what the full range of considerations is that influences their behavior, or how specific motivations affect particular recusal decisions.

Uncertainty about what drives recusal behavior is also fueled by the variability in the rate at which the justices recuse themselves from cases. Figure 2.1 reports the percentage of cases in which Supreme Court justices recused themselves between 1946 and 2010, based on data from the Supreme Court Database.[8] Overall, the justices recused themselves from about 2.1%

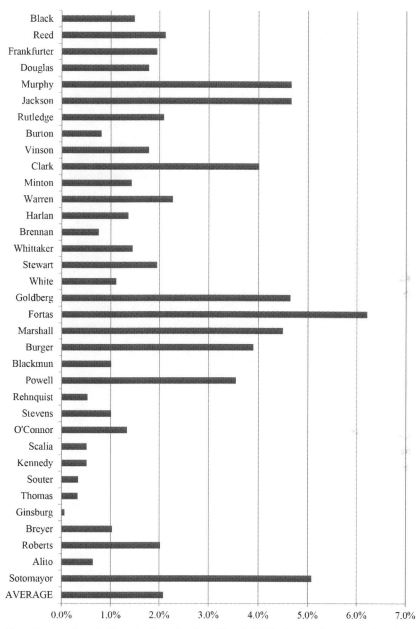

Note: Data are from the Supreme Court Database (Spaeth 2011). Justice Elena Kagan is excluded because she served only in the 2010 term, but in that year she sat out of 34.9% of cases.

Figure 2.1. Percentage of Cases in which Justices Recused Themselves, 1946–2010.

of cases, but there is much variation in the rate at which justices disqualified themselves. Justice Abe Fortas had the highest rate, withdrawing from 6.2% of cases, while Justice Ruth Bader Ginsburg had the lowest rate, at 0.06%. Of course, it is possible that this variation is attributable to differences in the rate at which potential conflicts of interest presented themselves. Some justices might, for example, have had more diverse stock portfolios than others, or they might have had a greater number of family members who were connected to cases coming before the Court. Yet the variability also reinforces the perception that recusals are discretionary and that the justices disqualify themselves at different rates based on how they balance various interests.

In this chapter, I elaborate on the various motivations that are likely to influence the justices' recusal practices, based on the justices' public statements and on what research has already taught us about judicial behavior. Then, in the next chapter, I theorize about how the justices are likely to balance these interests, and I test several empirical implications of the theoretical framework that I develop. While it is difficult to know what determines recusal decisions in specific cases unless the justices tell us, one can gain insight into the factors that influence their aggregate behavior by using systematic quantitative analysis. Such an analysis can help us to identify the range of potential factors that affect recusal decisions and gauge the approximate weight that the justices give to ethical considerations relative to other criteria.

Statutory Motivations for Recusals

The decision whether to disqualify oneself from a case is technically not voluntary. Federal judges, including Supreme Court justices, are covered by the recusal guidelines in 28 U.S.C. § 455, which is patterned after the American Bar Association's Model Code of Judicial Conduct. Other recusal statutes are either inapplicable to Supreme Court justices or limited in their application.[9] As revised in 1974, § 455 has two major provisions: section 455 (a), which requires judges to recuse themselves when their "impartiality might reasonably be questioned"; and section 455 (b), which describes categories of conduct that require recusal. These categories are explained in greater detail below. The purpose of the 1974 revisions was to reduce judicial discretion over disqualification by articulating an objective set of standards and clarifying that even the *appearance* of bias was sufficient grounds for a recusal.[10] Previously, the subjectivity in federal recusal law had permitted judges to prioritize a "duty to sit" over disqualification.[11] With the 1974 revisions, the duty to sit was repudiated by Congress and replaced, at least on the lower courts, with what one federal judge has described as a "robust disqualification regime."[12]

However, the justices have never conceded that Congress has the authority to regulate their recusal behavior, and the extent of the Court's compliance with the recusal statute remains unclear. Neither federal law nor the Judicial Conference's Code of Conduct for United States Judges requires Supreme Court justices to report the reasons for recusing themselves—or for declining to do so. The recusal decisions of lower court judges are reviewable by higher courts, but no tribunal reviews the recusal practices of Supreme Court justices, nor do the justices evaluate the decisions of their colleagues. As Chief Justice Roberts stated in his 2011 *Year-End Report*, "the Supreme Court does not sit in judgment of one of its own Members' decision whether to recuse in the course of deciding a case. Indeed, if the Supreme Court reviewed those decisions, it would create an undesirable situation in which the Court could affect the outcome of a case by selecting who among its Members may participate."[13]

Of course, violating the ethical rules is a potentially impeachable offense, and the threat of impeachment could be motivating at least some of the justices to be compliant. However, the more likely incentive for the justices to follow the recusal statute is their interest in preserving the Court's legitimacy. Researchers have long observed that the authority of courts depends on public confidence in the institution. Unlike the President and Congress, which have the powers of the sword and purse, respectively, Supreme Court justices lack institutional resources to secure compliance. It is for this reason that Alexander Hamilton referred to the judiciary as the "least dangerous" branch.[14] To be effective policy makers, the justices depend primarily on their reputations, certified by robust public confidence in the institution.

Among the ways that judges can enhance public confidence is with the use of legitimacy-conferring symbols and behaviors.[15] Symbols include the ceremonial trappings of the judiciary, such as the robes judges wear, the formal style of judicial proceedings, and the marble temples in which judges conduct their business. Behaviors include the practice of defending judgments in writing, the avoidance of *ex parte* communications, and the refusal to comment on issues that are likely to appear before the Court. Such activities help judges to cultivate and maintain the perception that they are principled, which in turn enhances legitimacy. Gibson and Caldeira have suggested that these types of symbols create a "positivity bias" that affects how citizens evaluate judges. "Legitimizing symbols likely activate preexisting loyalty toward the institution (where it exists)," they write, "as well as reinforce the understanding that courts are different from other political institutions." A frame of "judiciousness" is activated and, "for some, becomes the dominant frame for judging the events."[16]

Recusals have the potential to affect public confidence because they relate directly to the perception that the justices are principled. If the justices were to violate the federal recusal statute routinely, they would raise questions not simply about the substance of their policy choices but also about the integrity of the procedures that produced these choices. However, if the justices were compliant with the statutory guidelines, they would demonstrate that they respected the ethical rules and were committed to principles of impartial justice. For this reason, one might expect the justices to favor complying with the federal recusal statute except when other institutional or policy considerations weigh against disqualification.

A. Financial Conflicts of Interest

Perhaps the most important provision of the recusal statute, which tends to generate the most recusals, is § 455 (b) (4), which requires justices to recuse themselves when they have financial conflicts of interest. The section reads that a justice shall withdraw from a case when "he, individually or as a fiduciary, or his spouse or minor child residing in his household, has a financial interest in the subject matter in controversy or in a party to the proceeding."[17] Even if the financial stake is minimal, a justice is still expected to withdraw to avoid the appearance of bias. For example, Justice O'Connor frequently recused herself from cases because of her ownership of AT&T stock.[18] Chief Justice Roberts divested himself of Pfizer stock in 2010 to participate in two cases concerning that company after previously recusing himself from cases involving Pfizer.[19] In another case, the justices lacked a quorum after four justices recused themselves because of their investment holdings or other financial conflicts.[20]

This behavior suggests that the justices take financial conflicts of interest very seriously, and in fact the primacy of financial motivations for judicial disqualification is deeply rooted in the American legal tradition. It was the only basis for recusal under English common law,[21] and it was one of two grounds for recusal described in the original 1792 recusal statute.[22] Even Chief Justice John Marshall, who is notorious for having participated in

Marbury v. Madison despite his direct prior involvement with the controversy,[23] recused himself from *Martin v. Hunter's Lessee* because he had a financial stake in the dispute.[24] Today the concern about financial conflicts remains significant, and, as commentators have noted, it is the one area in which the justices appear to err most consistently on the side of recusal. Bassett observes that "a dichotomy currently exists between recusal for financial versus most non-financial interests," noting that "any doubts about potential bias resulting from a financial interest generally are resolved in favor of recusal, whereas any doubts about potential bias resulting from most non-financial interests tend to be resolved in favor of participating in the case."[25] Bleich and Klaus agree, commenting that "[t]he only consistent exception to the court's generally laissez-faire attitude toward disqualification continues to be John Marshall's sore point: money."[26]

While the current Supreme Court justices do not generally discuss the importance of financial conflicts of interest in their off-the-bench remarks, one can deduce their thinking about the subject from their opinions concerning the recusal practices of judges on other courts. Perhaps most noteworthy is *Caperton v. Massey*, which concerned the failure of a justice on West Virginia's high court to recuse himself from a dispute involving one of his top political contributors.[27] Justices on the Supreme Court of Appeals of West Virginia are selected in partisan elections and serve for twelve-year terms. Justice Brent Benjamin won his seat in 2004, supported by three million dollars in contributions made by Don Blankenship, who was the head of the A.T. Massey Coal Co., which had just suffered a fifty million dollar jury verdict for "fraudulent misrepresentation, concealment, and tortious inter-ference with existing contractual relations."[28] By all appearances, it seemed that Justice Benjamin had been bought and paid for with the expectation that he would reverse the jury's verdict when the case eventually came to him on appeal—and in fact he did just that, serving as the swing vote in a narrow 3-2 decision.[29]

Superficially, *Caperton* would seem to have few implications for recusal practices on the U.S. Supreme Court because it focuses on judicial elections. Supreme Court justices are not elected but appointed to life terms, so they do not receive campaign contributions. However, *Caperton* established broad principles that have implications for more than just state judicial elections. Perhaps most significantly, the justices ruled that the due process clauses of the U.S. Constitution require recusals in some circumstances.[30] The *Caperton* majority acknowledged that most recusal decisions are governed by statutes and judicial codes of conduct, but the justices also held that "there are objective standards that require recusal when the probability of actual bias on the part of the judge or decisionmaker is too high to be constitutionally tolerable."[31] For example, when judges stand to benefit financially from cases, principles of due process may be violated.[32] *Caperton* therefore provides some insight into the justices' views on recusals. All of the justices agreed that financial conflicts of interest are problematic. Even the dissenting justices in *Caperton* accepted the principle that "a judge may not preside over a case in which he has a 'direct, personal, substantial pecuniary interest.' "[33] Presumably, the justices would say that they hold themselves to the same standards and that any financial conflicts of interest that arise in their own cases would be grounds for disqualification.

Yet the fact that *Caperton* was closely divided—by a 5-4 vote—suggests that there is also ambivalence on the Court about expanding judicial oversight of recusal practices and second-guessing judges who decline to disqualify themselves. Chief Justice Roberts, in dissent, was wary of setting a precedent that would cause the public to question the impartiality of judges. "The end result," he said, "will do far more to erode public confidence in judicial impartiality than an isolated failure to recuse in a particular case."[34] Instead, Roberts suggested that it would be better to trust judges to make these determinations for themselves. "There is a presumption of honesty and integrity in those serving as adjudicators," he said. "All judges take an oath to uphold the Constitution and apply the law impartially, and we trust that they will live up to this promise."[35] Even the justices in the majority acknowledged that judicial intervention would not have been appropriate were it not for the "extraordinary" facts of *Caperton*.[36]

B. Pre-Bench Activities

In addition to cases presenting financial conflicts of interest, justices also recuse themselves from cases that relate to their pre-bench activities. Section 455 (b) (2-3) requires the justices to disqualify themselves from cases in which they have "served as lawyer in the matter in controversy" or "served in governmental employment and in such capacity participated as counsel, adviser or material witness concerning the proceeding."[37] Commonly, these types of conflicts arise from the justices' activities before they served on the Court. Writing on the subject of recusals in the 1950s, Anthony Lewis observed that Justice Tom Clark frequently recused himself because of his work as Attorney General in the Truman administration, and that Chief

Justice Earl Warren sat out of disputes relating to his work as the governor of California.[38] For a number of years, Justice William O. Douglas recused himself from cases involving the Securities and Exchange Commission, for which he had served as Chairman.[39] More recently, Elena Kagan has withdrawn from cases on which she had worked as the Solicitor General.

The justices have clarified that failure to withdraw from cases involving pre-bench activities can amount to constitutional violations of due process. In *Williams v. Pennsylvania*, the Supreme Court considered the matter of Chief Justice Ronald Castille of the Pennsylvania Supreme Court, who had declined to recuse himself from a case in which he had served as district attorney three decades earlier.[40] In his prior role, Castille had approved the trial prosecutor's request to pursue the death penalty against the defendant, Terrance Williams. Writing for a bare majority, Justice Kennedy concluded that Castille's subsequent participation in the case, this time as Chief Justice, was inappropriate. "Where a judge has had an earlier significant, personal involvement as a prosecutor in a critical decision in the defendant's case," he wrote, "the risk of actual bias in the judicial proceeding rises to an unconstitutional level."[41]

Although recusals generally involve conflicts with the justices' pre-bench activities, justices might occasionally anticipate conflicts with their *future* responsibilities. For example, Chief Justice Burger had to determine whether it was appropriate to participate in *United States v. Nixon*, concerning President Richard Nixon's release of audiotapes to Special Prosecutor Leon Jaworski, in light of the fact that Burger might later be called upon to preside over Nixon's impeachment trial.[42] Because the impeachment trial would depend, in part, on the validity of Nixon's claims that executive privilege shielded his activity, Burger risked deciding questions in *Nixon* that he would be asked to consider again in the later proceeding. As one commentator observed at the time, there is no substitute for the Chief Justice at an impeachment trial, and so it arguably would have been appropriate for Burger to avoid potential controversy by recusing himself from *Nixon*: "If Mr. Burger sits on the tapes case, it would be virtually impossible for him to disqualify himself later as presiding officer at any impeachment trial, both because of the constitutional mandate and because all of his colleagues, having participated in the earlier decision, would be equally ineligible."[43] Ultimately, Chief Justice Burger declined to recuse himself, but Nixon's resignation meant that the Chief Justice would have no role to play in an impeachment trial, so in the end no conflict of interest occurred.

C. Off-the-Bench Remarks

Additionally, section 455 (b) (3) requires recusal when the justices have "expressed an opinion concerning the merits of the particular case in controversy."[44] This provision might lead the justices to disqualify themselves when they have expressed views on particular disputes before the Court in off-the-bench remarks, confirmation hearings, or other contexts.[45] For example, Justice Scalia recused himself from *Elk Grove v. Newdow*, concerning the constitutionality of the words "under God" in the pledge of allegiance, after giving a speech in which he had been critical of the lower court's opinion.[46] Unlike the *Cheney* case, in which Scalia had made no public comments about the merits of the dispute, his remarks about the Ninth Circuit's opinion implied prejudgment and, to Scalia, warranted recusal.

To avoid the necessity of disqualifying themselves routinely, justices generally try to avoid making comments on cases or issues that are likely to appear before the Court. Indeed, the justices are often reticent to speak at their confirmation hearings about their views on constitutional questions for this reason.[47] However, there are limits to how far the justices can extend this policy. Because the same issues arise frequently on the Court, over time the justices develop paper trails on many subjects. These prior opinions cannot be the foundation for recusals or the Court could not conduct its business, even if a reasonable argument could be made that prior rulings prevent the justices from looking at subjects with fresh eyes when the same issues come before them. "Logically, a judge's recusing himself must relate to his personal interest in a particular case or person, not to his views on the legal issue in the case," wrote court reporter Anthony Lewis in the 1950s. "This is because any legal issue may keep recurring in the court's work, and there could be nothing improper in a view on it."[48]

The distinction between "personal" and "professional" views of a case can be difficult to parse. Some might say that justices should recuse themselves from cases when they have formed or expressed views on specific controversies independently of their formal review of the briefs, oral arguments, and other proceedings in the official records. However, this standard might be difficult to apply consistently. For example, Justice Ginsburg spent years as the director of the Women's Rights Project at the American Civil Liberties Union, arguing a number of leading women's rights cases before the Court. Her views on the appropriate standard for reviewing classifications based on sex under the Equal Protection Clause were clear when she advocated for the use of strict scrutiny as counsel in *Frontiero v. Richardson*.[49] It came as no surprise to Court watchers when, years later, in *United States v. Virginia*, Justice Ginsburg moved the intermediate scrutiny standard closer to strict scrutiny for sex-based classifications, ruling that states must have an "exceedingly persuasive justification" to make these distinctions.[50] Yet few would argue that Justice Ginsburg should have recused herself from *U.S. v. Virginia* because of her earlier advocacy work.[51] The point is defensible, but in practice it would unduly hamper the Court for Ginsburg to sit out of all sex discrimination cases.

Likewise, Clarence Thomas has made no secret of his opposition to affirmative action, due in part to his own experiences with these policies before arriving on the Court.[52] However, his comments on the issue have not stopped him from participating in affirmative action cases, most recently *Fisher v. University of Texas*.[53] One could maintain that the arguments against Justice Thomas's participation were at least as strong as the ones against Scalia's had been in *Newdow*, if not more so. Justice Scalia at least appeared to be expressing a professional judgment about the Ninth Circuit's decision, whereas Thomas's objections to affirmative action were grounded in his personal experiences. Yet, once again, the justices seem to recognize the infeasibility of recusing themselves from cases because of their general views about policies, however strong they might be. Instead, the justices reserve disqualification for occasions when they have expressed opinions about the particular disputes before the Court.

D. Family Connections

Other potential grounds for recusals are rooted in the justices' personal and family relationships. Recently, the political activities of Justice Thomas's wife, Ginni, have raised questions about whether justices should participate in cases when their spouses have commented about the merits.[54] In addition to her specific advocacy against the health care law, Ginni Thomas has a long history of lobbying for conservative causes, even founding the 501(c)(4) organization Liberty Central, which endorses Tea Party principles.[55] An argument could be made that these political activities reflect back on the justices and make it appear as though they have prejudged matters that are appearing before the Court.

Justice Thomas has consistently maintained that his wife's political behavior is not grounds for recusal, and his position on this issue is widely shared by commentators on and off the Court.[56] For the most part, the justices view their spouses' professional and political lives as separate from their own and do not recuse themselves from cases based on their activities. Justice Ruth Bader Ginsburg, for example, did not recuse herself from tax cases despite the fact that her husband, Martin Ginsburg, was a prominent tax lawyer. At the lower court level, Judge Stephen Reinhardt wrote an opinion striking down California's Proposition 8 even though his wife had worked for the ACLU and publicly favored same-sex marriage.[57]

An exception might occur when the spouses or children of justices stand to benefit financially from disputes that are before the Court. Ginni Thomas's affiliation with Liberty Central raised concerns not just because of her political advocacy but also because of the possibility that her husband was deciding cases involving one or more of the group's anonymous donors.[58] If these groups were, in effect, paying Ginni Thomas's salary, then there would have been serious ethical questions about her husband's participation, implicating § 455 (b)(4), which requires recusal for financial conflicts of interest. Because Liberty Central was not required to publicly disclose its donor list, the number of potential conflicts that Justice Thomas faced is unknown. However, the Supreme Court's Public Information Office reported that Mrs. Thomas did consult with the Court's legal office when she formed Liberty Central in 2009.[59]

Recusals might also be necessary when family members have affiliations with law firms that are arguing cases before the Supreme Court. During the 1980s, former Solicitor General Erwin Griswold and Washington lawyer Ernest Gellhorn noted that the frequency of these types of connections was threatening to create an excessive number of recusals. "It is . . . important that the rules governing judicial conduct do not needlessly bar a justice's participation when there is in fact no threat to fairness or public standards," they wrote.[60] Griswold and Gellhorn suggested that recusals should be limited to occasions when family members were in the same office or department within a firm that was working on a case, and not simply the same firm. The justices appeared to agree, and in their 1993 *Statement of Recusal Policy* they clarified that they would recuse themselves only when relatives had worked directly on cases at some stage of litigation or when relatives were partners who stood to benefit financially.[61] Applying the policy, Chief Justice Rehnquist declined to recuse himself from *Microsoft v. United States*, even though his son was a partner in a firm representing Microsoft, because the case involved a different legal matter. Rehnquist concluded that because "my son's personal and financial concerns will not be affected by our disposition of the Supreme Court's Microsoft matters," his recusal was not required.[62]

Institutional Considerations

In general, then, there is broad consensus about when recusals are warranted. When justices stand to benefit from cases financially, when their family members stand to benefit, when the justices have worked on cases previously, or when they have publicly commented about the merits of specific disputes pending before the Court, then the justices should disqualify themselves. What complicates matters—and what has created so much uncertainty about the recusal process—is that the justices have discretion about how to apply these broad principles to particular cases. The arguments in favor of recusal are not always clear-cut, and justices have other institutional and policy incentives that might discourage disqualification.

From an institutional standpoint, recusals can be problematic because they make it difficult for the justices to fulfill their responsibility to decide cases and controversies. This institutional commitment is usually expressed in terms of either a "duty to sit" or "rule of necessity," which have different emphases but share the same goals of enabling the justices to resolve disputes and promote clarity in federal law. The "duty to sit" was first articulated in the lower courts,[63] but it was endorsed at the Supreme Court level by then-Justice Rehnquist in a memorandum declining to recuse himself from *Laird v. Tatum*.[64] Conceding that his decision to participate in *Laird* was "a fairly debatable one" because he had testified before Congress about the Army surveillance program that was in dispute, Rehnquist nonetheless determined that the recusal statute did not require his disqualification, and that "a federal judge has a duty to *sit* where *not disqualified* which is equally as strong as the duty to *not sit* where *disqualified*."[65]

Rehnquist argued that the duty to sit was "even stronger" for Supreme Court justices than it was for lower court judges because there was "no way of substituting Justices on this Court as one judge may be substituted for another in the district courts."[66] Rehnquist said that the justices risked dividing evenly when recusals occurred, and there was no other court to step in and resolve the controversy. "The consequence attending such a result," he explained, "is, of course, that the principle of law presented by the case is left unsettled."[67] The failure to resolve legal disputes was "even more serious" when the circuits were divided, because then federal law would mean different things in different parts of the country. It would be untenable, he suggested, for there to be "one rule in Athens, and another rule in Rome."[68]

Although the 1974 revisions to the federal recusal statute were supposed to have replaced the duty to sit with an obligation for the justices to disqualify themselves when their "impartiality might reasonably be questioned," the justices have repeatedly asserted their commitment to *Laird*'s principles. Versions of *Laird*'s rationale appear in both the justices' 1993 *Statement of Recusal Policy*[69] and Roberts' 2011 *Year-End Report on the Federal Judiciary*.[70] Chief Justice Rehnquist relied on it in his memorandum declining to recuse himself from the *Microsoft* case,[71] and Justice Ginsburg endorsed the principle in off-the-bench comments.[72] These statements generally stop short of citing *Laird* directly, which is perhaps understandable given the amount of controversy that Rehnquist's memorandum generated at the time. As noted in the previous chapter, Congress's decision to amend the recusal statute in 1974 is traceable, at least in part, to Rehnquist's memorandum. However, *Laird*'s spirit clearly lives on. In his 2011 remarks before the House Appropriations subcommittee, Justice Breyer was explicit on this point, testifying that when making a recusal decision, "you have to remember you have a duty to sit."[73]

Some of the premises underlying the duty to sit have been challenged by legal commentators and empirical research about the Court. Bassett has observed that if the Court were to divide evenly, the result would not be "unusual or disastrous"; in fact, it would be no different from if the justices had never granted *certiorari* in the first place, which occurs in the vast majority of cases that come before the Court.[74] Ethically, however, the justices would find themselves on firmer ground if they followed the recusal statute more closely. As Stempel puts it, "Although it would be preferable if the Court always acted by majority and never made split affirmances of inconsistent cases, it does not follow from this observation that any such inconsistency justifies a relaxed view of judicial ethics and the recusal statute."[75]

Empirical work by Black and Epstein also casts doubt on the premises underlying the duty to sit.[76] They find that recusals do not frequently cause the justices to divide evenly, occurring less than 6% of the time when they were possible, which is below what one might expect if vote divisions occurred randomly.[77] It would seem, then, that recusals do not necessarily produce the institutional hardships that the justices have put forward. Black and Epstein speculated that the justices might be acting purposively to avoid the possibility of dividing evenly, suggesting "that a participating justice will cast a 'sophisticated' vote (in an apparent four-to-four case) to avoid a decision that may be even more distant from her policy preferences than the one issued by the five-to-three Court that she has agreed to join."[78]

In subsequent research, Black and Bryan find support for this hypothesis, with evidence showing "that ties are less likely when a decision is necessary to resolve a dispute in the lower courts and when cases are important to the executive branch."[79]

Indeed, one might argue that this approach is more appropriate when ethical questions arise. The duty to sit supposes that it is the responsibility of justices to minimize the hardships that their own recusals impose, but arguably this responsibility should fall to the other justices. It is by no means inevitable that a coalition of eight justices must divide evenly, regardless of how ideologically diverse they are. Some would say that, instead of encouraging justices who face ethical conflicts to participate anyway, the remaining justices should find a way to forge a consensus, prioritizing their duty to decide cases and controversies over their doctrinal preferences. Based on recent empirical research, it appears that the justices do frequently achieve this sort of consensus, but if so then the logic animating the duty to sit is questionable.

The "rule of necessity" is related to the duty to sit but applies primarily to circumstances in which the application of ethical guidelines would require most, or even all, of the justices to disqualify themselves from controversies. In *United States v. Will*, the justices clarified that the 1974 revisions to § 455 did not limit the application of the rule of necessity.[80] *Will* centered on the interpretation of statutes fixing the compensation of high-level federal officials, including judges. If the ethical rules were applied too stringently, no federal judge would have been available to hear the case at the trial or appellate level because all federal judges stood to benefit financially from the outcome of the dispute. The justices decided that such an interpretation went against the spirit of § 455. "The declared purpose of § 455 is to guarantee litigants a fair forum in which they can pursue their claims," Chief Justice Burger wrote for the majority. "Far from promoting this purpose, failure to apply the Rule of Necessity would have a contrary effect, for without the Rule, some litigants would be denied their right to a forum."[81]

The rule of necessity has received less criticism than the duty to sit, although some commentators maintain that the loss of a quorum is not enough to justify relaxing the ethical rules, particularly if the trade-off is to the Court's legitimacy.[82] When the Court lacks a quorum, the lower court's opinion is affirmed automatically, just as when the justices divide evenly. The Court might miss an opportunity to clarify federal law, but, once again, the consequences might not be all that severe. The litigants would have had at least one appeal, and, most likely, the justices could still address the underlying legal questions in a future case. In the interim, to solve the quorum issue, the justices could take steps to minimize their conflicts of interest, such as by divesting themselves of relevant financial holdings. Congress could also assign final jurisdiction to another court or else waive the application of the recusal statute.

Regardless of the actual severity of the institutional hardships imposed by recusals, the justices' comments suggest that they do take seriously both the "duty to sit" and the "rule of necessity" and that they balance these institutional considerations against the requirements of the federal recusal statute when ethical questions arise. To explain the variation in the justices' recusal behavior, one must therefore take into consideration not just whether any of the provisions of § 455 (a) or (b) are implicated, but whether the justices have reason to think that their disqualification will make the Court divide evenly or lack a quorum. Justices might be particularly wary of recusing themselves when cases present legal questions that have generated conflicts in the lower courts or have divided the justices themselves in the past.

Policy Considerations

Justices are also likely to have policy incentives that weigh on their decisions to participate in cases, particularly when the arguments in favor of recusing themselves are not conclusive. It is well established that the attitudes of the justices are the single best predictors of their votes on the merits.[83] As described by Segal and Spaeth, several institutional features of the Supreme Court encourage the justices to behave attitudinally, including the justices' lack of accountability to higher courts, the absence of meaningful court-curbing measures by the other branches, the lack of aspiration by the justices for higher office, and their almost complete control over their docket.[84] These institutional conditions, which are unique to the U.S. Supreme Court, free the justices to act on their sincere preferences much of the time and habituate them to approaching the Court's business this way.[85] While individual justices may vary in the extent to which they behave attitudinally, in the aggregate the evidence in favor of ideological voting is persuasive.[86]

It is reasonable to think that many of the same institutional characteristics that encourage preferential voting on the merits would lead the justices to behave attitudinally in the recusal context. Like their decisions on the merits, the justices' recusal decisions cannot be appealed to other tribunals. The justices do not stand for reelection, nor do they generally have aspirations for other offices, so their recusal practices are unlikely to affect their career ambitions. The threat of impeachment is also likely to seem remote.[87] Added to these incentives is the fact that the justices make their recusal decisions almost entirely in secret. On most occasions the public is not even aware that a recusal is a possibility unless the justices choose to tell them about it.

With their recusal decisions made in secret, with no oversight, and with no accountability for what they decide, the justices are likely to encounter few constraints that might curb preferential recusal behavior. The potential damage to the Court's legitimacy is, of course, still present, but unless the justices are in clear violation of the recusal statute, this cost might seem small when weighed against the benefits of participation. The justices must know—indeed, they have acknowledged—that their participation can change case outcomes. As Breyer stated in his 2011 testimony before the House Appropriations subcommittee, "there is no one to replace me if I take myself out, and that could change the result."[88] Breyer repeated this remark later the same year at the Aspen Ideas Festival.[89] The Court also implicitly recognized the policy consequences of recusals in their 1993 *Statement of Recusal Policy* in the context of discussing the possibility of litigants "strategizing" recusals, which occurs when parties seek the recusal of a particular justice by selecting a law firm where a justice's relative works.[90] Like litigants, the justices seemed to understand that case outcomes can change depending on who is sitting out.

If the justices care about the development of the law, and if they would like to see the law reflect their sincere policy preferences as much as possible, then one might expect the justices to avoid recusing themselves from cases too often. Otherwise, they risk ceding to others the resolution of important federal questions about which they have substantive policy concerns. This is not to suggest that justices will never disqualify themselves from cases in which they have policy interests. Many times the arguments in favor of recusal will be too strong, regardless of the justices' interest in participating. My suggestion is subtler: that often the arguments in favor of recusal are not decisive, and in these circumstances the justices will err on the side of participating when they have ideological incentives to do so. Indeed, it is quite possible that the justices do not realize the extent to which attitudes influence their judgments. As Cross observes in his study of the Supreme Court's use of originalist sources, "It is quite cynical to suggest that judges are intentionally violating legal requirements, and this doesn't fit with their self-perception." Instead, Cross suggests that attitudinal voting derives from "a natural tendency of people to favor information that confirms their preexisting beliefs."[91]

In other words, the justices' desire to participate in cases might influence their assessment of whether the arguments in favor of disqualification are weak or strong. Research on motivated reasoning has identified a "confirmation bias" in the selection and use of evidence, whereby "people tend to overweight positive confirmatory evidence or underweight negative disconfirmatory evidence."[92] As Kunda puts it, "People are more likely to arrive at those conclusions that they want to arrive at."[93] In the recusal context, justices might have a tendency to devalue evidence that would seem to favor recusal when they have strong policy reasons for participating. If justices anticipate that their absence will change the results, or if cases involve issue areas that are important to them, the arguments against recusal might start to appear more compelling to the justices. In this way, the justices' attitudes come to influence their judgments, even when they sincerely believe that they are applying the ethical rules objectively.

Conclusion

It would seem, then, that the testimony that Justices Kennedy and Breyer gave to the House Appropriations subcommittee was an accurate reflection of the various motivations that influence the justices when they are making recusal decisions. A summary of these motivations is provided in Figure 2.2. As the figure suggests, the justices do have incentives to follow the statutory recusal guidelines to promote their institution's legitimacy. However, the justices also have other institutional and policy motivations that might lead them to participate in cases anyway, particularly when the statutory arguments in favor of recusal are inconclusive. Institutional considerations serve

Motivation		Goal
Statutory Considerations	→	Legitimacy
Institutional Considerations	→	Legal Clarity
Policy Considerations	→	Ideology

Figure 2.2. Summary of Competing Motivations for Recusal Behavior.

to advance the goals of resolving disputes and promoting legal clarity, while policy considerations advance the justices' sincere ideological preferences.

One might therefore predict that variations in recusal behavior will be shaped by a combination of statutory, institutional, and policy incentives. Yet it remains unclear precisely how the justices balance these various interests. The justices themselves provide little guidance about how they draw the line, prompting a number of questions: When do the justices follow the statutory guidelines closely? Are there some provisions of the federal recusal statute that the justices prioritize over others? Under what circumstances are institutional or policy motivations more likely to prevail? And how could we determine, empirically, what factors are the most influential? I take up these questions in the next chapter.

3

An Analysis of the Justices'
Recusal Practices

The previous chapter ended with a puzzle. The justices' off-the-bench remarks, their behavior, and their formal memoranda and policy statements suggest that recusal practices reflect a combination of statutory, institutional, and policy motivations, but the extent of the justices' reliance on each consideration is unknown. Deepening the uncertainty is the fact that, with rare exceptions, the justices do not explain their recusal decisions, nor do they reveal when they have thought about recusing themselves from cases but did not. The puzzle, then, is to sort out exactly how these competing motivations influence particular recusal decisions.

The problem for the justices is that neither recusing nor declining to recuse oneself is costless. As discussed in the previous chapter, the justices risk damaging the Court's legitimacy when they ignore the federal recusal statute and participate in cases despite clear ethical conflicts. They also risk violating federal law. Justices therefore cannot decide *never* to recuse themselves from cases because they would jeopardize the Court's reputation. To the extent that the Court's power depends on public confidence in the institution, justices have incentives to withdraw from cases when necessary to protect the Court's legitimacy.[1] The fact that Chief Justice Roberts devoted his 2011 *Year-End Report* to the subject of recusals is instructive, suggesting that the Court's recusal practices were damaging the Court's reputation.[2] On the other hand, if the justices recused themselves from cases whenever they plausibly could, they would limit their capacity to pursue their other institutional and policy goals.

How, then, do justices reconcile these various interests? As I discuss below, the answer depends on the context. In general, one might expect the justices to go along with the statutory guidelines and to recuse themselves from cases when conflicts of interest arise. Adhering to the recusal statute advances judicial impartiality and promotes the Court's legitimacy by signaling that the justices are concerned about the integrity of their decision-making processes. However, the justices relax conformance with the statute when recusals threaten their other institutional and policy goals or when the application of the statute is unclear. Because federal law does not require the justices to explain their recusal decisions, the justices have the flexibility to evade professional recusal norms from time to time without damaging the Court's reputation, as long as they do not make it a regular practice. Disregarding the recusal statute routinely would make the Court appear unprincipled and, in this way, could hurt its legitimacy.

A Theoretical Decision-Making Framework

Figure 3.1 presents a theoretical decision-making framework describing how justices are likely to approach the question of whether to disqualify themselves from cases, based on the review of existing law and scholarship that I presented in the previous chapter. Consistent with that review, when constructing the framework, I began with the assumption that recusal decisions are not simply the result of what the justices would like to do or what they think the law requires, but reflect a balance of competing motivations and constraints. Justices accommodate recusal procedures and norms in the pursuit of their other legal and policy goals.

This is not to say that there are not some justices, or indeed many, who sincerely wish to abide by ethical rules. Surely there are. Yet even these justices are likely to have other goals and responsibilities as well. As I discussed in the previous chapter, the justices are motivated by the duty to sit, which is itself a professional commitment that can be in tension with the justices' ethical obligations. The justices might also have policy goals that will be affected by their recusal activity. The task for the justices, then, is to maximize the attainment of their institutional and policy goals within the constraints of the statute, recognizing that strictly following the ethical rules will not always be in the best interests of the justices or the institution.

Figure 3.1 outlines the decision-making process in some detail. As a first step, the justices are likely to determine whether an alleged conflict

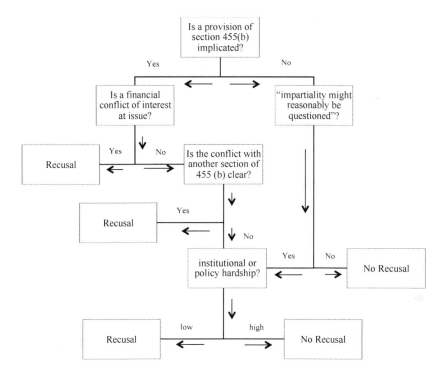

Figure 3.1. Recusal Decision Tree.

of interest is within the scope of one of the specific provisions of § 455 (b). Section 455 (a) is an unlikely starting place because it is less precisely defined, requiring the justices to recuse themselves when their "impartiality might reasonably be questioned." Because it is not immediately apparent whether a potential conflict of interest is within the scope of § 455 (a), the justices have stated that applying this provision of the statute requires them to inquire into whether "a reasonable observer who is informed of all the surrounding facts and circumstances" would call the justice's impartiality into question.[3] By contrast, the provisions of § 455 (b) are more detailed, describing specific conditions in which recusals are warranted. It is likely, then, that a justice would begin with the more clearly outlined categories in § 455 (b), looking to see whether an alleged conflict is covered by one of its provisions before proceeding to the more general inquiry under § 455 (a).

From there, it is likely to matter which provision of § 455 (b) is implicated because they will not all prompt equal concerns about the Court's legitimacy. Section 455 (b) (4), which requires disqualification when a justice "has a financial interest in the subject matter in controversy," is the most likely provision to generate a recusal because of how damaging perceptions of financial corruption can be to public confidence in the Court.[4] The previous chapter described how, since the early days of the republic, justices have disqualified themselves because of financial conflicts.[5] It remains the one area in which they most consistently err on the side of disqualification.[6] I therefore expect that if an ethical conflict arises under § 455 (b) (4), then a justice will be the most likely to withdraw from a case.

If a different provision of § 455 (b) is at issue, then disqualification is less likely to be automatic but will depend on whether a justice is in clear violation of the recusal statute. When a conflict with the statute is clear, a recusal is more likely to occur because of the potential damage to the Court's legitimacy.[7] For example, if a justice has worked on the same case as counsel at an earlier stage of litigation, it will be clear to all that if the justice participates, the justice will be in violation of § 455 (b) (2), which requires a recusal when a judge has "served as lawyer in the matter in controversy." The justice will almost certainly withdraw from the case to avoid damaging public confidence in the Court. Similarly, if a justice has expressed an opinion on the precise question before the Court, either as a lower court judge or in off-the-bench remarks, a recusal is likely to follow because § 455 (b) (3) requires judges to recuse themselves when they have "expressed an opinion concerning the merits of the particular case in controversy." To behave otherwise would put the justice in clear violation of the statute.

Many potential conflicts, however, are not this straightforward. If § 455 (b) is not clearly applicable, or if a justice is weighing a recusal decision under § 455 (a), then other institutional and policy considerations will come into play and may frequently prove decisive. The next step, then, is for a justice to assess the impact of a recusal on these other goals. When the institutional or policy hardships imposed by a recusal are likely to be small, a justice might choose to withdraw from a case to reinforce the impression that the Court is generally in compliance with the recusal statute. If, for example, a justice expects a dispute to be resolved unanimously, then the institutional costs of recusal will seem low. When an area of law is doctrinally less important to a justice, or if a justice does not expect a recusal to affect the outcome of the dispute, the justice also might err on the side of recusal.

The considerations will change, however, when a justice anticipates that the institutional or policy costs of a recusal are severe or even moderate. If, for example, a justice has reason to expect that a case will divide evenly because of a recusal, then the justice will have an incentive to participate. A justice will also be reluctant to withdraw from a case that is doctrinally important, or when a justice anticipates that participating in a dispute will change the case's disposition or the rule that the majority opinion establishes. A recusal might still occur anyway in these circumstances, depending on the controversy, but in the absence of a clear violation of the statute, the incentives to participate may carry more weight.

Some Examples

Consider, for example, how one might use the decision framework in Figure 3.1 to help explain several recent recusal decisions on the Supreme Court, beginning with Justice Kagan's participation in the health care dispute.[8] When questions arose about whether Kagan should disqualify herself, her first step would have been to determine precisely how the federal recusal statute applied. Because the controversy centered on whether she had worked on the case as the Solicitor General, the inquiry fell within the scope of § 455 (b). However, it was not § 455 (b) (4), which might have prompted an automatic disqualification if there was any reason to suspect that Kagan would benefit financially from the outcome of the case. Instead, it was § 455 (b) (3), which requires a recusal when a judge has previously worked on a case as government counsel. In the past, this same provision prompted Kagan to recuse herself from cases in which her participation as Solicitor General was clear, including several cases from that same term.[9]

Yet in the health care case, it was far from clear—at least to outsiders—what Kagan's previous role had been. Many commentators assumed that she had worked on the case because she was the Solicitor General when the legal defenses for the Affordable Care Act were first developed.[10] Email records from the period reinforced the impression that Kagan had played some role, even if it was only a peripheral one,[11] but the evidence was not conclusive, and at her confirmation hearings Kagan testified that her participation had not been direct.[12] Still, Kagan might have recused herself anyway if the policy stakes in the case had not been so high. At issue was not some routine dispute, but the central legislative accomplishment of the president who appointed her. Moreover, Kagan had strong reasons to suspect that the Court would divide evenly without her participation.[13] Without a clear violation of the recusal statute, and with the institutional and policy costs of recusal heightened, Kagan chose to participate.

In contrast, several years earlier, the recusal statute was clearly implicated when Justice Scalia decided to withdraw from *Elk Grove v. Newdow*.[14] The case centered on the question of whether the words "under God" in the Pledge of Allegiance violated the Establishment Clause, and in remarks delivered in January 2003 at a Religious Freedom Day rally sponsored by the Knights of Columbus, Scalia directly criticized the Ninth Circuit's decision, in effect previewing what his opinion on the merits would be. "The establishment clause was once well understood not to exclude God from the public forum and political life," he said.[15] Scalia therefore ran up against § 455 (b) (3), which requires a recusal when a justice has "expressed an opinion concerning the merits of the particular case in controversy."[16] Despite the importance of the *Newdow* case, and the potential for the Court to divide evenly without his participation, the clarity of the conflict with the recusal statute forced Scalia to withdraw.

Later that term, however, Scalia declined to recuse himself from *Cheney v. U.S. District Court*, even though he had gone duck hunting with Vice President Cheney shortly before the Court granted *certiorari* in the case.[17] Unlike in *Newdow*, no provision of § 455 (b) clearly applied.[18] Justices are not prohibited from maintaining friendships with parties who might one day appear before the Court. Scalia therefore evaluated the recusal motion under the general terms of § 455 (a), inquiring whether his "impartiality might reasonably be questioned," and found no violation. He also implied that there would be institutional costs to the Court if he bended to media pressure and disqualified himself anyway, writing that, "recusing in the face of such charges would give elements of the press a veto over participation of any Justices who had social contacts with, or were even known to be friends of, a named official. That is intolerable."[19] The lack of a clear violation of the recusal statute, together with the institutional costs of disqualification, led Scalia to deny the motion.

Empirical Implications

The preceding analysis presents a general framework describing how statutory, institutional, and policy incentives are likely to influence recusal behavior. The framework suggests a number of hypotheses for systematic quantitative analysis. However, there are obstacles to conducting such an inquiry. The major methodological challenge is that we do not have a full catalog of the occasions on which justices had cause to recuse themselves, nor do we know when justices have thought about recusing themselves but did not. Indeed, these data might be undiscoverable. We do have records of when litigants have filed recusal motions on the Supreme Court, but these motions are uncommon, so they do not provide a complete record of when recusals were possible.[20] We therefore cannot directly compare circumstances in which justices recused themselves with occasions when they merely considered doing so.

However, it is possible to examine the cases in which recusals have occurred to see if they exhibit characteristics that one would expect to observe if the justices were following the decision framework in Figure 3.1. For example, if the framework is correct, then recusals should be more common when justices have financial conflicts of interest or when the recusal statute is clearly applicable, and they should be less frequent when justices expect cases to divide evenly, or when they have policy incentives to participate. If we find that recusals occur when we expect them to, then we can be more confident that justices are behaving consistently with the theoretical framework, even if we do not know the full range of cases in which recusals were possible. I detail these empirical implications and propose specific hypotheses below.

A. Statutory Considerations

The first implication of Figure 3.1 is that recusals will be the most common when disputes affect the financial holdings of the justices. The framework indicates that justices err on the side of recusing themselves when they have financial conflict of interests, so logically one might expect to observe a disproportionately larger number of recusals in cases that involve financial matters. Specifically, one might hypothesize that recusals will occur more frequently when a business, corporation, or financial institution is a party before the Court. If there is a correlation between recusals and the presence of one of these organizations as the petitioner or respondent, it is hard to think of an explanation for the finding except that financial conflicts of interest are prompting the justices to recuse themselves, and that the justices are therefore following the recusal statute:

> H_1: *Justices are more likely to recuse themselves from cases when a business, corporation, or financial institution is listed as the petitioner or respondent.*

The justices should also be more likely to withdraw from cases when they own stock in one of the companies appearing before them, or when one of their other assets is affected by a dispute:

> H_2: *Justices are more likely to recuse themselves from cases when a company in which they have a direct financial interest is a named party in a dispute.*

For the past several decades, the justices have reported their stock holdings and other assets in their financial disclosure reports. If the justices were to participate in cases involving companies in which they had ownership stakes, they would be in clear violation of the recusal statute. Even when their financial interests are minimal, the mere appearance of impropriety should be enough to lead justices to recuse themselves from these cases more often than not.

A second implication of the framework in Figure 3.1 is that recusals will be more likely when conflicts with the federal recusal statute are clear. Many of the clearest conflicts occur when justices have "served as lawyer in the matter in controversy," "served in governmental employment and in such capacity served as counsel, adviser or material witness concerning the proceeding," or "expressed an opinion concerning the merits of the particular case in controversy." In other words, the statute is the most clearly applicable when justices have already participated in cases in some capacity. For example, Justice Kagan recused herself from dozens of cases in which she participated as Solicitor General, consistent with the practice of other former solicitors general who served on the Court. For many years after his appointment, Justice William O. Douglas recused himself from cases involving the Securities and Exchange Commission, for which he had served as Chairman;[21] and Chief Justice Earl Warren disqualified himself from cases that touched upon his service as Governor.[22]

In most circumstances, this behavior occurred before the justices were appointed to the Court. It is therefore reasonable to predict that recusals will occur more frequently at the beginning of a justice's term, when litigation is more likely to relate to pre-bench activities. As a justice's years of service increase, the likelihood that there will continue to be conflicts declines:

> H_3: *Justices are less likely to recuse themselves as their term in office increases.*

Relatedly, I expect that over time the relationship between years of service and recusals will become attenuated. An additional year of service will be less influential as the temporal distance from pre-bench conflicts becomes increasingly remote and the chances that the justices will decide cases that involve these activities becomes less likely:

H_4: *Over time, the relationship between years of service and recusals is likely to become attenuated.*

Two forms of previous work experience are particularly likely to prompt recusals and should be considered separately. First, as I noted above, several justices had been solicitors general before becoming justices.[23] Because the Solicitor General represents the federal government in the Supreme Court, one might expect former solicitors general to have participated in cases that come before the Court, prompting these justices to recuse themselves more frequently:

H_5: *Justices are more likely to recuse themselves from cases when they have previously served as the Solicitor General.*

Also more likely to recuse themselves are justices who have had federal appellate experience because they may have already served as judges in the proceedings below. For example, Chief Justice Roberts recused himself from *Hamdan v. Rumsfeld*, concerning the Bush administration's use of military commissions to try detainees as Guantanamo Bay, because he had served on the three-judge panel on the D.C. Circuit that reviewed the case:

H_6: *Justices are more likely to recuse themselves from cases when they have had federal appellate experience before becoming justices.*

Because the effects of these particular forms of service on recusal behavior are also likely to diminish over time, I hypothesize that there will be statistically significant interactions between years of service and a justice's prior work experience as a judge or the Solicitor General.

B. Institutional Considerations

The next implication of Figure 3.1 is that when the recusal statute does not clearly apply and the justices have discretion about whether to sit out, they will decline to recuse themselves if the institutional incentives to participate are strong or even moderate. As discussed above, the justices are motivated by a duty to sit that is grounded in their concern about how their absence from disputes will impair the capacity of the Court to decide cases and controversies. Participation promotes clarity in the law, which is a goal that the justices are known to pursue in other contexts, such as the agenda-setting stage[24] and the decision on the merits.[25] The justices have expressed particular concerns about dividing evenly,[26] so one might expect the justices to feel that their participation is the most needed when they think cases will be close.

That is to say, when cases are likely to be *divisive*, recusals should be less common. Even if a justice cannot predict the final vote on the merits with precision at the time of a recusal decision, the justice will probably still have a good sense of whether a case is likely to be close. For example, when a case presents a question that has divided the lower courts, a justice might expect the same question to be divisive on the Supreme Court:

> H_7: *Justices are less likely to recuse themselves from cases when the legal questions have generated conflicts in the lower courts.*

Conflicts among the lower courts indicate that multiple resolutions are possible, either because the law is unclear or the legal questions are ideologically divisive.[27] Either way, justices are likely to feel that their participation is necessary to bring clarity to the law, causing them to avoid recusing themselves in these circumstances. Similarly, when a judge below has dissented, the justices might feel that their participation is warranted:

> H_8: *Justices are less likely to recuse themselves from cases when one of the judges in the court below has dissented.*

Just as a conflict among the lower courts is an indicator of a case's divisiveness, so too is the presence of a dissent.[28] As Edelman et al. explain, "the presence of a dissent in a lower court decision is a strong indication that reasonable people could disagree about the right answer in a case and might tend to diverge along ideological lines."[29] Justices might predict that they will be less likely to achieve consensus in these cases, encouraging them to participate.

Even when justices do not expect cases to be close, they might still feel a responsibility to resolve controversies in important areas of law. For example, when cases are salient, recusals might be less common because salient cases are more likely to present important questions of federal law that the justices wish to clarify. The justices might also anticipate having difficulty achieving consensus in salient cases. Corley et al. observe that "cases with a high degree of salience to external political actors and the public are salient to the justices as well and therefore more likely to expose divisions among them."[30] If salient cases are more divisive, then justices might perceive a greater possibility of dividing evenly if they were to sit out:

H_9: *Justices are less likely to recuse themselves from salient cases.*

In contrast, I expect recusals to be more likely to occur in statutory cases. In matters of constitutional interpretation, the justices are the final authorities, and this heightened institutional responsibility is likely to create incentives for justices to participate in order to clarify important questions of law. However, statutory cases are open to revision by Congress, so the stakes are likely to be lowered somewhat.[31] Corley et al. have also suggested that statutory cases are less divisive than constitutional cases: "The language of statutes is generally more detailed and less ambiguous than the language of the Constitution, which makes it easier for judges to determine legislative intent and plain meaning when interpreting them."[32] Altogether, these considerations suggest that justices will have fewer incentives to participate in statutory cases:

H_{10}: *Justices are more likely to recuse themselves from statutory cases.*

C. Policy Considerations

A final implication of Figure 3.1 is that justices will be less likely to recuse themselves from cases when their participation advances their policy goals. Specifically, I expect the justices' incentives to recuse themselves to vary depending on their distance from the Court's median justice. Much literature has focused on the question of which justice plays the most pivotal role in determining the Court's policy output. Some research has focused on the Court's median because that justice determines the disposition of case outcomes,[33] while other research has focused on the role of the median member of the signing coalition in determining the content of majority opinions.[34] Still other research has suggested that the median justice varies depending on the issue area[35] and that the pivotal "swing" justice in a case is not necessarily the Court's median.[36]

When it comes to understanding the justices' recusal practices, I focus on the Court's median because justices are less likely to know the identity of other pivotal justices at the time when they are making recusal decisions. In general, justices decide whether to recuse themselves from cases before the oral arguments have occurred. At that time, the best heuristic that justices can use to determine whether their policy goals will be threatened by recusals is the identity of the Court's median.[37] Specifically, I expect that justices who are close to the Court's median will be less likely to recuse themselves from cases. These justices, by virtue of their proximity to the median, will see their votes as pivotal to the disposition, particularly if the median justice does not vote as expected. Research by Enns and Wohlfarth suggests that the swing justice on the Court is not necessarily always the median,[38] so it would be reasonable for justices who are close to the Court's median to anticipate that their votes could be decisive:

H_{11}: *Justices are less likely to recuse themselves from cases when they are close to the Court's median.*

I also anticipate, for different reasons, that justices who are far from the Court's median will have incentives to participate, and that they will therefore be less likely to recuse themselves from cases. Justices who are far from the Court's median will not expect their preferences to be reflected in the proceedings otherwise. By participating, justices at the ideological extremes of the Court will shift coalition medians toward them, and, if they are in the majority, affect the scope of the majority opinions the Court produces:[39]

H_{12}: *Justices are less likely to recuse themselves from cases when they are far from the Court's median.*

It is the justices in between these two extremes, neither close to the Court's median nor at the ideological poles, who will withdraw at the baseline rate. These justices are not close enough to the Court's median to expect case dispositions to turn on their judgments; they might even lie outside the minimum coalitions necessary for obtaining specific outcomes. Yet neither are they far enough away to feel like outliers whose views will be unrepresented unless they participate.

Finally, I expect that the likelihood of a recusal will vary based on the justices' attitudes toward the lower court's decision. The more strongly that a justice disagrees with the holding of the lower court, the less likely it is that a justice will withdraw from the dispute:

H_{13}: *Justices will be less likely to withdraw from cases the more strongly they disagree with the lower court's decision.*

Justices who disapprove of the decision below on ideological grounds will have strong incentives to participate in order to review, and potentially reverse, the judgment. A recusal might seem especially costly because, were the Court to divide evenly, the lower court's opinion would be automatically affirmed, preserving the policy outcome the justices oppose.

Research Design

To test my hypotheses, I relied on an enhanced version of the Supreme Court Database.[40] Originally developed by Harold Spaeth, the database is a comprehensive archive of Supreme Court decisions dating from 1946 to 2010 that contains information on a broad range of case attributes, including the justices' voting behavior. The database can also be augmented with additional measures, such as the data on recusal behavior that is the focus of this study. Because my unit of analysis is the justice, I used the justice-centered data, which include separate entries for every justice who participated in each case.[41]

The dependent variable is a dichotomous variable measuring whether a justice sat out of a dispute. It is based on the Vote variable in the Supreme Court Database, which records how a justice voted on the merits. When the value of Vote is listed as missing ("."), it indicates that a justice was on the bench but did not participate. An examination of these cases in Lexis confirms the accuracy of the coding. For example, in *Howsam v. Reynolds*, the Vote entry for Justice O'Connor is listed as missing in the Supreme Court Database, and the headnotes in Lexis indicate that "O'CONNOR, J., took no part in the consideration or decision of the case." Later that same term, in *PacifiCare Health Systems v. Book*, Justice Thomas's Vote is missing, and the Lexis headnotes confirm that he "took no part in the consideration or decision of the case." I coded the dependent variable "1" when a justice did not participate and "0" otherwise. The mean value of the recusal variable is 0.0208, which means that justices on average sit out of about 2.1% of cases.

Because I am only interested in recording circumstances in which justices voluntarily recused themselves from cases, it was necessary to isolate entries in which justices withdrew because of illness or because they were appointed after the oral arguments occurred. Votes in these cases are also recorded as "." in the Supreme Court Database but needed to be recoded to "0." To identify these cases, I followed procedures developed by Black and Epstein,[42] recoding cases to "0" when the date of a justice's appointment came after the oral argument.[43] Cases were also recoded to "0" when justices withdrew from at least four cases on consecutive dates of oral argument because this behavior is consistent with illness.[44]

The first set of independent variables test hypotheses relating to statutory motivations for recusals. The BUSINESS PETITIONER/RESPONDENT variable is coded "1" when the petitioner *or* the respondent is a business, corporation, or financial institution; "2" when *both* the petitioner and the respondent are financial institutions; and "0" when neither is. I expect the BUSINESS PETITIONER/RESPONDENT variable to be positively correlated with the dependent variable. It is based on the PETITIONER and RESPONDENT variables in the Supreme Court Database, which classify petitioners and respondents by type.[45] Measuring the specific financial holdings of the justices was limited by the fact that justices have been filing financial disclosure reports for only a portion of the study period. Instead of truncating the data, the examination of the justices' financial holdings is featured in a separate analysis later in the chapter.

The YEARS OF SERVICE variable is a count of the number of years that a justice served on the Court at the time of his or her vote. I expect YEARS OF SERVICE to be negatively correlated with recusals. I also included a squared version of this variable (YEARS OF SERVICE)^2 to test the hypothesis that the effects of years of service become attenuated over time. The SOLICITOR GENERAL variable is a dummy variable recording whether a justice previously served as the Solicitor General.[46] The FEDERAL APPELLATE EXPERIENCE variable records whether a justice served on the U.S. Courts of Appeals.[47] I expect both variables to be positively associated with recusals. I also included two interaction terms in order to assess whether time diminishes the influence of a justice's experience as the Solicitor General (YEARS OF SERVICE* SOLICITOR GENERAL) or a federal judge (YEARS OF SERVICE* FEDERAL APPELLATE EXPERIENCE).

The second set of variables focuses on institutional reasons for recusals. CONFLICT is a dummy variable based on the certReason variable in the Supreme Court Database, assigned a value of 1 when the justices have reported division or uncertainty in the courts below.[48] DISSENT BELOW is the lcDisagreement variable from the same database, coded 1 when there is mention in the majority opinion of a dissent in the court below. I expect

Table 3.1. Summary of Variables

Variable	Coding	Direction
Dependent Variable		
RECUSAL	1 = a justice voluntarily withdraws from a dispute (excluding illness and appointment effects)	
	0 = a justice does NOT withdraw voluntarily	
Statutory Considerations		
BUSINESS PETITIONER/ RESPONDENT	2 = BOTH the petitioner and the respondent are a business, corporation, or financial institution	
	1 = EITHER the petitioner or the respondent is a business, corporation, or financial institution	+
	0 = NEITHER the petitioner or the respondent is a business, corporation, or financial institution	
YEARS OF SERVICE	a continuous variable measuring the number of years that a justice has served	−
SOLICITOR GENERAL	1 = a justice previously served as Solicitor General	
	0 = a justice has NOT served as Solicitor General	+
FEDERAL APPELLATE EXPERIENCE	1 = a justice has served on the U.S. Courts of Appeals	
	0 = a justice has NOT served on the Courts of Appeals	+
Institutional Considerations		
CONFLICT	1 = the justices report a division or uncertainty in the courts below	
	0 = the justices do NOT report division or uncertainty	−
DISSENT BELOW	1 = the justices mention a dissent in the courts below	
	0 = the justices do NOT mention a dissent	−

continued on next page

Table 3.1. Continued

Variable	Coding	Direction
CASE SALIENCE	1 = a case is featured on the front page of the *New York Times*	−
	0 = a case is NOT on the front page of the *New York Times*	
STATUTORY	1 = a case involves statutory interpretation	+
	0 = a case does not involve statutory interpretation	
Policy Considerations		
IDEOLOGICAL DISTANCE FROM COURT MEDIAN	a continuous variable measuring the absolute value of the difference between the ideology score of a justice and the median justice for the Court that term (using the Martin-Quinn scores)	variable
IDEOLOGICAL DISTANCE FROM LOWER COURT	a continuous variable measuring the strength of a justice's agreement with the lower court decision	+

both variables to be negatively associated with recusals. CASE SALIENCE is based on Epstein and Segal's measure of whether a case was featured on the front page of the *New York Times*.[49] I expect it also to be negatively associated with recusals.[50] The STATUTORY variable is a dummy variable adapted from the LAWTYPE variable in the Supreme Court Database, coded 1 when a case involves a matter of statutory interpretation, with the expectation that it will be positively associated with recusals.[51]

The final group of variables focuses on policy-oriented motivations for recusals. The IDEOLOGICAL DISTANCE FROM COURT MEDIAN variable is based on measures developed by Martin and Quinn and represents the absolute value of the difference between the ideology scores of a justice and the median justice for the Court that term.[52] Because I expect the effects of ideological distance to change as the distance from the median increases, I modeled it as a third-order polynomial, which best fits the data. These effects are captured by the inclusion of two additional variables, (IDEOLOGICAL DISTANCE)^2 and (IDEOLOGICAL DISTANCE).^{3} I generated the IDEOLOGICAL DISTANCE FROM LOWER COURT variable by multiplying each justice's Martin-

Quinn score and the ideological direction of the lower court's decision.[53] Positive values indicate agreement with the decision, while negative values signal disagreement.

Results

The results of the analysis are presented in Table 3.2 in three columns. Because the dependent variable is dichotomous, I used logistic regression.[54] Model A presents the key explanatory variables, while Model B introduces the interaction terms and Model C is robust to the introduction of justice dummy variables, the coefficients for which are not reported. With a few exceptions, the results are consistent with expectations. Looking first at the statutory variables, the results indicate that justices are more likely to recuse

Table 3.2. Logit Model of Recusals, 1946–2010

	Model A	Model B	Model C
Statutory Considerations			
BUSINESS PETITIONER/RESPONDENT	0.402***	0.406***	0.418***
	(0.052)	(0.052)	(0.053)
YEARS OF SERVICE	−0.184***	−0.173***	−0.155***
	(0.012)	(0.013)	(0.017)
(YEARS OF SERVICE)²	0.005***	0.005***	0.005***
	(0.000)	(0.000)	(0.001)
SOLICITOR GENERAL	1.216***	2.084***	−0.721
	(0.084)	(0.144)	(0.538)
(YEARS OF SERVICE)*			
(SOLICITOR GENERAL)	—	−0.126***	−0.103***
	—	(0.020)	(0.022)
FEDERAL APPELLATE EXPERIENCE	−0.166*	−0.519***	0.855
	(0.075)	(0.105)	(0.643)
(YEARS OF SERVICE)*			
(FEDERAL APPELLATE EXPERIENCE)	—	0.044***	0.006
	—	(0.010)	(0.014)

continued on next page

Institutional Considerations			
CONFLICT	−0.663***	−0.657***	−0.659***
	(0.108)	(0.108)	(0.108)
DISSENT BELOW	−0.112	−0.103	−0.100
	(0.086)	(0.086)	(0.087)
CASE SALIENCE	0.140	0.141	0.145
	(0.097)	(0.098)	(0.099)
STATUTORY	0.420***	0.434***	0.440***
	(0.070)	(0.070)	(0.071)
Policy Considerations			
IDEOLOGICAL DISTANCE FROM COURT MEDIAN	−0.692***	−0.696***	−0.599***
	(0.115)	(0.112)	(0.122)
(IDEOLOGICAL DISTANCE)^2	0.197***	0.209***	0.213***
	(0.045)	(0.044)	(0.051)
(IDEOLOGICAL DISTANCE)^3	−0.015**	−0.016***	−0.018***
	(0.005)	(0.004)	(0.005)
IDEOLOGICAL DISTANCE FROM LOWER COURT	0.009	0.022	0.027
	(0.015)	(0.015)	(0.016)
Chief Justice			
VINSON	−0.124	−0.041	0.796**
	(0.124)	(0.124)	(0.279)
WARREN	0.193*	0.197*	0.289
	(0.081)	(0.082)	(0.158)
REHNQUIST	−0.707***	−0.619***	−0.404
	(0.097)	(0.128)	(0.219)
ROBERTS	−0.631**	−0.979***	−0.610
	(0.212)	(0.231)	(0.479)
Constant	−3.135***	−3.174***	−2.709***
	(0.112)	(0.118)	(0.136)
Chi-square	784.660***	1036.210***	1261.770***
Pseudo R^2	0.083	0.089	0.110

*p < 0.05; **p < 0.01; ***p < 0.001   N = 73,811

Note: Model A includes all variables except the interaction terms; Model B introduces the interaction terms; and Model C includes dummy variables for each justice (the coefficients for which are not reported).

themselves from cases when a business, corporation, or financial institution is the petitioner, respondent, or both (BUSINESS PETITIONER/RESPONDENT). The effects of this variable are presented in Figure 3.2, which reports the probability of a recusal for selected values of the statutory variables.[55] When a business interest is not before the Court (BUSINESS PETITIONER/RESPONDENT = 0), the likelihood of a recusal is about 1.2%, but when at least one business interest is represented as either the petitioner or the respondent (BUSINESS PETITIONER/RESPONDENT = 1), the likelihood increases to 1.9%. When both the petitioner and the respondent represent business interests (BUSINESS PETITIONER/RESPONDENT = 2), the likelihood of a recusal is about 2.8%, a total difference of about 1.6 percentage points. The effect is substantively small, but it should be remembered that the baseline probability of a recusal is low to begin with, at about 2.1%.

Larger substantive effects are generated by the number of years that a justice has served on the bench (YEARS OF SERVICE). Figure 3.2 on page 56 illustrates that when justices are first appointed, they recuse themselves from about 12.8% of cases, but by their tenth year they disqualify themselves from just 3.8% of cases. By twenty years, the recusal rate falls to 0.8%. Substantively, this finding makes sense because many of the clearest conflicts of interest derive from pre-bench activities. As time increases, and these activities become more remote, there is less of a chance that they will have an impact on the justices' current caseload. Table 3.2 also affirms that the effects of years of service become attenuated with time, as indicated by the fact that the (YEARS OF SERVICE)^2 variable is statistically significant and signed opposite from the YEARS OF SERVICE variable.[56] This finding is consistent with expectations because one would not expect the difference between the first and second years of service to be the same as the difference between the tenth and eleventh years. Indeed, Figure 3.2 illustrates this trend. Between zero and five years of service, the likelihood of a recusal drops by 5.6 percentage points, but between ten and fifteen years of service, the likelihood falls by just 1.9 percentage points.

Table 3.2 also reports that justices who have served as the SOLICITOR GENERAL are more likely to recuse themselves from cases and that the interaction between the SOLICITOR GENERAL and the YEARS OF SERVICE variables is also significant. Substantively, this finding suggests that the importance of having served as the Solicitor General decreases as the amount of time since the experience becomes remote. Figure 3.2 shows that in the first year of service, a former Solicitor General is 8.8 percentage points more likely to withdraw from cases, but by the tenth year the likelihood changes by just 1.3

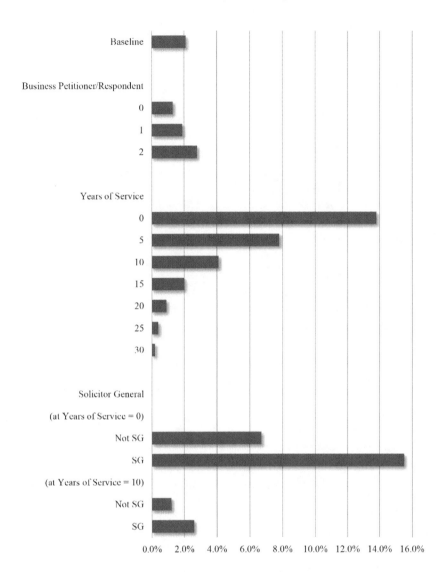

Figure 3.2. Probability of a Recusal, Statutory Considerations.

percentage points. These results should be interpreted with caution, however, because they are not robust to the introduction of the justice dummy variables.

Contrary to expectations, FEDERAL APPELLATE EXPERIENCE does not increase the likelihood that justices will withdraw from cases. Columns A and B of Table 3.2 suggest that there is a statistically significant relationship, but in the opposite direction as hypothesized. That is to say, justices with prior experience as federal appellate judges are *less* likely to recuse themselves from cases. The reason for this result is not immediately clear. It is possible that prior judicial experience familiarizes justices with federal recusal requirements, leading them to behave in ways that minimize the possibility of conflicts of interest. For example, former judges might know how to structure their financial affairs to avoid having direct ownership stakes in financial organizations that litigate frequently in the federal courts. These possibilities can be explored in future research. It must be noted, however, that the coefficient for FEDERAL APPELLATE EXPERIENCE is not robust to the introduction of justice dummies.

Turning to institutional considerations, two of the variables in Table 3.2 do not attain statistical significance (CASE SALIENCE and DISSENT BELOW). However, two other variables (CONFLICT and STATUTORY) do perform as hypothesized and are robust to the introduction of the justice dummies. Their effects on the probability of a recusal are reported in Figure 3.3. The data show that when there is a CONFLICT reported in the courts below, justices are less likely to disqualify themselves from cases, decreasing the rate of recusal from about 1.6% to 0.8%. Substantively, this finding suggests that justices avoid withdrawing from cases that they expect to be divisive.

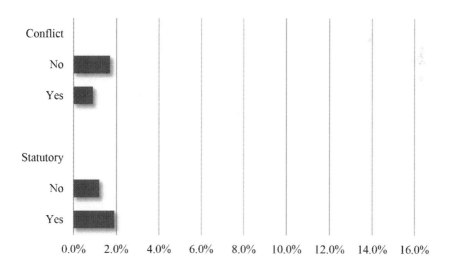

Figure 3.3. Probability of a Recusal, Institutional Considerations.

Figure 3.3 also indicates that there is a significant association between recusals and STATUTORY cases. When cases involve statutory interpretation, the likelihood of a recusal increases from 1.2% to 1.8%. The most likely explanation for this finding is that justices feel that their participation is less necessary because, unlike constitutional cases, statutory decisions are open to revision by Congress. The justices might also have an easier time achieving consensus in statutory cases, for reasons discussed above, easing concerns about dividing evenly.[57]

Looking next at policy-based explanations for recusal practices, Table 3.2 finds support for the influence of ideology on the justices' behavior. While I found no relationship between recusals and the strength of a justice's disagreement with the court below (IDEOLOGICAL DISTANCE FROM LOWER COURT),[58] the IDEOLOGICAL DISTANCE FROM COURT MEDIAN variable is statistically significant, as are the squared (IDEOLOGICAL DISTANCE)^2 and cubed terms (IDEOLOGICAL DISTANCE).^{3} The effects of these variables are illustrated in Figure 3.4.[59] Because the MEDIAN IDEOLOGICAL DISTANCE variable was modeled as a third-order polynomial, the graphical representation

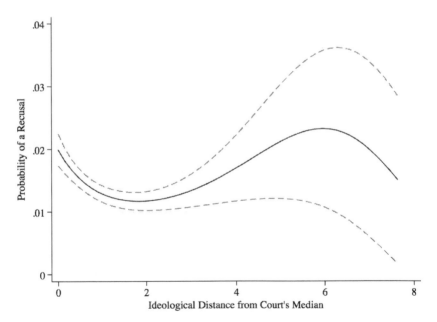

Note: Dashed lines represent the 95% confidence interval. The baseline likelihood of a recusal is 0.0208.

Figure 3.4. Probability of a Recusal, Policy Considerations.

of the marginal effects is curvilinear and changes directions twice. Initially, the likelihood of a recusal decreases as a justice's ideological distance moves away from the Court's median. This trend is consistent with my expectation that justices who are close to the Court's median will be less likely to recuse themselves from cases because their proximity to the median enhances their sense of influence over the case disposition. Justices near the center of the Court might anticipate that they could serve as the swing vote if the median justice does not vote as expected, which would give them control over the disposition. Alternatively, justices who are close to the median might expect to serve as part of a minimum winning coalition, increasing their incentives to participate.

As the ideological distance increases further, the effect of ideology changes and the probability of a recusal increases, leveling out near the baseline probability of about 2.1%. This trend is also consistent with expectations because justices who are neither close to the Court's median nor far from it lack special incentives to participate, instead disqualifying themselves at the baseline rate. Finally, as the ideological distance from the Court's median increases to its furthest point, the likelihood of a recusal drops again, falling below the baseline. These justices, at the ideological extremes of the Court, are likely to feel that their participation is needed for their attitudes to be represented. Interestingly, an implication of Figure 3.4 is that median justices recuse themselves from cases more frequently than other justices near the center of the Court. This finding is counterintuitive but might reflect the fact that other justices simply have greater incentives to participate than median justices, who withdraw at the baseline rate.

Finally, Figure 3.5 on page 60 examines how recusal rates have varied based on the chief justice. It shows, surprisingly, that recusals have become less frequent over time, with the rate of recusal lower on the Rehnquist and Roberts Courts than under Warren and Vinson.[60] One might have expected recusals to have become more common, not less, after Congress amended the federal recusal guidelines in 1974, especially because a key purpose of the amendments was to encourage recusals by removing the presumption of the "duty to sit." The explanation for this finding is not immediately clear. It is possible that the federal recusal statute has had a formative impact on the justices, giving them a better understanding of how to organize their affairs in order to avoid conflicts of interest. However, it is also possible that justices simply prioritize different goals over conformance with the recusal statute. We know, for example, that Justice Rehnquist supported the duty to sit doctrine, as indicated by his opinion in *Laird v. Tatum*.[61]

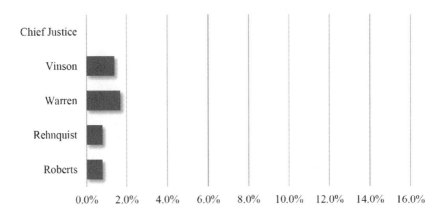

Figure 3.5. Probability of a Recusal, by Chief Justice.

Quite possibly, after he became Chief Justice, Rehnquist took measures to discourage recusals in spite of the statute, and these trends have persisted on the Roberts Court. Whatever the explanation, justices today are less likely to withdraw from cases than they once were.

Financial Conflicts of Interest: Further Investigations

The results above indicate that Supreme Court justices pursue a variety of statutory, institutional, and policy-based motivations when deciding whether to withdraw from disputes. The evidence from Table 3.2 provides initial confirmation that the justices adhere to the statutory guidelines with respect to financial conflicts of interest, showing that the justices are more likely to withdraw from cases when business interests appear before the Court. However, the data establish at best only an indirect link between the justices' financial holdings and recusal behavior. Given the primacy of financial conflicts in the recusal statute and in the justices' own discourse about their behavior, further investigation of the relationship is warranted.

The financial disclosure reports are imperfect records of the justices' holdings because they cover a limited number of years, with records unavailable before 1980. They also underreport the extent of the justices' financial interests. The reports typically do not mention subsidiary companies, for example, even when these companies are appearing before the Court. In

2008, Justice Alito was criticized for declining to recuse himself from a case concerning ABC Inc. despite owning stock in ABC's parent, Walt Disney Co.[62] Alito's financial disclosure report listed only the Disney stock. These limitations can make the reports somewhat unreliable for assessing whether justices are recusing themselves from cases when they should be.

Nevertheless, the reports offer at least two kinds of information about the justices that can be used to evaluate their recusal practices. To begin with, the reports provide data on the justices' net worth. Figure 3.6 on page 62 details the median net worth of all Supreme Court justices serving from 1980 to 2010, with the figures converted to 2010 dollars. The data show that the financial holdings of the justices are highly variable. The wealthiest justice, Ruth Bader Ginsburg, had a net worth of about $20 million, while Justice Thurgood Marshall's net worth was frequently quoted as $0, with a median of about $36,500 for the period. Overall, the median net worth for all justices was $1.5 million. It is possible that justices who have a higher net worth are more likely to withdraw from cases because they are more likely to have broad portfolios of investments with the potential to present conflicts of interest.

To test this hypothesis, Table 3.3 on page 63 estimates a logit model using only data from after 1980, when the financial disclosure reports became available. The model includes a new variable, NET WORTH, which measures each justice's annual net worth in millions, as reported in their financial disclosure reports. To keep the data comparable, the figures were converted to 2010 dollars. The model also includes all of the variables that were statistically significant in Table 3.2, with coefficients robust to the introduction of justice dummies. The results indicate that, contrary to expectations, there is no relationship between the NET WORTH of the justices and their recusal practices, although the other explanatory variables do continue to perform as expected in the post-1980 model. The effect of business interests litigating before the Court remains significant (BUSINESS PETITIONER/RESPONDENT), as do the effects of years of service (YEARS OF SERVICE, YEARS OF SERVICE),[2] ideology (IDEOLOGICAL DISTANCE FROM COURT MEDIAN, IDEOLOGICAL DISTANCE,[2] IDEOLOGICAL DISTANCE[3]), and the presence of a conflict in the lower federal courts (CONFLICT). The effects of the STATUTORY variable diminish somewhat in the new model, but on the whole, the results in Table 3.3 affirm once again that the decision to withdraw from a case reflects a combination of statutory, policy, and institutional incentives.

Although the justices' recusal activity is not correlated with their net worth, there still could be a connection to the justices' assets, which

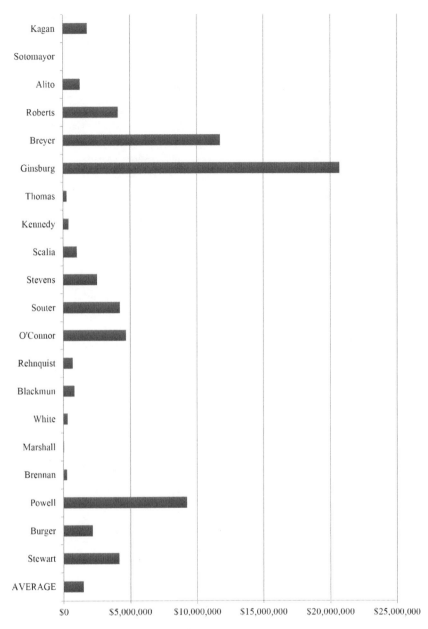

Note: Net worth is reported in 2010 dollars.

Figure 3.6. Median Net Worth of Supreme Court Justices, 1980–2010.

Table 3.3. Logit Model of Recusals, 1980–2010, with the Justices' Net Worth

Statutory Considerations

BUSINESS PETITIONER/RESPONDENT	0.562***
	(0.097)
NET WORTH	−0.102
	(0.065)
YEARS OF SERVICE	−0.144***
	(0.039)
(YEARS OF SERVICE)^2	0.003*
	(0.001)

Institutional Considerations

CONFLICT	−0.788***
	(0.174)
STATUTORY	0.294*
	(0.139)

Policy Considerations

IDEOLOGICAL DISTANCE FROM COURT MEDIAN	−1.247**
	(0.395)
(IDEOLOGICAL DISTANCE)^2	0.547**
	(0.200)
(IDEOLOGICAL DISTANCE)^3	−0.062*
	(0.027)
Constant	−1.416**
	(0.641)
Chi-square	453.360***
Pseudo R^2	0.129

$^*p < 0.05$; $^{**}p < 0.01$; $^{***}p < 0.001$ N = 31,918

Note: Results are robust to the inclusion of justice dummy variables (the coefficients for which are not reported).

are also listed in the reports. Specifically, one might expect justices to be more likely to withdraw from cases when they have a financial stake in a company that is appearing before them. To conduct this second analysis, I compiled a list of every asset that the justices reported in their financial disclosure reports during a ten-year period, 2004 to 2014. The same assets could be listed multiple times if they were owned by different justices or if the same justices owned them in multiple years. In total, there were 2,302 assets reported for the ten justices included in the sample over the ten-year period.[63] The justice who had the greatest number of holdings was Breyer, with 673 for the decade, followed by Roberts (509) and Alito (337). I then conducted a search of all Supreme Court cases from the period to see if any of the listed companies appeared as named parties.

It turns out that it was very uncommon for a listed company to appear before the Court, at least at the merits stage.[64] Table 3.4 reports that only nine cases from 2004 to 2014 met the criteria. Probably this finding is no accident because the justices are known to divest themselves of stock when they expect companies to appear before them.[65] The small number of cases makes it infeasible to conduct a systematic quantitative analysis of the justices' behavior, so I used a qualitative approach to identify whether the affected justices withdrew from the disputes. The findings are reported in Table 3.4. At first glance, the results would appear to suggest that the justices are not following the recusal guidelines because they participated in more than half of the listed cases. In five of the nine cases in Table 3.4, the justices declined to recuse themselves from disputes even though one of the named parties was on their financial disclosure reports.

A closer examination of the justices' assets, however, mediates these concerns. In both of the cases in which Chief Justice Roberts participated, the listed assets were mutual funds.[66] The Wachovia assets owned by Justice Stevens included bank accounts and a mutual fund. Justice Kennedy owned a life insurance policy though Metropolitan Life. It is not clear that recusals were warranted in these circumstances. To begin with, the performance of a mutual fund generally depends on the success of the securities held in the fund, not the owners of the fund itself. Were Chief Justice Roberts to rule in favor of Janus Capital Group, it is not clear that the securities held in his Janus Fund would do any better because those companies were not before the Court.[67] Moreover, it does not appear that the federal recusal statute even applies in these situations. Section 455(d)(4)(i) states, "Ownership in a mutual or common investment fund that holds securities is not a 'financial interest' in such securities unless the judge participates in the

Table 3.4. Listed Assets Appearing as Named Parties, 2004–2014

Case	Listed Asset	Justice	Recusal?
BP American Production Co. v. Burton (2006)	BP	Breyer	Yes
Exxon Shipping Co. v. Baker (2008)	Exxon Mobil	Alito	Yes
Gabelli v. SEC (2013)	Gabelli EI Fund	Roberts	No
Janus Cap. Grp. v. First Derivative Traders (2011)	Janus Fund	Roberts	No
Metropolitan Life Insurance Co v. Glenn (2008)	Metropolitan Life	Kennedy	No
Microsoft Corp. v. AT&T Corp. (2007)	Microsoft	Roberts	Yes
Microsoft Corp. v. I4I Limited Partnership (2011)	Microsoft	Roberts	Yes
Wachovia Bank v. Schmidt (2006)	Wachovia	Stevens	No
Waters v. Wachovia Bank (2007)	Wachovia	Stevens	No

management of the fund." In none of the cases listed in Table 3.4 did any of
the justices participate in the management of the funds, so there would have
been no grounds for a recusal, at least as far as the statute was concerned.
Therefore, in all five cases in which the justices participated, their behavior
was consistent with the requirements of the recusal statute.

It is true that Justice Alito ran into some trouble during his Supreme
Court confirmation hearings for having participated in cases involving Vanguard, but the problem may have been of his own making. In 1990, when
he was being confirmed for a seat on the U.S. Court of Appeals for the
Third Circuit, Alito had pledged to withdraw from Vanguard cases because
he had invested in Vanguard mutual funds. Although the recusal statute
did not require this pledge, the fact that he made it created problems for
Alito when, in 2002, he participated in a case involving Vanguard and ruled
in the company's favor. During his confirmation hearings to the Supreme
Court, Alito was criticized for the ethical lapse, but the concerns do not
appear to have been based on his mutual fund investments per se but the
fact that he had broken his word. "You made a pledge to the Senate, and
effectively to the American people," said Senator Ted Kennedy, "that you
were going to recuse yourself."[68] In his defense, Alito stated in a letter to
Senate Judiciary Committee Chairman Arlen Specter that his 1990 pledge
had probably been ill-advised. "My intention was to state that I would
never knowingly hear a case where a conflict of interest existed," he wrote.
"As my service continued, I realized that I had been unduly restrictive."[69]

Although Table 3.4 reports that the justices have not withdrawn from
cases because of their mutual fund holdings, it does show that justices recused
themselves from all four of the cases in which they directly owned stock in
the listed companies. Justice Breyer withdrew from one case involving BP;[70]
Justice Alito recused himself from a case involving Exxon Mobil;[71] and Chief
Justice Roberts sat out of two disputes in which his Microsoft stock was
implicated.[72] In these cases, the justices had direct ownership stakes in the
companies before them, and the value of those interests might have changed
depending on how they ruled. Even if the justices stood to gain very little,
they would have clearly violated the recusal statute if they had participated.

It would appear, then, that the justices do adhere to the letter of the
recusal statute with regard to their financial interests. The justices do not
withdraw from cases because of their investments in mutual funds, savings
accounts, or life insurance policies, but they do recuse themselves when
they own stock in the companies appearing before them. The distinction
is defensible and grounded in the plain language of the recusal statute,

but it also suggests that the justices do not go further than what the law requires. Unless the justices have direct ownership in a company, the duty to sit prevails and the justices participate.

Conclusion

Altogether, the results of the quantitative analysis are consistent with the theoretical decision framework presented in Figure 3.1. The trends in the data suggest that justices do follow the statutory guidelines for recusals set out in 28 U.S.C. § 455, particularly when the recusal statute is clearly implicated. Justices are more likely to disqualify themselves from cases when businesses, corporations, and financial institutions are before the Court, which is what one would expect to observe if the justices were recusing themselves regularly because of financial conflicts of interest. The justices are also more likely to withdraw from cases in their initial years of service, when their pre-bench activities are more likely to relate to their work as justices. These findings provide evidence that the justices are generally compliant with federal recusal guidelines, at least when the guidelines most clearly apply. On the occasions when one would expect justices to have the most conflicts, we find a greater number of recusals.

However, the analysis has also found, consistent with the theoretical framework, that institutional and policy motivations influence recusal behavior. The results indicate that the justices take the "duty to sit" seriously and are less likely to withdraw from divisive cases, particularly cases that present questions that have generated disagreements in the lower federal courts. Participating in these cases enables the justices to fulfill their institutional responsibility to resolve disputes and bring clarity to federal law. Yet the behavior is also in tension with the objectives of the recusal statute. By its terms, 28 U.S.C. § 455 indicates that recusal decisions should be influenced only by a justice's sincere evaluation of whether the justice is biased or likely to appear biased by participating in a dispute. Because the justices participate disproportionately in conflict cases, the implication is that the justices are not strictly following the statutory criteria and may be participating in some cases despite their biases.

Normatively, it is not necessarily problematic if the justices avoid recusing themselves for institutional reasons. Participating in divisive cases serves the public by resolving important questions of law. However, the finding that recusal behavior is also correlated with the justices' policy preferences may be more troubling. The results indicate that justices who are close to the Court's median are less likely to recuse themselves from cases, most likely because they know that case dispositions, which are typically set by the median justice, could turn on their participation. Justices who are very far from the Court's median are also less likely to disqualify themselves because these justices are more likely to feel that their views about cases will not be represented unless they participate. These findings are consistent with the predictions of the theoretical framework and previous research on judicial behavior, but they are in tension with the statutory requirements as well as norms of judicial ethics. While some might argue that it is permissible for justices to deemphasize ethical guidelines in favor of other institutional responsibilities, fewer would say that justices should participate in cases simply to achieve their policy goals. Indeed, the findings lend support to critics who maintain that the recusal process requires more transparency and accountability.[73] I detail these arguments in the final chapter. Before considering the proposals for reforming the recusal process, however, in the next two chapters I examine the consequences of the justices' recusal behavior for law and policy.

4

The Impact of Recusals on
Supreme Court Policy Making

The previous chapter demonstrated that the justices do not attend exclusively to statutory and ethical criteria when making recusal decisions. However, the consequences of this behavior for law and policy are not immediately clear. One can make the case that it is inherently important to know whether judges are behaving ethically because a foundational principle of the American legal system is its commitment to impartial justice.[1] The fact that the justices sometimes waver from this principle might be enough to support proposals for reform, as I discuss in the final chapter. Yet many of the justices' critics suggest that the effects of recusal behavior run much deeper, shaping public perceptions of the Court as well as case outcomes.

Three claims in particular have penetrated into media commentary about recusal behavior. The first is that recusal misconduct influences public confidence in the Court. For example, when Justice Kagan chose to participate in the health care dispute, commentators routinely stated that the Court's legitimacy was threatened.[2] "If there is any chance that the public will perceive her to have prejudged the case, or rubber-stamped the views of the President who appointed her," wrote the editorial page of the *Wall Street Journal*, "she will damage her own credibility as a Justice and that of the entire Court."[3] A few years earlier, questions about the Court's legitimacy were likewise front and center when Justice Antonin Scalia declined to recuse himself from the *Cheney* case.[4] "There is a real danger that his participation will damage the court's reputation," wrote the editorial page of the *New York Times*.[5] Opinion writers at the *Los Angeles Times* agreed. "Judicial disqualification is a serious matter for the U.S. Supreme Court," they wrote, "which depends on public confidence for its legitimacy. . . . The reputation of the Supreme Court is at stake."[6] The assumption underlying these comments was that public confidence in the Court was related to the justices' recusal practices, and that Scalia's participation would damage public confidence by making the justices appear unprincipled.

A second claim is that recusals influence judicial efficiency, making it more difficult for the justices to achieve consensus on the merits. For example, during the *Cheney* controversy, the editorial page of the *Wall Street Journal* opposed Justice Scalia's recusal because of the possibility of creating an evenly divided court. "There are only nine Justices," the editor wrote, "and if one or another has to recuse himself or herself every time some newspaper ethicist cries 'appearance,' we'll soon be getting a lot more 4-4 no-decisions."[7] Similarly, critics maintain that too many recusals will damage judicial efficiency by making the justices lack a quorum. The editorial page of the *New York Times* in 2008 urged the justices to divest themselves of stock after the recusal of four justices made it impossible for the Court to decide one of its cases.[8] "Plainly, the public would be better served if justices put their money in mutual funds, government securities or certificates of deposit instead of inviting conflicts by investing in publicly traded companies with matters coming before the court."[9]

The third and perhaps most serious charge is that recusal misconduct harms judicial integrity. Indeed, for many editorial writers during the *Cheney* controversy, the leading concern was that Justice Scalia was compromising the Court's impartiality. The *Los Angeles Times* commented that Scalia's participation in the case raised questions about the Court's "ability to be fair,"[10] while the *St. Louis Post-Dispatch* accused Scalia of being "blind to the requirements of justice."[11] The implication of these editorials was that, with an improperly constituted Court, the justices would make a decision that was biased, or at least different from what would have happened if a recusal had occurred. Recusals have this potential because the composition of the Court can affect judicial decision making throughout the process, including at three key points: the decision to grant *certiorari*, the conference vote on the merits, and the assignment of the majority opinion. Because the Supreme Court is a collegial body whose members have influence over each stage of the decision-making process, minor shifts in the Court's membership can affect which side wins and how broadly the rules accompanying judgments are worded.

Not everyone agrees, however, that recusals are likely to bring about these consequences, at least not routinely. Indeed, some legal commentary suggests that editorial writers have been intentionally misleading, putting forward unfounded speculation about the consequences of recusals in order to secure the disqualification of justices they dislike. Through repetition, these claims have gained a semblance of authenticity despite having no empirical foundation. "Demands that Justice Kagan and Thomas recuse themselves from deciding the constitutionality of the Affordable Care Act were not made to protect the integrity of the Court," writes Kristen Henke, "they were partisan attempts to gain an advantage when the Affordable Care Act came before the Court."[12] Henke accuses editorial writers of creating a "manufactured crisis."[13] Recusals almost invariably have minor consequences, she suggests, but because they occasionally do tip case outcomes, partisans seek them to obtain advantages in court.

Trends in public opinion research and in media commentary about recusals support this perception. Opinion polls gauging public attitudes about recusal behavior are uncommon, but in 2000 the *Los Angeles Times* conducted a poll asking Americans whether they supported the recusal of Justices Scalia and Thomas from *Bush v. Gore*.[14] The reasons advanced were that Justice Scalia's sons worked for law firms representing George W. Bush and that Justice Thomas's wife was on the Bush transition team. The poll was conducted in December 2000, shortly after the Supreme Court decided the case, when the issue was still highly salient and popular attitudes about it were fresh.[15] The trends, which are reported in Figure 4.1 on page 72, indicate that a plurality of Americans supported the recusals of Justices Scalia and Thomas, but considerations of policy shaped their responses. Among Bush voters, only 25.3% supported recusal, but among Gore voters, support was at 70.1%. It would appear, then, that for many voters, politics influenced their attitudes about recusals. Gore voters supported the disqualification of Justices Scalia and Thomas because these justices had ruled against their favored candidate.

Since that time, media commentary about recusals has followed a similar pattern, with support for disqualification correlated with the ideologies of the justices and the editorial writers themselves. Figure 4.2 on page 73 reports the number of editorials supporting the recusal of Supreme Court justices in six major newspapers since 1990.[16] Three of the newspapers had more liberal editorial pages, and three had more conservative pages.[17] In the traditionally liberal newspapers, editorial writers tended to support the recusal of conservative justices: liberal newspapers produced twenty-six editorials supporting the recusal of conservative justices, while conservative papers generated only sixteen such editorials. Similarly, editorials calling for the recusal of liberal justices were more likely to appear in newspapers

As you may know, Supreme Court Justice Antonin Scalia's sons work for law firms which represented George W. Bush in both the Florida and U.S. Supreme Court cases. The wife of Supreme Court Justice Clarence Thomas works with the Bush transition team. Her duties include accepting applications for people seeking employment in the Bush administration. Do you think that Justices Scalia and Thomas should have recused themselves, that is, not taken part in the court's deliberation because of an appearance of impropriety due to these relationships, or not?

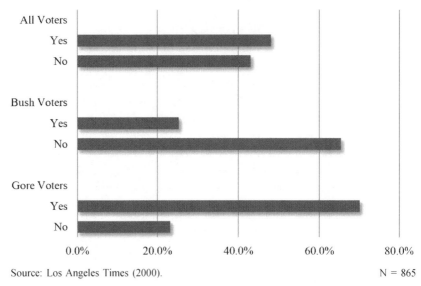

Source: Los Angeles Times (2000).   N = 865

Figure 4.1. Public Attitudes about the Recusal of Justices Scalia and Thomas, December 2000.

with conservative editorial pages. Liberal papers published four editorials supporting the recusal of liberal justices, compared to seven such editorials in conservative newspapers. The differences are not large, but the trends are suggestive. Editorial writers sought the recusal of their ideological opponents on the bench.

It should be little surprise, then, that during the *Cheney* controversy, one of the most consistent advocates of Scalia's recusal was the editorial page of the *New York Times*. Repeatedly, the paper demanded his disqualification, declaring that it was necessary to "protect the Supreme Court's integrity and legitimacy."[18] It can be no accident that a paper known for its liberal editorials was one of Scalia's biggest detractors, nor is it surpris-

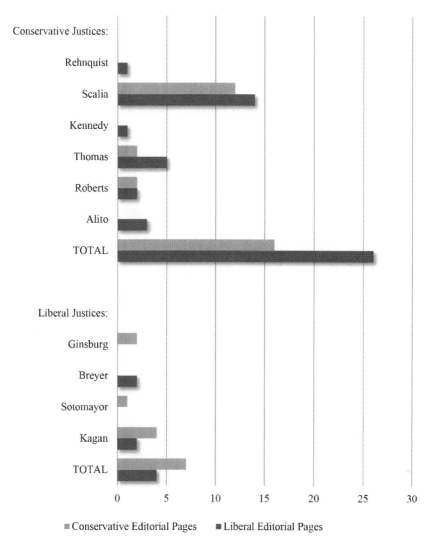

Conservative Justices:
Rehnquist
Scalia
Kennedy
Thomas
Roberts
Alito
TOTAL

Liberal Justices:
Ginsburg
Breyer
Sotomayor
Kagan
TOTAL

0   5   10   15   20   25   30

▨ Conservative Editorial Pages   ■ Liberal Editorial Pages

Note: Conservative editorial pages were the *Wall Street Journal*, *Chicago Tribune*, and *Los Angeles Times*. Liberal pages were the *New York Times*, *Washington Post*, and *St. Louis Post-Dispatch*.

Figure 4.2. Number of Editorials Favoring Recusals in Six Major Newspapers, 1990–2012.

ing that the conservative-leaning *Wall Street Journal* came to his defense. The latter argued that "merely being friends with federal officers shouldn't require Justices to recuse themselves from cases" and that it was "a shame that so many editors stooped to invoking 'ethics' in the name of what was really just a political hit job."[19] The arguments for and against Justice Scalia's disqualification align with what we already know about the political leanings of the two editorial pages.

Naturally, none of the editorial writers put forward blatantly partisan justifications for supporting or opposing recusals. They all expressed concerns about how recusal behavior would influence public confidence in the Court, judicial integrity, and the Court's efficiency. Yet the rhetoric they used followed predictable formulas. When writers argued in favor of recusals, they discussed how a justice's participation would harm public confidence in the Court and judicial integrity. When they opposed recusals, they described the administrative hardships that recusals cause. These trends are illustrated in Figure 4.3.[20] The data show that by far the most commonly expressed concern was that improper recusal behavior would harm judicial integrity. This concern was raised by 76.5% of editorial writers who favored the recusal of a justice but only 29.0% of writers opposing disqualification. Recusal supporters also commonly wrote about the potential for recusal behavior to damage public confidence in the Court, making this claim in 31.4% of editorials supporting recusals, compared to just 6.5% of editorials opposing them. By

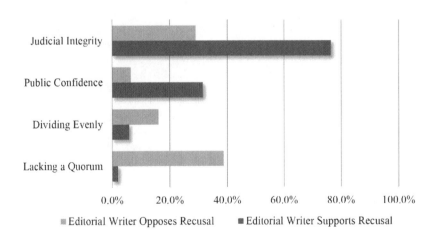

Figure 4.3. Reasons Advanced for Supporting/Opposing Recusals by Editorial Writers in Six Major Newspapers, 1990–2012.

contrast, recusal opponents emphasized the possibility that the Court would divide evenly when a justice was absent, making this argument 16.1% of the time. Recusal supporters rarely discussed this possibility, mentioning it in only 5.9% of their editorials. Opponents of recusals also said that disqualifications would cause the Court to lack a quorum, raising the point in 38.7% of their editorials, compared to 2.0% of editorials favoring recusals.

Overall, then, it would seem that editorials about recusals have followed a consistent rhetorical pattern designed to persuade readers to support the outcomes the writers favored, not to give a balanced discussion of the advantages and disadvantages of recusals. Indeed, the impression generated by the data is that media commentators have been opportunistic in their support of recusals, favoring them for reasons that have little to do with the explanations they put forward. The data give weight to doubts expressed by Henke and others about whether many of our assumptions about the effects of recusals are valid. Minimally, it would seem that popular discourse about recusals is steeped in a lot of myths.

And yet this does not mean that the concerns are baseless. We simply do not know enough about the consequences of recusals to disentangle the myths from the reality. In the next two chapters, I examine the consequences of recusals to gauge the scope of their impact on law and policy. The focus of this chapter is on the effects that recusals have on the Court's policy output, evaluating whether recusals influence case outcomes, the assignment of majority opinions, and the ideological composition of majority coalitions. Then, in the next chapter, I evaluate the impact of recusals on public confidence in the Court, the Court's administrative efficiency, and the Court's docket. As the analyses will show, media commentary about the consequences of recusals is almost certainly overstated, but it is not without some foundation. Recusals can shape legal policy, just not to the extent that media commentators would have us believe.

Measuring Bias on the Supreme Court

As discussed above, a leading concern expressed by the Supreme Court's critics is that recusal misconduct produces biased outcomes. The idea that the Court's impartiality might be compromised is problematic for several reasons, not the least of which is that bias, or its appearance, could erode public confidence in the Supreme Court.[21] I explore this possibility in the next chapter. The other concern is more normative and grounded in an expectation that litigants in the American legal system deserve authoritative case resolutions that are free of bias. Recusal misconduct threatens this presumption by eliminating one of the preconditions for impartial justice: a decision-making tribunal composed of disinterested adjudicators. When this condition is not met, the litigants arguably have not received a "fair" or "just" result.

In empirical terms, it is difficult to know what an unjust result would look like, but if recusal misconduct does create bias, then at the very least one would expect the Court to produce systematically different case outcomes when recusals occur. Moreover, one should expect the impact of recusals not to be idiosyncratic, but consistent with the justices' known preferences. The disqualification of conservative justices should tilt Supreme Court policies in more liberal directions, while the recusal of liberal justices should make policies more conservative. If these types of ideological shifts happen when recusals occur, then it is defensible to conclude that recusals affect the ideological content of legal policy and that the failure of justices to recuse themselves biases legal policy in the direction of the justices' sincere preferences.

The theoretical assumption underlying the analysis, then, is that if recusal behavior influences Supreme Court policy making, it is primarily via the ideological preferences of the recusing justices. I make this assumption because of the overwhelming evidence that Supreme Court justices vote consistently with their sincere policy preferences.[22] Although attitudinal voting is less pervasive at other levels of the federal judiciary,[23] it is the single best predictor of case outcomes on the U.S. Supreme Court.[24] In addition to influencing the final vote on the merits, policy considerations are known to guide the drafting of majority opinions[25] and the composition of the Court's docket,[26] among other factors. In light of this research, it is reasonable to assume that the best way to observe the effects of recusals is by studying their impact on the ideological direction of the Court's policy output, with regard to both case dispositions and opinion content.

This approach is also defensible because when commentators speak of bias, it is often with the justices' ideology in mind. For example, when the editorial page of the *Wall Street Journal* questioned Justice Kagan's decision to participate in the health care dispute, it remarked, "We're confident that Mr. Obama knows exactly the kind of reliable liberal vote he's getting."[27] Similarly, a commentator in the *Los Angeles Times* suggested that Justice Scalia declined to recuse himself from the *Cheney* case in order to advance the political agenda of a conservative administration. Unless Justice Scalia recused himself, the commentator warned, it "would be the most politically activist court of modern times because its prevailing philosophy would be to green-light the actions of this wildly activist president."[28] My focus on ideological bias is therefore grounded in how editorial writers themselves have described the impact of recusals.[29]

At the merits stage, there are at least three opportunities for recusals to influence Supreme Court policy making. The first is by changing the direction of the Court's judgment. Research suggests that case outcomes are typically set at the Court's median,[30] so if a recusal shifts the location of the median to the right or the left, then it can change the result, depending on which justice sits out.[31] For litigants, this effect is perhaps the most consequential because case dispositions determine who wins and loses disputes. If we find that recusals systematically shift the direction of case dispositions, then litigants will have good reason for concluding that the failure of justices to withdraw from cases will affect their chances of winning.

A second potential impact of recusals is on who writes the majority opinion. Although litigants might consider the opinion writer to be less consequential than the case disposition, the majority opinion can have a lasting impact on the development of the law by describing the rule that governs the outcome. The majority opinion sets the precedent that will guide litigants and lower court judges in future cases. For this reason, it is important to know who gets to write the majority opinion and whether the disqualification of a justice has any influence on this choice. If it turns out that recusals systematically shift the ideologies of majority opinion writers to the right or the left, then there could be a real impact on the contents of legal policies.

A third, and related, potential influence of recusals is on the median ideology of the majority coalition. Research on judicial behavior suggests that coalition medians have an even greater impact on the contents of majority opinions than opinion writers do.[32] Because majority opinions are negotiated documents that represent the views of the Court's majority, they are not simply reflective of the opinion writer's sincere preferences.[33] To hold majority coalitions together, opinion writers circulate drafts and accommodate suggestions from other members, and in this way the opinions come to reflect the consensus of the group.[34] One might expect, then, that if recusals systematically shift coalition medians, then they will change the group dynamics and influence the scope of the precedents that the Court establishes.

In the rest of this chapter, I examine the impact of recusal behavior on case dispositions, the assignment of majority opinions, and the ideological composition of majority coalitions. If recusals do not affect Supreme Court policy making in any of these areas, then it will be difficult to maintain that the failure of justices to recuse themselves biases policy. However, if there is a connection between disqualification and the Court's policy content, then recusal misconduct will have more serious implications. The failure of justices to recuse themselves would have the potential to change case outcomes and the scope of the precedents that the Court establishes.

Research Design

To gauge the impact of recusals on Supreme Court policy making, I once again used the Supreme Court Database, augmented with my own original data.[35] Unlike the previous chapter, in which I used justice-centered data with one entry per voting justice, in this chapter I used the case-centered data because I am interested in knowing the impact of recusal behavior on general case characteristics, not individual justice votes. Specifically, I am interested in learning the impact that recusal behavior has on case dispositions, the ideology of majority opinion writers, and the ideology of coalition medians. These characteristics vary by the case, not the voting justice, so it was appropriate to use the version of the database with only one entry per case.

I used three dependent variables to capture the influence of recusal behavior on Supreme Court policy making. The first dependent variable, CASE OUTCOME, is a dichotomous variable measuring the ideological direction of the Court's decision, based on the DECISIONDIRECTION variable in the Supreme Court Database. It is coded 1 when the direction of Supreme Court's decision is conservative, and 0 otherwise. The second dependent variable, OPINION WRITER IDEOLOGY, is a continuous variable measuring the ideology score for the majority opinion writer. To measure ideology, I used the Martin-Quinn scores, with positive values associated with more conservative justices.[36] The final dependent variable also uses the Martin-Quinn scores to measure the MEDIAN IDEOLOGY OF THE MAJORITY COALITION. For all three dependent variables, I expect the recusal of a conservative justice to move Supreme Court policy in a more liberal direction, while the recusal of a liberal justice will move policy in a conservative direction.

To measure the ideology of recusing justices, it was necessary first to identify cases in which justices recused themselves, using the same procedures that I employed in the previous chapter.[37] Once recusing justices were identified, I classified them as being conservative when they were to the right of the Court's median, and liberal when they were to the left of the median, based on the Martin-Quinn scores. Because Martin-Quinn scores vary from term to term, it was possible for the same justice to be classified as conservative one year and liberal another, depending on his or her voting record relative to the rest of the Court. From these data, I generated two dichotomous variables, CONSERVATIVE RECUSAL and LIBERAL RECUSAL.[38] I expect the CONSERVATIVE

Recusal variable to be negatively associated with the dependent variables, and the Liberal Recusal variable to be positively associated with them.[39]

Along with the principal independent variables, I included a series of control variables for each model. For case outcomes, I controlled for the Court's median (Court Median Ideology) because research suggests that case dispositions on the Supreme Court are typically set by the median justice.[40] I also included the Court Median Ideology variable when modeling the third dependent variable, Median Ideology of the Majority Coalition. However, for the second dependent variable, which measures the ideology of the majority opinion writer (Opinion Writer Ideology), I controlled for the ideology of the majority opinion assigner (Opinion Assigner Ideology) and the median of the majority coalition (Median Ideology of the Majority Coalition) because research indicates that these alternative measures better predict who writes the majority opinion than the Court's median.[41] I identified the majority opinion assigner using the Supreme Court Database, and based Median Ideology of the Majority Coalition on the median ideology score of the majority coalition in each case. For all of these variables, I measured ideology using the Martin-Quinn scores.[42]

Additionally, in each of the three models, I controlled for the ideological direction of the lower court's decision (Lower Court Direction), as reported in the Supreme Court Database.[43] I expect the variable to be negatively correlated with each of the three dependent variables.[44] I also introduced dummy variables for each chief justice, with Justice Burger excluded as the baseline category, and clustered standard errors by natural court. Because the first dependent variable, Case Outcome, is dichotomous, I used logistic regression. For the other two dependent variables (Opinion Writer Ideology, Court Median Ideology), which are measured on continuous scales, I used ordinary least squares regression.

Results

The results indicate that recusals in fact do influence law and policy, but not necessarily in the manner—or with the magnitude—that editorial writers suggest. To begin with, I do not find strong evidence that recusals affect case dispositions. Table 4.1 on page 80 models the likelihood that the Supreme Court will produce a conservative outcome, and while it reports some evidence of a direct correlation between case outcomes and recusal behavior, the effects are limited. The data indicate that the recusal of a conservative justice (Conservative Recusal) makes it less likely that the

Table 4.1. Logit Model of Case Outcomes, 1946–2010

	All Cases	Civil Liberties Cases	Other Issue Areas	Salient Cases	Non-Salient Cases
CONSERVATIVE RECUSAL	-0.248**	0.104	-0.343***	-0.400	-0.234*
	(0.091)	(0.180)	(0.086)	(0.325)	(0.100)
LIBERAL RECUSAL	-0.001	0.278	-0.128	0.484	-0.085
	(0.077)	(0.142)	(0.140)	(0.274)	(0.097)
COURT MEDIAN IDEOLOGY	0.280***	0.504***	0.064	0.635***	0.237***
	(0.073)	(0.130)	(0.084)	(0.200)	(0.073)
LOWER COURT DIRECTION	-0.887***	-1.150***	-0.675***	-0.524***	-0.929***
	(0.092)	(0.095)	(0.101)	(0.155)	(0.101)
VINSON	-0.081	-0.085	-0.072	-0.402*	-0.048
	(0.138)	(0.099)	(0.196)	(0.173)	(0.169)
WARREN	-0.530***	-0.438**	-0.522***	-0.549*	-0.521***
	(0.092)	(0.158)	(0.095)	(0.260)	(0.077)
REHNQUIST	-0.016	0.022	-0.034	-0.261*	0.032
	(0.079)	(0.101)	(0.087)	(0.123)	(0.099)
ROBERTS	-0.077	-0.120	-0.009	-0.426*	-0.008
	(0.125)	(0.193)	(0.085)	(0.195)	(0.112)

Constant	0.455***	0.547***	0.356***	0.040	0.516***
	(0.082)	(0.136)	(0.076)	(0.171)	(0.083)
Wald chi^2	191.140***	331.430***	207.430***	107.950***	187.290***
Pseudo R^2	0.062	0.097	0.036	0.061	0.063
N	8330	4302	4028	1060	7185

$^*p < 0.05$; $^{**}p < 0.01$; $^{***}p < 0.001$

Court will produce a conservative outcome. Across all cases, a conservative recusal decreases the likelihood that the Court will produce a conservative ruling from 48.1% to 42.0%, a moderate but not insubstantial effect.[45] However, the relationship does not obtain in civil liberties cases or in salient cases. Case outcomes are affected by the recusal of conservative justices only in low-salience cases and in cases that do not involve civil liberties issues.

The finding that recusals affect case outcomes only in certain contexts is not altogether surprising when one considers that justices are selective about when they disqualify themselves. The previous chapter found that justices avoid recusing themselves from important cases in which their votes are likely to affect the outcomes, so it stands to reason that the effects of recusal behavior would be muted in these cases. Another interesting trend in Table 4.1 is that case outcomes are affected by the recusal of conservative justices only. The recusal of liberal justices (LIBERAL RECUSAL) does not have a similar effect on case dispositions.[46] The reason for this trend is not immediately apparent from the data, but a likely explanation is that the ideology of the Court has tended to be conservative throughout much of the study period, so the recusal of conservative justices has had more potential to tip the balance of power on the Court.[47]

With regard to opinion assignments, recusals appear to have had no effect, at least not directly. As Table 4.2 shows, opinion assignment is almost entirely a function of the MEDIAN IDEOLOGY OF THE MAJORITY COALITION, more so than even the ideology of the majority opinion assigner (OPINION ASSIGNER IDEOLOGY). Neither conservative (CONSERVATIVE RECUSAL) nor liberal recusals (LIBERAL RECUSAL) affect the ideology of the majority opinion writer, not in the general model nor in any of the categories of cases examined. One can therefore safely conclude that recusals do not have any direct impact on opinion assignments.

Yet Table 4.3 on page 85 shows that the justices' recusal behavior does influence the ideological composition of the majority coalition. Indeed, the data suggest that this effect may be the most consistent influence on the Court's policy output. The coalition median changes in response to both conservative (CONSERVATIVE RECUSAL) and liberal recusals (LIBERAL RECUSAL), and the relationship is robust across different case types. It would be reasonable to conclude, then, that the primary effect of a recusal is to alter the ideological makeup of the majority coalition. When a conservative justice withdraws from a case, the coalition becomes more liberal, and when a liberal justice sits out, the coalition becomes more conservative.

The consequences of this effect for law and policy are not trivial. The majority opinion describes the legal rule and establishes the precedent for lower

Table 4.2. Regression Model of Majority Opinion Writer Ideology, 1946–2010

	All Cases	Civil Liberties Cases	Other Issue Areas	Salient Cases	Non-Salient Cases
CONSERVATIVE RECUSAL	-0.062 (0.100)	0.090 (0.150)	-0.027 (0.129)	0.350 (0.217)	-0.118 (0.095)
LIBERAL RECUSAL	-0.184 (0.110)	-0.009 (0.092)	-0.206 (0.145)	-0.199 (0.249)	-0.221 (0.122)
OPINION ASSIGNER IDEOLOGY	0.019 (0.026)	0.052 (0.030)	0.002 (0.026)	0.062 (0.063)	0.014 (0.024)
MEDIAN IDEOLOGY OF THE MAJORITY COALITION	0.932*** (0.050)	0.920*** (0.054)	0.904*** (0.060)	0.887*** (0.084)	0.941*** (0.055)
LOWER COURT DIRECTION	-0.099** (0.030)	-0.088* (0.038)	-0.121 (0.063)	-0.031 (0.117)	-0.109*** (0.026)
VINSON	-0.229** (0.070)	-0.499*** (0.039)	0.118 (0.136)	-0.244* (0.102)	-0.224* (0.082)
WARREN	0.021 (0.078)	-0.150 (0.078)	0.265 (0.146)	-0.304* (0.143)	0.062 (0.095)

continued on next page

Table 4.2. Continued

	All Cases	Civil Liberties Cases	Other Issue Areas	Salient Cases	Non-Salient Cases
REHNQUIST	0.037	−0.077	0.223	−0.221	0.067
	(0.180)	(0.109)	(0.278)	(0.127)	(0.199)
ROBERTS	0.438***	0.169**	0.794***	0.275*	0.447***
	(0.083)	(0.049)	(0.142)	(0.122)	(0.090)
Constant	−0.174*	0.042	−0.470**	0.094	−0.206**
	(0.064)	(0.058)	(0.139)	(0.098)	(0.074)
F	407.690***	272.490***	248.780***	66.490***	203.730***
R^2	0.223	0.295	0.164	0.309	0.205
N	8314	4292	4022	1060	7169

$*p < 0.05; **p < 0.01; ***p < 0.001$

Table 4.3. Regression Model of Majority Coalition Median Ideology, 1946–2010

	All Cases	Civil Liberties Cases	Other Issue Areas	Salient Cases	Non-Salient Cases
CONSERVATIVE RECUSAL	-0.352***	-0.380***	-0.330***	-0.432**	-0.337***
	(0.064)	(0.084)	(0.066)	(0.150)	(0.062)
LIBERAL RECUSAL	0.255***	0.335***	0.213***	0.411**	0.208***
	(0.054)	(0.082)	(0.050)	(0.143)	(0.052)
COURT MEDIAN IDEOLOGY	0.756***	0.798***	0.721***	0.724***	0.751***
	(0.056)	(0.039)	(0.084)	(0.104)	(0.051)
LOWER COURT DIRECTION	-0.136***	-0.213***	-0.063*	-0.066	-0.147***
	(0.022)	(0.039)	(0.031)	(0.068)	(0.024)
VINSON	-0.217	-0.216	-0.200	-0.366	-0.197
	(0.215)	(0.180)	(0.240)	(0.348)	(0.204)
WARREN	-0.281***	-0.212***	-0.313***	-0.390**	-0.268***
	(0.059)	(0.049)	(0.083)	(0.120)	(0.053)
REHNQUIST	0.136*	-0.132*	-0.136*	-0.332*	-0.100*
	(0.053)	(0.053)	(0.062)	(0.130)	(0.045)
ROBERTS	0.112	0.024	0.229	-0.121	0.094
	(0.079)	(0.038)	(0.128)	(0.117)	(0.060)

continued on next page

Table 4.3. Continued

	All Cases	Civil Liberties Cases	Other Issue Areas	Salient Cases	Non-Salient Cases
Constant	0.192***	0.218***	0.158**	0.146	0.204***
	(0.034)	(0.027)	(0.051)	(0.090)	(0.035)
F	127.560***	294.510***	54.030***	28.370***	154.170***
R^2	0.296	0.285	0.317	0.208	0.301
N	8324	4296	4028	1060	7179

*$p < 0.05$; **$p < 0.01$; ***$p < 0.001$

courts to apply. The way an opinion is written therefore has strong potential to influence the future development of the law.[48] To put it more precisely, when all of the other variables are held at their mean values, the recusal of a conservative justice causes the ideology of the coalition median to decrease from a value of 0.328 to about –0.024.[49] Substantively, this shift is the equivalent of the coalition median changing from Justice Stewart (0.323), White (0.324), or O'Connor (0.326) to Justice Breyer (–0.033), Ginsburg (-0.025), or Stevens (–0.024).[50] Even if the case disposition does not change, one might expect the Court to produce a very different majority opinion with such a change in the coalition median. Similarly, when a liberal justice sits out, the ideology of the majority coalition median shifts from 0.297 to 0.552, the equivalent of the median shifting from Justice Clark (0.260) or Blackmun (0.270) to Justice White (0.526) or Stewart (0.553).[51] The change is moderate but could still have an impact on the scope of the opinion that the Court produces.

Conclusion

Overall, the data suggest that recusals do influence law and policy, but their impact is the strongest on opinion content. Although recusals affect case outcomes from time to time, it is only in specific circumstances, such as when justices who are routinely members of the majority coalition sit out. The more typical impact is on the median ideology of the majority coalition, which affects the substance of the rule that the majority announces. This effect is not inconsequential, however. By shaping legal policy, recusals affect subsequent litigation,[52] the manner in which lower court judges resolve disputes,[53] and even how Supreme Court justices decide future controversies.[54] In these ways, recusals can influence the subsequent development of the law.

Media commentators are therefore correct to think that advocating for the recusal of specific justices can have policy consequences. If liberal editorial writers from newspapers such as the *New York Times* push for the recusal of conservative justices—and conservative writers seek the recusal of liberal ones—it is rational for them to do so. However, there are limits to what one should expect recusals to achieve. The findings suggest that recusals are only likely to change case outcomes when justices who would otherwise be in the majority sit out. Particularly on the Rehnquist and Roberts Courts, the recusal of conservative justices has mattered more than the recusal of liberal ones. Perhaps it is for this reason that, as Figure 4.2 showed, media commentators in recent years have more actively sought the recusal of conservative justices.

The results of the quantitative analysis suggest a complex response to the question that opens the chapter: Does recusal misconduct produce bias? On the one hand, the answer would seem to be yes. If, as the findings suggest, recusals do have policy consequences, then it must also be true that the failure of justices to recuse themselves from cases has policy consequences as well. One could argue that when justices participate in cases in error, and it changes the outcome, the Court has reached the "wrong" result. But is this form of bias something about which, normatively, we should be concerned? Can we say that judicial integrity is seriously impaired when the justices seek to maintain their influence over legal policy by participating in important cases? These questions are more difficult to answer.

After all, justices vote based on their sincere policy preferences routinely.[55] We usually know, or suspect, the justices' ideological leanings at the time of their confirmation hearings, but we do not typically think of the justices as biased simply because they vote consistent with these preferences.[56] We expect the justices to influence policy in ways that reflect the ideologies of their appointing presidents—indeed, we elect presidents with this expectation in mind.[57] If the bias that is produced by a recusal decision is merely the preservation of the current ideological status quo, then judicial integrity might not be jeopardized. It is not necessarily unethical for justices to take into account how their absence will change the outcome and the legal principle that the Court's opinion establishes. Arguably, it advances the interests of the constituents who appointed and confirmed the justices to the Court.

Reasonable people will disagree about the ethical implications of these findings, and about the need for reform, but one thing the data do make clear is that the policy consequences of recusals are not nearly as great as commentators have made them out to be. In fact, I suspect that, outside the legal community, few who write about recusals are really worried about judicial ethics at all.[58] In the media, at least, most talk about recusals seems to be less about judicial integrity and more about power, with advocates seeking to change the composition of the Court in order to secure the legal outcomes they favor. As the data from the beginning of the chapter illustrate, debates over the recusal of specific justices have become another form of partisan wrangling, with the reasons put forward designed to achieve specific policy objectives. If it turns out that some of these reasons have truth to them, it does not necessarily mean that the process is broken or that reforms are needed, but that the rhetoric is plausible enough to make it persuasive. Any serious reform proposals will need to distinguish the real concerns about judicial ethics from the politics.

5

Other Consequences of Recusals

The previous chapter concluded that the impact of recusals on law and policy is limited, but commentators have also suggested that recusals have other consequences that should be considered before discussing proposals for reform. For example, recusals might affect the Court's efficiency, making the justices less capable of resolving disputes by increasing the likelihood that they will divide evenly. Or perhaps recusal misconduct influences public confidence in the Court and thus threatens the Court's legitimacy. Alternatively, recusals might affect the amount of bargaining and accommodation that occurs behind the scenes during the opinion-writing process; or maybe recusals are influential at the *certiorari* stage, depriving petitioners of the votes that they need to secure grants and have cases placed on the docket.

Because there has been so little systematic research on recusals, we do not know how credible these possibilities are, so in this chapter, I examine the evidence for them, making use of the best available data. I find that, in each instance, there is some foundation for supporting the hypothesized effect, both theoretically and empirically. However, I also find, once again, that the consequences of particular recusal decisions have been limited. Although recusals do have some impact on the Court's efficiency, legitimacy, bargaining activity, and docket, it is only in specific circumstances and not to the extent that commentators have claimed.

Dividing Evenly

One potentially negative consequence of recusals is that they might increase the probability that the justices will divide evenly. Critics frequently point to the possibility of dividing evenly as a reason to oppose the recusal of particular justices,[1] and the justices themselves have stated that they resist withdrawing from cases for this reason.[2] Indeed, it is one of the primary rationales behind the "duty to sit."[3] The concern is that, with only eight justices present, the Court is at risk of being unable to attain a majority. The lower court's opinion is affirmed automatically and the Court's opinion has no authority as precedent, leaving unaddressed the underlying legal questions that prompted the justices to grant *certiorari* in the first place. Because many of these questions have divided the lower federal courts,[4] the inability of the justices to answer them yields inconsistencies in federal law. The same federal statutes or constitutional provisions come to mean different things in different parts of the country.

From the standpoint of due process, one can also make the case that when the justices divide evenly, the litigants are denied the final appeal that they have been promised. Worse for petitioners, they are denied a likely victory because the Supreme Court tends to reverse the lower court decisions it reviews. Table 5.1 reports the dispositions of all cases in which recusals occurred and the justices reached the merits, based on the Supreme Court Database.[5] It shows that the justices reversed, vacated, or remanded prior judgments, in whole or in part, in 62.9% of cases. It would seem, then, that dividing evenly is indeed consequential and that petitioners have good reason to believe that they would have won their appeals if all of the justices had participated.

Yet, as previous scholars have recognized, dividing evenly rarely occurs. In their study of the justices' recusal practices, Ryan Black and Lee Epstein found that dividing evenly is not just uncommon; it occurs less frequently than one would expect if voting distributions were assigned randomly after

Table 5.1. Merits Dispositions Following Recusals, 1946–2010

Disposition	Frequency	Percent
Affirmed	303	31.4
Reversed	221	22.9
Reversed and Remanded	235	24.4
Vacated	6	0.6
Vacated and Remanded	111	11.5
Affirmed and Reversed (or Vacated) in Part	34	3.5
Other	55	5.7
TOTAL	965	100.0

a recusal.[6] My own fresh investigation of the question confirms these findings. Table 5.2 lists the vote breakdown of all cases from 1946 to 2010 in which a recusal occurred and in which eight justices were present.[7] The data show that by far the least common voting outcome was a 4-4 vote, happening in just 55 cases, or 7.5% of the time when dividing evenly was possible. By contrast, the justices voted unanimously 41.9% of the time, and they voted with just a single dissent in another 15.2% of cases.[8] Consistent with Black and Epstein, then, I find that dividing evenly is by no means an inevitable occurrence. The justices' tendency is to find consensus, not to leave important questions of federal law unaddressed.

Of course, one might respond that it is not trivial for the justices to divide evenly 7.5% of the time. Critics could also point out that, although dividing evenly is rare, the risk of dividing evenly is more common. Table 5.2 reports that the justices have come close to dividing evenly—with a vote of 5 to 3—in about 17.6% of cases. Arguably these "near misses" should also be taken into account when assessing the Court's potential to divide evenly. When the cases with 5-3 votes are added to the cases in which the justices voted 4-4, the data suggest that the justices have been in danger of dividing evenly in more than a quarter of the cases in which recusals have occurred. When looked at in this way, the risk of dividing evenly is not small, and it becomes understandable that the justices would take measures to prevent it.

Additionally, one might expect the likelihood of dividing evenly to vary depending on which justice withdraws from a dispute. The previous chapter found that recusals primarily influence case outcomes only when conservative justices disqualify themselves. The explanation for this finding was that, in recent years, conservative justices have more frequently been members of the majority coalitions, which has made their recusals more consequential

Table 5.2. Vote Distributions Following Recusals, 1946–2010

Disposition	Frequency	Percent
4-4	55	7.5
5-3	130	17.6
6-2	132	17.9
7-1	112	15.2
8-0	309	41.9
TOTAL	738	100.0

Note: Table 5.2 includes only cases in which eight justices were in the majority coalition.

in determining who wins and loses disputes. For similar reasons, one might expect that the Court would also be at greater risk of dividing evenly when recusing justices are to the right of the Court's median. When conservative justices sit out, they are more likely to be taking votes away from majority coalitions, increasing the chances that the Court will deadlock.

These tendencies are affirmed in Table 5.3. It reports that when a liberal justice withdraws from a dispute, the Court votes 4-4 in about 5.4% of cases, below the baseline rate of 7.5%.[9] However, when a justice to the right of the Court's median sits out, the likelihood of dividing evenly increases to 9.6%. These trends become stronger when one examines only data from the Rehnquist and Roberts Courts, when there was a relatively stable 5-4 conservative majority for much of the period. Since 1986, the likelihood of dividing evenly has been 15.4% when conservative justices have recused themselves, compared to 5.7% when liberal justices have sat out.[10] It would seem, then, that there is a reasonable chance that recusals will cause the Supreme Court to divide evenly, but only if the justices who disqualified themselves were likely to have voted with the majority coalition in the first place.

Table 5.3. Vote Distributions Following Recusals, by Justice Ideology

A. Recusal of a Conservative Justice

Disposition	Frequency	Percent
4-4	25	9.6
5-3	42	16.2
6-2	48	18.5
7-1	41	15.8
8-0	104	40.0
TOTAL	260	100.0

B. Recusal of a Liberal Justice

Disposition	Frequency	Percent
4-4	16	5.4
5-3	52	17.6
6-2	49	16.6
7-1	44	14.9
8-0	135	45.6
TOTAL	296	100.0

Note: Table 5.3 includes only cases in which eight justices were in the majority coalition.

The aftermath of Justice Scalia's death in spring 2016 is a case in point. Although it was technically not a recusal, Scalia's sudden departure left the majority coalition without a member for a sustained period, putting in doubt the Court's ability to forge consensus in major cases. In some cases, such as *Zubik v. Burwell*, which concerned the Affordable Care Act, the justices were able to agree on a compromise,[11] but in other cases the Court divided evenly, including a major case concerning public unions.[12] In the latter case, the Court had been widely expected to reach a conservative judgment with Scalia on the Court, but after his death, the conservative governing coalition was a vote short of what it needed.[13]

To provide a more rigorous test of the hypothesis that dividing evenly depends on the ideology of the recusing justice, Table 5.4 models the

Table 5.4. Logit Model of Dividing Evenly, 1946–2010

	Model A	Model B	Model C
RECUSAL	2.854***	—	—
	(0.438)	—	—
CONSERVATIVE RECUSAL	—	2.099***	1.604**
	—	(0.448)	(0.600)
LIBERAL RECUSAL	—	1.264**	1.248**
	—	(0.405)	(0.398)
MEDIAN RECUSAL	—	2.272***	2.255***
	—	(0.317)	(0.311)
IDEOLOGICAL DIVERSITY	0.502	0.631	0.613
	(0.390)	(0.422)	(0.397)
CASE SALIENCE	–2.601**	–2.720**	–2.782**
	(0.945)	(0.959)	(1.005)
POST REHNQUIST	0.008	–0.160	–0.768*
	(0.348)	(0.307)	(0.377)
(CONSERVATIVE RECUSAL)*	—	—	2.215**
(POST REHNQUIST)	—	—	(0.755)
Constant	–3.880***	–3.508***	–3.291***
	(0.899)	(0.935)	(0.861)
Chi-square	161.470***	215.610***	227.570***
Pseudo R^2	0.314	0.283	0.295

*$p < 0.05$; **$p < 0.01$; ***$p < 0.001$ N = 8,245

Note: Table 5.4 also controls for issue area, the coefficients for which not reported.

likelihood of dividing evenly using logistic regression. The database is the same one used in the previous chapter, based on an augmented version of the Supreme Court Database.[14] The dependent variable is a dichotomous variable coded 1 when the Court divided evenly and 0 otherwise.[15] The principal independent variables measure whether justices who withdrew from disputes were to the right of the Court's median (CONSERVATIVE RECUSAL), to the left of it (LIBERAL RECUSAL), or at the median (MEDIAN RECUSAL).[16] Because I expect the effect of a CONSERVATIVE RECUSAL to be stronger in the Rehnquist and Roberts Courts, I created an interaction term using CONSERVATIVE RECUSAL and another variable measuring whether a case occurred after Rehnquist was confirmed as Chief Justice (POST REHNQUIST). I also introduced several control variables. The IDEOLOGICAL DIVERSITY variable assesses whether dividing evenly occurs because of ideological heterogeneity on Supreme Court coalitions. It was measured by calculating the standard deviations of the ideologies of all of the justices who participated in each case, based on their Martin-Quinn scores.[17] I expect diverse coalitions to have harder times achieving consensus, so I anticipate that the IDEOLOGICAL DIVERSITY variable will be positively associated with dividing evenly. Additionally, I controlled for CASE SALIENCE and issue area.[18] Reported coefficients have standard errors clustered by natural court.[19]

Table 5.4 presents the results in three columns. Column A features a summary variable measuring whether a recusal of any sort occurred (RECUSAL); Column B takes the ideology of the recusing justices into account; and Column C introduces the interaction term. The data show that, in all circumstances, the disqualification of justices increases the likelihood of dividing evenly. However, the magnitude of the effect depends on the ideology of the justice who sat out. As reported in column B, the recusal of justices to the right of the Court's median (CONSERVATIVE RECUSAL) has had a larger substantive influence on dividing evenly than the recusal of a liberal justice (LIBERAL RECUSAL), but the largest substantive effect has been generated by the recusal of the median justice (MEDIAN RECUSAL). When all other variables are held at their mean values, the recusal of a conservative justice increases the likelihood of dividing evenly by 1.9%, and the recusal of a liberal justice increases the likelihood by 0.7%.[20] The recusal of the median justice increases the chances of dividing evenly by 2.3%.[21]

The primacy of the median justice is not altogether surprising in light of the fact that the median justice determines case dispositions and is thus frequently a member of the majority coalition.[22] Yet, as column C affirms, the effect of a conservative recusal is also important and has become even more influential on the Rehnquist and Roberts Courts. The interaction term is significant and signed positively, indicating that the effect of the CONSERVATIVE RECUSAL variable intensifies when the POST REHNQUIST variable assumes a value of 1. More precisely, before Rehnquist's confirmation as Chief Justice, a conservative recusal increased the likelihood of dividing evenly by about 1.1%, but after Rehnquist's confirmation, the magnitude of the effect increased to 5.3%. These trends are consistent with the hypothesis that the impact of conservative recusals has become stronger during the Rehnquist and Roberts Courts, when there has been a relatively stable 5-4 conservative majority.

The findings affirm that recusals do increase the likelihood that the justices will divide evenly, particularly when members of the Court's conservative majority have disqualified themselves. The recusal of the median justice also increases the likelihood of dividing evenly. However, as Black and Epstein observed, the likelihood of dividing evenly remains small.[23] In most cases, a recusal increases the chance of dividing evenly by just one or two percentage points, which might be consequential to the litigants in the affected cases, but is not necessarily indicative of a broader problem. It is by no means the case that recusals always cause the Court to divide evenly. Indeed, it is much more common for the justices to seek consensus.

Those who would criticize the justices for recusing themselves unnecessarily must therefore recognize that dividing evenly is not typical. More often than not, the administrative efficiency of the Court is not impaired when recusals occur. At the same time, it should be remembered that the justices are selective about when they withdraw from disputes. As Chapter 3 showed, the justices tend to participate in divisive cases, and this behavior has surely had an impact on the rate at which the Court divides evenly. If the justices were less selective about when they recused themselves, and if they were more willing to withdraw from divisive cases, then most likely the Court would divide evenly with greater frequency.

Legitimacy

Another potential impact of recusals is on public attitudes about the Court. Recusal behavior could have a negative impact on public confidence if the public comes to believe that the justices are not withdrawing from cases when they should be or that the justices' recusal practices are otherwise unethical. Alternatively, recusals could have an indirect connection to public attitudes if the public disapproves of how other justices on the Court behave when they are short a member. Confidence in the Court might decline, for example, when the justices choose to divide evenly following a recusal instead of finding compromise.

As discussed in the previous chapter, commentators frequently link recusals to legitimacy, alleging that confidence in the Supreme Court will decline unless the justices follow the statutory and ethical recusal guidelines.[24] These claims are potentially quite serious because the justices require legitimacy to govern effectively. Without it, the public might be unwilling to comply with court decisions, particularly decisions that they oppose.[25] Public judgments about legitimacy have been described variously as "diffuse support"[26] and "loyalty,"[27] or what Gibson refers to as "a fundamental commitment to an institution and a willingness to support the institution that extends beyond mere satisfaction with the performance of the institution at the moment."[28] Legitimacy is therefore concerned with public attitudes about judicial institutions rather than just their policy output. When recusal practices are said to threaten legitimacy, the implication is that the public believes that the Court is not "acting appropriately and correctly, within its mandate."[29] The justices say that preserving legitimacy is important to them,[30] and it is the most likely reason why they tend to follow the federal recusal statute.

However, we do not actually know whether recusals and legitimacy are related. On the one hand, it is reasonable to think that there could be a connection because recusals directly relate to the institutional performance of the Court. Research has established that legitimacy is shaped by the public's perception that the justices are principled decision makers.[31] This research has found that although citizens understand that ideology influences judging, they still expect the justices to be principled. When citizens think of judges as little more than "politicians in robes," confidence in the Court declines.[32] If recusal misconduct creates the perception that the justices are biased, then legitimacy could be threatened because the public would have less foundation for believing that the justices were deciding cases in a principled, sincere fashion.

Yet there are also reasons to be doubtful that the relationship between legitimacy and recusals is as strong as commentators suggest. Time and again, the legitimacy of the Supreme Court has proven to be robust, capable of withstanding short-term bursts of disapproval of the justices' behavior.[33] For example, following *Bush v. Gore*,[34] many commentators assumed that the Court's legitimacy would be damaged because the decision was so salient and considered to be partisan by so many. However, research did not find a sustained negative impact on legitimacy. On the contrary, "institutional loyalty predisposed most Americans to view the decision as based on law and therefore legitimate."[35] While there is evidence that unpopular decisions can produce temporary declines in public confidence,[36] over the long term the Court's legitimacy has been resilient.[37] If a decision as salient and polarizing as *Bush v. Gore* has not caused long-term declines in public confidence in the Court, then it might be unreasonable to expect recusals to be any more damaging, given how much less salient they generally are.

My own investigation of the question suggests that the connection between recusals and legitimacy is most likely limited. Figure 5.1 charts public attitudes about the Supreme Court from June 2003 to November 2004, encompassing a period of about six months before and after Justice Scalia declined to recuse himself from the *Cheney* decision.[38] Given the salience of this controversy, if recusal misconduct has any effect on aggregate levels of public confidence, then one would expect to observe it here. However,

Please tell me how much confidence you, yourself have in the U.S. Supreme Court?

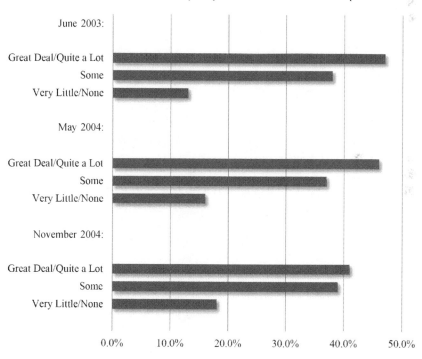

Source: Gallup   N = 1,029 (May 2003); 1,002 (June 2004); 885 (November 2004)

Figure 5.1. Public Confidence in the Supreme Court, 2003–2004.

there is no evidence that Scalia's behavior had a negative impact on public attitudes about the Court. In June 2003, six months before the Cheney story broke, approximately 47% of Americans said that they had either a "great deal" or "quite a lot" of confidence in the Supreme Court; and by May 2004, two months after Justice Scalia issued his memorandum declining to recuse himself from the *Cheney* case, the confidence levels had not changed. The number of respondents expressing a "great deal" or "quite a lot" of confidence in the Supreme Court was about 46%. The following November, confidence was down to about 41%, but there is little reason to suppose that the decline was directly attributable to *Cheney* or that it signaled a collapse of public confidence in the Court.[39]

It is true that the question employed in the survey is not an ideal measure of public confidence. The best measures do not ask respondents directly about their levels of confidence in the Court but instead try to gauge loyalty to the institution by asking them whether they support doing away with the Court or reducing its jurisdiction, among other similar indicators.[40] It is unclear whether the survey question used in Figure 5.1 captures institutional loyalty the same way that these other measure do or if it simply records job approval.[41] Yet even if the measure is imperfect, the fact that the *Cheney* decision appears to have been associated with no change in public attitudes about the Supreme Court should give pause. The Court's job approval ratings are generally less stable and more subject to short-term fluctuations than legitimacy is.[42] Because public attitudes about the Supreme Court were basically flat throughout the *Cheney* controversy, it seems doubtful that legitimacy was damaged in a meaningful way.

Of course, it is possible that only certain members of the public had their confidence in the Supreme Court shaken by Scalia's participation in *Cheney*. For example, one might hypothesize that Democratic respondents would have been more likely to oppose Scalia's participation and therefore reported less confidence in the Court following the *Cheney* controversy. Yet, once again, the evidence does not suggest that Scalia's behavior had much of an effect. Figure 5.2 breaks down the trends in public confidence by the party identification of respondents and shows that, for Republicans, confidence levels were generally stable, with about 56% of respondents reporting a "great deal" or "quite a lot" of confidence in June 2003 and about 53% reporting support at these levels in May 2004. Among Democrats, however, confidence in the Supreme Court actually increased, from 44% in June 2003 to 47% in May 2004. These figures are within the margin of error, so they suggest that there was essentially no change in public opinion that could be attributable to *Cheney*.

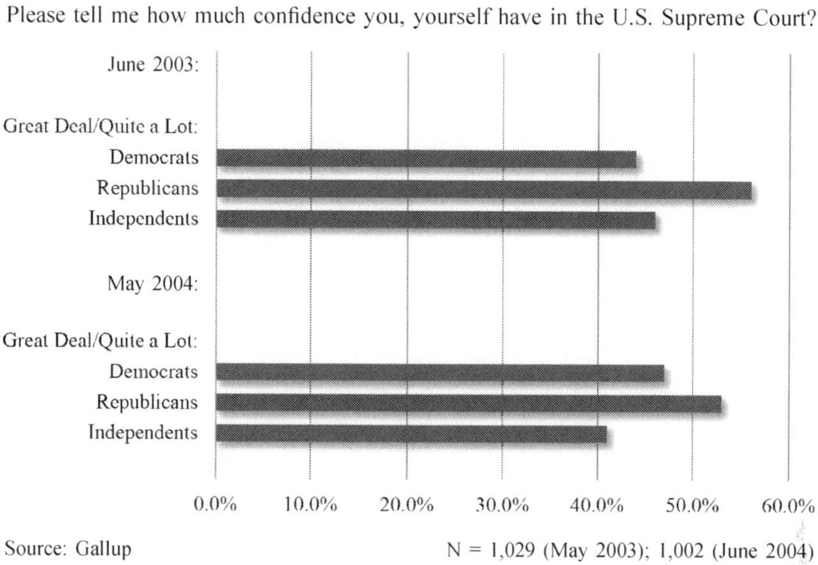

Please tell me how much confidence you, yourself have in the U.S. Supreme Court?

Figure 5.2. Public Confidence in the Supreme Court, by Party Identification, 2003–2004.

Alternatively, it is possible that the effect only would have been observable among knowledgeable respondents. Because it was necessary for respondents to have known about the *Cheney* incident for it to have influenced their behavior, respondents who were more attentive to the news may have been more likely to have declining confidence in the Supreme Court. Unfortunately, the survey did not ask respondents to report directly whether they were attentive to the news, but if we use their education levels as proxies, Figure 5.3 on page 100 reports that while there was no change in confidence levels among less educated respondents, there was a decline in confidence among respondents who were college educated. In June 2003, 63% of respondents had a "great deal" or "some confidence" in the Supreme Court, and by May 2004, confidence levels had fallen to 57%. Obviously the decline is small, and it is difficult to know whether it is directly attributable to *Cheney* or some other events that might have occurred in the intervening months, but the results do indicate that educated respondents experienced a decline in positive feelings about the Court during the study period.

Yet, even if we assume that the trends in Figure 5.3 are attributable to the *Cheney* decision and not some other phenomenon, the most that

Please tell me how much confidence you, yourself have in the U.S. Supreme Court?

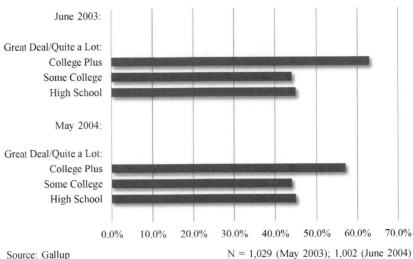

Source: Gallup   N = 1,029 (May 2003); 1,002 (June 2004)

Figure 5.3. Public Confidence in the Supreme Court, by Education Level, 2003–2004.

one can conclude from the data is that recusal misconduct might cause a decline in confidence among respondents who are knowledgeable about the Court's behavior. General levels of confidence were still flat throughout the period, which makes it difficult to conclude that the *Cheney* controversy had a meaningful impact on public attitudes overall. Moreover, it is fair to question how frequently the Court's recusal behavior is likely to be salient even to educated respondents. No other recusal decision has matched the visibility of *Cheney*, before or since, although the controversy over Kagan and Thomas's participation in the health care case was arguably close. Most of the time, recusals have much lower visibility. It is hard to imagine that the Court's recusal behavior would influence public confidence levels in these routine circumstances because the *Cheney* decision itself appears to have had such a minor impact on public attitudes about the Court.

This is not to suggest that public confidence in the Court is "bulletproof"[43] or that the justices have no reason to be concerned about the potential for recusal misconduct to influence public opinion. Justices still have incentives to appear as principled decision makers, and their recusal behavior surely contributes to this impression. Yet the obstacles to influence are substantial, requiring the public to know about potential recusals, to conclude that the justices have behaved inappropriately, and for the public's concerns over judicial misconduct to supersede their well-established institutional loyalty to the Court. Given these obstacles, it is probably unreasonable to expect a single recusal decision to do lasting damage to the Court, although a series of questionable recusal decisions might undermine public confidence.

An exception might occur if justices refused to disqualify themselves from controversies in which they stood to benefit financially. As I discussed in Chapters 2 and 3, the justices have been mostly scrupulous about recusing themselves from cases in which they have financial conflicts of interest. In fact, none of the recent recusal controversies on the Court has involved these types of financial conflicts.[44] It is possible that the reason the justices have been so careful to adhere to the letter of the statute in these cases is that financial conflicts have greater potential to erode public confidence. Research on judicial elections has shown that money can have a corrosive effect on public confidence in other contexts. For example, research has found that campaign contributions hurt legitimacy by creating the appearance of "a *quid pro quo* relationship between the donor and the judge."[45] When judges rule in favor of their major campaign donors, as occurred most infamously in *Caperton v. Massey*,[46] the public has reason to suspect that the judges are not basing their decision on principles but personal gain.

Supreme Court justices do not participate in election campaigns, but other types of financial conflicts could have similarly corrosive effects. If the justices started voting for companies in which they had investment interests, the public might have difficulty trusting their motives, so it would be reasonable for the justices to take special precautions in these cases. However, once again, the potential damage to legitimacy should not be overstated. Most likely, a single bad recusal decision will not cause public confidence in the Court to collapse, even when financial misconduct has occurred. The Court's legitimacy is simply too resilient to be damaged so easily. Moreover, because most recusal deliberations occur in secret, the public is unlikely to possess the information that it needs to evaluate the justices' behavior. Lacking a factual record, the arguments in favor of recusal will only rarely be clear, giving the public less cause to believe that the justices are behaving in an unprincipled or insincere fashion.

A different but related possibility is that recusals indirectly affect public confidence by making the Court less efficient. For example, confidence in the Court might decline when the justices divide evenly. Although the analysis in the previous section showed that dividing evenly is relatively uncommon after a recusal, it is still possible that the public responds negatively when it does happen. If the public believes that it is the responsibility of the Supreme Court to produce an authoritative judgment on the cases it reviews, then the failure of the justices to produce consensus could cast doubt on the Court's ability to do its job. In this way, a recusal could still lead to a loss of public confidence, not because the recusal itself was unethical, but because the remaining justices failed to respond appropriately to the situation.

To study these effects, I conducted a survey of public attitudes about the Supreme Court in the months following Justice Scalia's death in spring 2016, when the Court had only eight members and the possibility of dividing evenly was high. I began by asking respondents whether they approved or disapproved of the Court dividing evenly.[47] The exact question wording along with the distribution of responses are presented in Figure 5.4. Surprisingly, respondents indicated that they approved of the Court dividing evenly, and by a wide margin. Only 28.6% disapproved, compared to 53.3% who thought "the justices should do what they think is right, even if they end up deadlocked." It seems unlikely, then, that the Supreme Court would suffer a decline in public confidence for its failure to find compromise following a recusal because most of the public approves of the justices dividing evenly.

Nevertheless, it is still possible that the justices experienced a decline in confidence among those respondents who did disapprove of the Court becoming deadlocked. The next few figures explore this relationship using several different measures of public attitudes about the Court. Figure 5.5 looks at the Court's job approval rating. It shows that the justices in general enjoyed a 56.5% approval rating among those surveyed, but for respondents who were opposed to the Court dividing evenly, the approval rating was

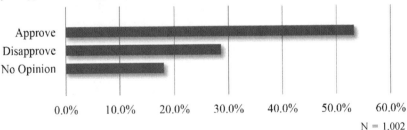

At least once this term, the Supreme Court became deadlocked because they were short a member. When the justices split 4-4, the lower court's decision becomes final and the Supreme Court's decision has no authority. Some people think that Supreme Court justices should work harder to find a compromise when they are short a member so that they do not divide evenly. But other people think the justices should do what they think is right, even if they end up deadlocked. What do you think? Do you approve or disapprove of the Court dividing evenly?

N = 1,002

Figure 5.4. Respondent Attitudes about Dividing Evenly, June 2016.

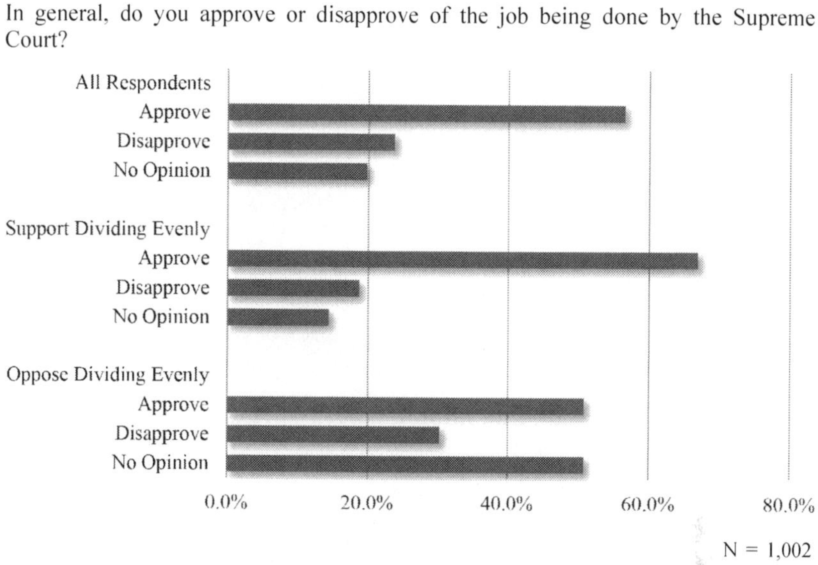

In general, do you approve or disapprove of the job being done by the Supreme Court?

Figure 5.5. Supreme Court Approval Rating, June 2016.

lower, at 50.9%. In contrast, supporters of the Court reported a much higher approval rating, at 66.9%. It is unknown from the survey whether the Court's approval rating was shaped by respondents' attitudes about dividing evenly or not.[48] Quite possibly, the relationship was reversed, and respondents who already disapproved of the Court were less likely to give them the benefit of the doubt when it came to dividing evenly. Minimally, though, Figure 5.5 establishes that there is a connection between public attitudes about dividing evenly and the Court's general approval rating.

This relationship becomes clouded, however, when more direct measures of legitimacy are employed. Figures 5.6, 5.7, and 5.8 (on pages 104 and 105) report the answers to three questions that have long been used by researchers who study Supreme Court legitimacy.[49] Of the three, only the first reveals a possible connection to public attitudes about dividing evenly.[50] Figure 5.6 finds some variation in respondents' reactions to the statement "If the Supreme Court started making a lot of decisions that most people disagree with, it might be better to do away with the Supreme Court altogether." Altogether, 4.1% of respondents strongly agreed with this statement, compared to 6.3% of respondents who disapproved of the Court dividing evenly. It is possible, then, that the justices do suffer some marginal institutional repercussions when they become deadlocked.

If the Supreme Court started making a lot of decisions that most people disagree with, it might be better to do away with the Supreme Court altogether.

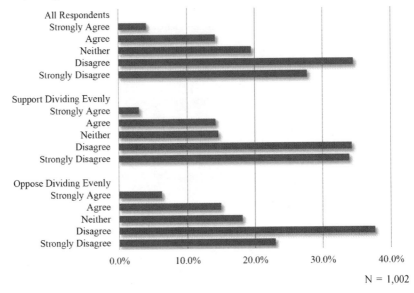

Figure 5.6. Supreme Court Legitimacy (Measure 1), June 2016.

The right of the Supreme Court to decide certain types of controversies should be reduced.

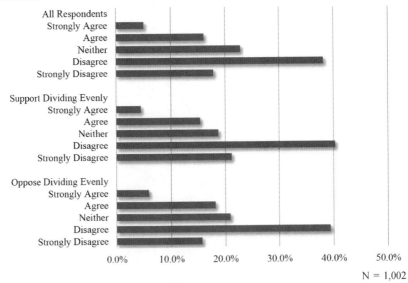

Figure 5.7. Supreme Court Legitimacy (Measure 2), June 2016.

The Supreme Court can usually be trusted to make decisions that are right for the country as a whole.

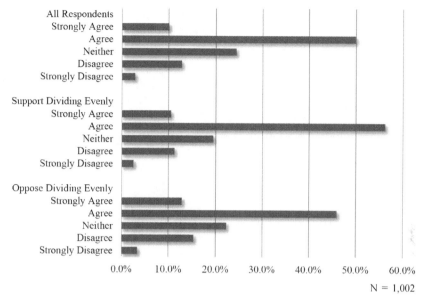

N = 1,002

Figure 5.8. Supreme Court Legitimacy (Measure 3), June 2016.

Yet the answers to the other two questions report no meaningful differences among respondents. Figure 5.7 shows that even respondents who disapproved of the Court dividing evenly were unlikely to agree with the statement "The right of the Supreme Court to decide certain types of controversies should be reduced." Just 5.9% of those who opposed the Court dividing evenly agreed strongly with this statement, compared to 5.1% of respondents in general. Similarly, there was little variation in reactions to the statement "The Supreme Court can usually be trusted to make decisions that are right for the country as a whole." Figure 5.8 shows that 3.5% of the respondents who were opposed to the justices dividing evenly disagreed strongly with this statement, compared to 2.9% of respondents generally. Although the trends are in the expected direction, the magnitude of the relationship is much too weak to be substantively meaningful.

These conclusions are reinforced in Table 5.5, which models the relationship between respondents' attitudes about dividing evenly and their general attitudes about the Court. The analysis employs two dependent variables. The first (S.C. APPROVAL) is a dummy variable recording respondents' approval rating of the Court, as reported in Figure 5.5. The second (S.C. LEGITIMACY) is a legitimacy index, which was generated by combining respondents' answers to the three survey questions in Figures 5.6 to 5.8.[51] The principal independent variable (DIVIDING EVENLY) is a dummy variable measuring whether respondents approved of the Court dividing evenly. Both of the models control for respondents' IDEOLOGY, PARTY IDENTIFICATION, SEX, BIRTH YEAR, race (ASIAN, BLACK, HISPANIC, WHITE), HOUSEHOLD INCOME, and EDUCATION LEVEL.[52] Because the S.C. APPROVAL variable is dichotomous, logistic regression was employed for the first analysis, while negative binomial regression was used for the second analysis of S.C. LEGITIMACY, which was measured as a count variable.[53]

The findings in Table 5.5 are consistent with the trends observed in the previous figures. Respondents who approved of the Court dividing evenly (DIVIDING EVENLY) were also more likely to approve of the job that the Supreme Court was doing (S.C. APPROVAL), but there was no measurable impact on the Court's legitimacy (S.C. LEGITIMACY). At most, then, one can conclude that people who were unhappy about the Court becoming deadlocked were also more likely to be unhappy with the Court's overall job performance. There is no evidence that the Court has suffered any institutional damage from dividing evenly.

Bargaining and Accommodation

A third potential consequence of recusals is that they cause the justices to engage in more bargaining activity at the opinion writing stage. The justices might circulate a greater number of opinion drafts, for example, or accommodate more suggestions from colleagues. Unlike the other consequences of recusals examined in this chapter, increased bargaining activity is not necessarily bad for the Court. The justices have institutional incentives to command a majority and produce a single opinion that will guide lower courts and litigants in future cases.[54]

Evidence of bargaining activity would also be consistent with the finding, from earlier in the chapter, that the justices divide evenly less frequently than one would expect when recusals occur. Perhaps the reason that the justices are able to find consensus is that they are making greater efforts to compromise behind the scenes. These tendencies might be the strongest when the chances of dividing evenly are high, such as when the initial conference vote is close or when members of the majority coalition have withdrawn. In recent years, the recusal of a conservative justice might be particularly likely to generate increased bargaining activity.

Table 5.5. The Impact of Dividing Evenly on Public Attitudes

	S.C. Approval	S.C. Legitimacy
DIVIDING EVENLY	0.857***	0.007
	(0.245)	(0.014)
LEGITIMACY	0.501***	—
	(0.047)	—
S.C. APPROVAL	—	0.244***
	—	(0.022)
IDEOLOGY	–0.000	–0.007***
	(0.039)	(0.002)
PARTY IDENTIFICATION	–0.283**	0.004
	(0.105)	(0.005)
SEX	–0.394	0.019
	(0.307)	(0.019)
BIRTH YEAR	0.014	–0.003***
	(0.013)	(0.001)
ASIAN	1.538*	–0.012
	(0.764)	(0.074)
BLACK	0.912	0.042
	(0.824)	(0.059)
HISPANIC	1.603*	0.001
	(0.659)	(0.074)
WHITE	1.490*	0.041
	(0.697)	(0.067)
HOUSEHOLD INCOME	0.022	0.006
	(0.053)	(0.003)
EDUCATION LEVEL	–0.162	0.022*
	(0.139)	(0.010)
Constant	–34.568	7.435***
	(25.225)	(1.138)
Chi-square	160.870***	470.770***
Pseudo R^2	0.271	0.035

$^*p < 0.05$; $^{**}p < 0.01$; $^{***}p < 0.001$ N = 690

Note: The first column models Supreme Court approval rating using logistic regression, while the second column uses negative binomial regression to model legitimacy. Robust standard errors are clustered by state.

Such behavior occurred in the months following Justice Scalia's death, when the justices found themselves with only eight members for a sustained period of time. Reports suggested that there were greater efforts at compromise on the Court, even if not all of the justices were committed to it.[55] According to newspaper coverage from the period, the justices who were the most willing to collaborate were the four at the center of the Court: Kennedy, Breyer, Roberts, and Kagan. Less agreeable to compromise were the justices at the far left, Ginsburg and Sotomayor, and the far right, Alito and Thomas. As a whole, however, the institution managed to find consensus and divide evenly less frequently than expected.

In fact, research on opinion writing indicates that justices routinely work together to craft majority opinions, and not just when their membership is down. Work by Forrest Maltzman, James Spriggs, and Paul Wahlbeck has shown that bargaining and accommodation is a regular part of the opinion-writing process.[56] This bargaining activity tends to increase when opinion writers are having trouble building or maintaining majority coalitions. We know, for example, that justices are more likely to circulate additional opinion drafts when majority coalitions are small, when they are ideologically diverse, or when the opinion writers themselves are ideologically distant from the other members of the coalition.[57]

No doubt a recusal intensifies these effects, and the regular determinants of bargaining activity become stronger when the possibility of dividing evenly accelerates the need for consensus. One might expect, for example, that if the justices ordinarily circulate a greater number of opinion drafts when they expect a case to be close, then they should be even more likely to do so when a justice has withdrawn from a dispute, especially if that justice was likely to have been a member of the majority coalition. In other words, one might expect to observe a statistically significant interaction between recusals and the other determinants of bargaining activity.

To test for these effects, Table 5.6 presents the results of a negative binomial regression model of opinion circulation during the years 1969 to 1985, with data from the Burger Court database.[58] The dependent variable is a count of the number of opinion drafts that majority opinion writers circulated during this period. The principal independent variables measure whether there was a recusal in the case by a justice to the right of the Court's median (CONSERVATIVE RECUSAL), to the left of the median (LIBERAL RECUSAL), or at the center of the Court (MEDIAN RECUSAL). The model also includes three additional variables that have been used in studies of bargaining activity.[59] The first counts the number of justices in the majority coalition (SIZE OF MAJORITY COALITION), with the expectation that when

Table 5.6. Negative Binomial Model of Majority Opinion Draft Circulation, 1969–1985

	Model A	Model B
Conservative Recusal	0.034	0.425*
	(0.040)	(0.204)
Liberal Recusal	–0.048	–0.054
	(0.046)	(0.047)
Median Recusal	–0.093	–0.100
	(0.085)	(0.086)
Case Salience	0.055**	0.055**
	(0.019)	(0.019)
Size of Majority Coalition	–0.065***	–0.062***
	(0.007)	(0.008)
(Conservative Recusal)* (Size of Majority Coalition)	—	–0.067**
	—	(0.025)
Author Distance	0.002	0.003
	(0.013)	(0.013)
(Conservative Recusal)* (Author Distance)	—	0.007
	—	(0.020)
Coalition Diversity	–0.043*	–0.043*
	(0.017)	(0.018)
(Conservative Recusal)* (Coalition Diversity)	—	0.010
	—	(0.061)
Constant	1.765***	1.745***
	(0.064)	(0.064)
Chi-square	268.990***	308.150***
Pseudo R^2	0.314	0.022

$*p < 0.05$; $**p < 0.01$; $***p < 0.001$ N = 1,888

Note: Table 5.6 also controls for justice, the coefficients for which are not reported.

coalitions get larger, fewer opinions will circulate because less negotiation is needed to build or maintain a majority.[60]

The next two variables measure the ideological distance of an opinion writer from the other justices in the majority coalition (Author Distance), as well as the ideological diversity of the majority coalition (Coalition

Diversity), using the Martin-Quinn scores.[61] Specifically, the Coalition Diversity variable measures the standard deviation of the Martin-Quinn scores for all of the justices in the majority coalition. It is expected that as opinion writers become more distant from the other justices in their coalitions, and as these coalitions become more ideologically diverse, justices will circulate additional drafts. The need for compromise will be greater because coalitions will be harder to keep together.

Contrary to expectations, however, the effects of recusals on bargaining activity appear to be limited. Column A of Table 5.6 finds no independent effects of recusal activity on the circulation of opinion drafts.[62] Neither the recusal of a conservative justice (Conservative Recusal) nor that of a liberal justice (Liberal Recusal) or a justice at its center (Median Recusal) increases the number of draft opinions circulated.[63] A recusal by itself, therefore, does not appear to increase bargaining activity. However, Column B suggests that there is a statistically significant interaction between a conservative recusal and one of the other determinants of bargaining activity, the size of the majority coalition. Specifically, the data show that the effects of coalition size intensify when a conservative recusal occurs.[64]

These trends are illustrated in Table 5.7, which estimates the average number of opinions that circulate as the size of the majority coalition expands. When a case is close, with only five justices supporting the outcome, the

Table 5.7. Estimated Number of Majority Opinion Drafts Following a Recusal

A. Recusal of a Conservative Justice

Size of Majority Coalition	Estimated Number of Drafts
5	4.1
6	3.1
7	2.9
8	2.6

B. Recusal of a Liberal or Median Justice

Size of Majority Coalition	Estimated Number of Drafts
5	3.5
6	3.0
7	3.0
8	2.8

number of drafts that a majority opinion writer circulates varies depending on whether a conservative justice has withdrawn. Conservative recusals result in the circulation of approximately 4.1 opinion drafts, compared to 3.5 drafts when a conservative recusal has not occurred.[65] The effect is not large, but it is statistically significant and suggests that opinion writers do treat the recusal of a conservative justice differently from other recusals. However, the effects of conservative recusals break down as the size of the majority coalition gets larger. When the size of the majority coalition increases by just one vote, from five justices to six, the presence of a conservative recusal has virtually no effect on bargaining, increasing the number of circulations from 3.0 to 3.1 opinions.

The fact that only conservative recusals affect circulation rates makes sense given that the Court had a conservative majority throughout the Burger Court years, which is the period covered in the database. During these years, the justices at the center of the Court were Harlan (1970), White (1971–1974, 1979–1982), Stewart (1975–1976), Blackmun (1977–1978), and Powell (1984–1985).[66] Although majority coalitions in these years were not as conservative or as stable as they would later become on the Rehnquist and Roberts Courts, the ideological composition of the Court was still more conservative than it had been in the Warren Court years. The implication, then, is that recusals can affect bargaining activity, but only in specialized circumstances. Recusals sometimes prompt justices to circulate additional drafts to forge consensus, but only in close cases and when a justice from the majority coalition has withdrawn. Still, the findings indicate that the justices do take extra steps to avoid becoming deadlocked when dividing evenly is most likely to occur.

The Court's Docket

A final possible impact of recusals is on the Court's docket by denying petitioners the votes that they need to have their petitions for *certiorari* granted. By tradition, four justices must agree to review a case before they place it on the docket. This practice is known as the Rule of Four.[67] Justices have stated that, more often than not, there is consensus about whether cases merit review, so the Rule of Four does not come into play too often. Yet when it does, the disqualification of a justice has the potential to determine whether a case is granted. Indeed, some justices and commentators have stated that a recusal prior to the *certiorari* stage is essentially a vote against the petitioner.[68] However, we do not actually know how likely it is that recusals will cause votes on *certiorari* petitions to turn out differently.

To investigate the effects of recusals on the Court's docket, I examined the papers of Justice Harry Blackmun, available in the *Digital Archive of the Papers of Justice Harry A. Blackmun*.[69] Ordinarily the Supreme Court does not release information about how justices voted on *certiorari* petitions. This information is included only in the justices' private notes. Fortunately, Justice Blackmun kept meticulous records, including docket sheets for the 1986 to 1993 terms. Using these records, it is possible to identify which cases were nearly granted and whether the participation of an absent justice would have made a difference. To that end, I examined the docket sheets for every case in the archive in which the Court denied *certiorari* and one or more of the justices disqualified themselves. I identified appropriate cases using LexisNexis and then pulled the corresponding docket sheets from the Blackmun Archive. Altogether, there were 267 cases that met these criteria.

As it turns out, in the vast majority of cases, there is no reason to think that the recusal made a difference. Blackmun's notes reveal that in just 7 of the 267 cases (2.6%) was the vote close, and in only a few of these cases does it appear likely that the participation of the absent justice would have resulted in a grant. These cases are summarized in Table 5.8. Complicating the analysis is the fact that in a large proportion of the cases, the docket sheets include no record of a vote. I have interpreted these blank docket sheets as circumstances in which petitions were dismissed without a formal vote or discussion,[70] but one cannot know for certain what the votes in these cases were, and it is possible that in a few circumstances Blackmun

Table 5.8. Close *Certiorari* Votes Following Recusals, 1986–1993

Case	Recusing Justice(s)	Conference Vote
Dow Jones v. Simon (1988)	Stevens	3-5
Keane v. U.S. (1989)	Stevens	3-5
Wallace v. Arizona (1990)	O'Connor	2-6
Minnesota Mining & Mfg Co. v. Freeman (1990)	Blackmun	2-6
Lewis v. Adamson (1990)	O'Connor, Kennedy	3-4
Willner v. Barr (1991)	Thomas	2-2-3*
Smith v. United States (1991)	Thomas	3-5

*In *Willner v. Barr*, two justices cast "Join-3" votes.

Note: Data are from the *Digital Archive of the Papers of Justice Harry A. Blackmun*.

simply omitted to record the votes. However, previous research that has relied on the Blackmun papers suggests that he was a good record keeper, so it is defensible to assume that if a case was nearly granted *certiorari*, or if it generated discussion in conference, then Blackmun would have made a note about it. Indeed, Blackmun routinely recorded the conference votes for cases in which he had disqualified himself.[71] Still, Table 5.8 is most accurately interpreted as recording those cases in which Blackmun's notes indicate that the *certiorari* votes were close.

Examining these cases in more depth, the first one listed, *Dow Jones v. Simon*, is one in which the disqualification of a justice is likely to have made a difference.[72] The case concerned the constitutionality of gag orders prohibiting prosecutors, defendants, and defense counsel from speaking to the press. The Supreme Court ruled in *Nebraska Press Assn. v. Stewart* that similar gag orders that were issued directly to the press unconstitutionally infringed upon First Amendment principles of no prior restraint,[73] but the circuits were divided over whether to extend *Nebraska's* holding to trial participants who wanted to speak to the press.[74] Justices White, Brennan, and Marshall were prepared to reach the merits in *Dow Jones* and even filed a dissent from the denial of *certiorari*, but they were unable to attract a fourth vote. It is impossible to know how the absent justice, Stevens, would have voted, but in the *Nebraska* case, Stevens joined White, Brennan, and Marshall in seeking a more vigorous defense of First Amendment principles than the majority opinion had provided.[75] It is reasonable to expect that Stevens would have voted once again with the three other justices to grant *certiorari* in *Dow Jones* and to reverse the lower court opinion, which had refused to extend the *Nebraska* holding. I therefore predict that Stevens's participation would have made a difference in the *Dow Jones* case, resulting in a grant of *certiorari*.

Justice Stevens also disqualified himself from the second case listed in Table 5.8, but in this case I do not predict that his recusal affected the result. In *Keane v. United States*,[76] Thomas Keane sought to have a mail fraud conviction vacated following the Supreme Court's decision in *McNally v. United States*,[77] which limited the scope of the federal mail fraud statute. The Seventh Circuit refused,[78] and Blackmun's notes indicate that three of the justices who had voted with the majority in *McNally*—Brennan, Marshall, and Blackmun—voted to grant *certiorari*, no doubt to reverse the Seventh Circuit's decision. Justice Stevens, however, had dissented in *McNally*,[79] in an opinion joined by Justice O'Connor, who voted against granting *certiorari* in *Keane*. I therefore expect that if Stevens had participated in *Keane*, he would have once again aligned with O'Connor and denied *certiorari* to avoid the possibility of extending *McNally's* rationale any further.

Similarly, in the next two cases, it appears unlikely that the participation of the absent justices would have impacted the *certiorari* decisions. In *Wallace v. Arizona*,[80] a death penalty case in which Justice O'Connor recused herself, four of the justices originally expressed interest in holding the case over for further discussion, according to Justice Blackmun's notes, but two of these justices—Blackmun and Stevens—ultimately voted against *certiorari*. Only Justices Brennan and Marshall dissented from the denial, using familiar language that they typically employed in death penalty cases.[81] None of their more conservative colleagues expressed support for the petition, so there is little reason to suppose that Justice O'Connor would have supported a grant if she had participated or that her participation would have persuaded Blackmun or Stevens to join Brennan and Marshall. I therefore classified this case as one in which the recusal made no difference. Similarly, in *Minnesota Mining & Manufacturing Company v. Freeman*,[82] Justice Blackmun's notes indicate that only Justices White and Black cast firm votes in favor of a grant. Justice O'Connor initially voted to pass, which might possibly have signaled indecisiveness about her eventual decision to deny *certiorari*. Yet, once again, there is little evidence that the participation of the absent justice, Justice Blackmun, would have prompted O'Connor to vote for *certiorari*, or that Blackmun would have joined her.

A case in which a disqualification is much more likely to have made a difference is *Lewis v. Adamson*.[83] Justices O'Connor and Kennedy both disqualified themselves from the case, which involved an inmate whose sentence of forty-eight to forty-nine years was changed to a death sentence by the presiding judge. The Ninth Circuit reversed this judgment along with the Arizona statute that permitted the sentencing judge to impose the death penalty in the first place.[84] In the initial conference vote on the *certiorari* petition, there were five votes to grant and vacate the Ninth Circuit's opinion in light of the Supreme Court's holdings in three other cases.[85] However, the two more liberal justices in the coalition—Brennan and Marshall—changed their votes, leaving only Rehnquist, White, and Scalia in favor of granting the petition. It seems highly likely that if O'Connor and Kennedy had participated, they would have joined their conservative colleagues. Both O'Connor and Kennedy had joined the other conservatives in the three cases cited in the dissent of denial of *certiorari* in *Adamson*. Indeed, O'Connor had written the majority opinion in one of them.[86] I therefore predict that the participation of either Justice O'Connor or Justice Kennedy would have resulted in a grant and perhaps a summary reversal.

Less clear is how *Willner v. Barr* would have turned out.[87] In conference, only Justices Stevens and O'Connor clearly favored a grant, while Justices White and Kennedy cast Join-3 votes.[88] Justice Thomas was out, and it is uncertain whether he would have provided the third vote needed to persuade either White or Kennedy to vote in favor of the petition. However, the grant was opposed by Thomas's closest ideological allies on the Court, Justices Rehnquist and Scalia. I therefore expect that Justice Thomas would have voted along with his conservative colleagues and denied the petition, which suggests that his disqualification did not matter. For similar reasons, I expect that Thomas's absence from *Smith v. United States* also made no difference.[89] Blackmun's notes indicate that there were initially five votes in *Smith* for granting *certiorari* and vacating the lower court opinion, but in opposition were three of the more conservative justices: Rehnquist, Scalia, and White. Kennedy and Stevens eventually switched their votes, resulting in a denial of the petition. Because, once again, I expect Thomas to have voted with the conservatives, I predict that Thomas's disqualification made no difference.

Altogether, then, of the seven cases during the 1986 to 1993 terms in which recusals plausibly could have affected the Court's decision to grant *certiorari*, only two appear to have mattered. The effects of recusals on the Court's docket therefore appear to be negligible. Between 1986 and 1993, the Court disposed of 42,786 cases, which means that the disqualification of a justice appears to have adversely affected petitioners in only about 0.00005% of them.[90] Even if Blackmun's notes missed a few cases, it would be very difficult to conclude that recusals have a meaningful impact on the Court's docket or that petitioners have any cause to be concerned that a disqualification will hurt their chances for a grant.

Conclusion

Media commentators would have us believe that there is much at stake when recusal controversies arise, and occasionally these concerns are justified, but the truth is that only rarely is a single recusal decision likely to have significant consequences. This is not to say that a recusal is never impactful. Depending on which justice sits out, it is possible that the outcome of a case could change or that the Court could divide evenly. Even more rarely, a recusal could affect a *certiorari* vote. However, it is unusual for a recusal to be so decisive. As the previous chapter demonstrated, it is more common for a recusal to influence the contents of the majority opinion than a case disposition or a *certiorari* grant.

There is also little reason to be concerned that recusal behavior will damage the Court's legitimacy. Most recusals are simply not salient enough for the public to notice, and the evidence of recusal misconduct is seldom clear, especially because the justices conduct their deliberations in secret, with no public records available. This does not mean that recusal misconduct has no potential to influence legitimacy. It is possible that if the justices abandoned their reliance on the federal recusal statute and made a series of poor ethical decisions, then legitimacy might be damaged. Yet it seems unlikely that the justices would behave this way, and even if they did, the justices have been effective at shielding their recusal behavior from public scrutiny and defending their decisions to participate when controversies have arisen.

To be sure, the situation might well be different in another regulatory environment. If the justices had to record the reasons for their recusal decisions, then public awareness of recusal misconduct could increase, potentially reducing legitimacy. However, it seems more likely that the justices would simply adapt to the increased public scrutiny, either becoming more attentive to the statutory criteria or sharpening their defenses for their behavior. The question is whether imposing additional burdens on the justices is worth it if the tradeoff is reducing the justices' discretion to prioritize other considerations, such as the duty to sit, over the ethical criteria when the need arises. In the final chapter, I enter this debate, describing some of the most commonly advanced proposals for reform and evaluating their costs and benefits.

6

Proposals for Reform

The evaluation of proposals for reforming the recusal process has, until now, been limited by the lack of systematic evidence about the causes and consequences of judicial disqualifications. The silence of Supreme Court justices has exacerbated this problem, inviting unflattering speculation about their motives and perhaps fueling demands for reform when none is needed. The findings in this book inform this debate and provide evidence that supports the claims of both reformers and their opponents. However, my own perspective is that, on balance, the arguments in favor of reform are not compelling. After reviewing the data, I am led to conclude that the potential benefits of reform are too modest and come at the risk of needlessly burdening the Court.

It is not that reformers lack cause for doubting the justices' commitment to the ethical guidelines. The findings in this book quite clearly suggest that the justices are willing to subordinate ethical commitments to their other institutional and policy goals. Indeed, the justices themselves have indicated that they do.[1] In Chapter 3, I found evidence that the justices still apply the duty to sit doctrine, despite the 1974 revisions to the federal recusal statute that were meant to abolish the presumption. Commentators are therefore correct to state that the justices have at times conducted their business as though the 1974 revisions never happened.[2] I also found that justices participate in cases when they have policy incentives to stay, withdrawing less frequently when they are close to the center of the Court or at the ideological extremes. Advocates for reform could point to these findings and make the case that the justices are not strictly following the federal recusal statute and that reforms are therefore needed.

On the other hand, the justices do seem to follow the recusal statute when the arguments in favor of recusal are the clearest. My review of the justices' financial disclosure reports in Chapter 3 revealed that the justices withdraw from cases when they own stock in the companies appearing before them. The quantitative analysis in the same chapter found that recusals occur more frequently when business interests are before the Court, as well as in the justices' early years of service, when cases are more likely to relate to pre-bench activities. If, in other cases, the justices are less likely to recuse themselves, it could be that the arguments in favor of recusal are less clear and the justices therefore have more discretion about whether to sit out. My research has uncovered no egregious examples of judicial misconduct. There is no evidence that the justices have tried to bend the ethical rules to advance their own personal or financial self-interest. As noted above, the justices are diligent about recusing themselves when these types of conflicts arise, despite the fact that any gains that they would receive from cases are likely to be small.[3] When the justices place less emphasis on ethics, their goal is generally to ensure the resolution of cases and controversies, as they were appointed and confirmed to do. It is true that the justices also seek to resolve cases consistently with their sincere policy preferences, but it is not necessarily unethical for justices to be so motivated if presidents appoint them with the expectation that they will shape legal policy in this manner.[4]

Nor does recusal misconduct routinely produce the sort of adverse consequences that would heighten the need for reform. On the contrary, my research has found that, for the most part, recusals do not have a substantial impact on law and policy. Case outcomes do not generally turn on the disqualification of particular justices, nor do the justices frequently divide evenly because of them. There is also little foundation for concluding that recusals affect the Court's docket or that recusal behavior has much influence on public attitudes about the Court. The more typical effect of a recusal is modest, incrementally altering the scope of the majority opinion by shifting the median ideology of the majority coalition to the right or left.

This is not to say that there are never exceptional cases in which a justice's recusal behavior has made a difference. Surely Justice Kagan's participation in the health care dispute fits this description. Had she chosen to recuse herself from the *Sebelius* case, the Court's resolution of the constitutionality of the Affordable Care Act almost certainly would have turned out differently. However, it is unusual for a single recusal decision to have so much influence, and even in the *Sebelius* case, it is by no means clear that Justice Kagan erred by participating. Many commentators maintained that Justice Kagan's decision to participate was justified and that demands for her disqualification were motivated primarily by politics.[5]

It is difficult, then, to identify a problem that reforms are supposed to solve, especially if one accepts the view that judicial ethics is just one of several goals that justices might legitimately pursue. Abiding by the statutory recusal guidelines is important, but so too is resolving cases and controversies. Supreme Court justices have found a way to pursue multiple goals simultaneously, maintaining a flexible set of decision criteria that are attentive to ethical considerations but not shackled by them, so that they can participate in cases when public policy needs are the most heightened. The justices maintain this flexibility, in part, by refusing to codify their practices and by keeping their deliberations over recusals private.

Yet, it would be disingenuous to suggest that the justices have been completely silent on the subject of ethics. In fact, they do sometimes comment about it,[6] and when controversies about their practices arise, they are willing to defend their recusal decisions in writing, as Justice Scalia did in his *Cheney* memorandum,[7] and as Chief Justice Roberts did in his 2011 *Year-End Report*, following the controversy over the participation of Justices Thomas and Kagan in the health care dispute.[8] There is simply no evidence to suggest that the justices are corrupt, or that they are in any way seeking to undermine the public interest through their recusal practices.

Nevertheless, supporters of reform can point to at least four reasons for taking their proposals seriously. The first is that it is necessary for the justices to be proactive about the Court's legitimacy because, in recent years, public support for the Court has been declining. Although historically confidence in the Court has been high, over the past decade citizens who report a "great deal" or "quite a lot" of confidence in the Court has fallen, from a high of 50% in 2001 to a low of about 30% in 2014.[9] These trends are illustrated in Figure 6.1 on page 120. There is no reason to suppose that this decline is directly attributable to the justices' recusal behavior. As I discussed in Chapter 5, the potential for recusal misconduct to influence legitimacy is most likely limited.[10] Yet if public sentiment is down, it might still benefit the Court to take precautions that would reinforce the impression that the justices are principled decision makers.[11]

A second justification for reforming the recusal process is that greater transparency could assist litigants and lawyers with filing recusal motions. Without clear guidelines, litigants have disincentives to file motions because they are wary of offending justices by accusing them of misconduct. "A less than compelling, and thus unsuccessful, recusal request could cause the

Please tell me how much confidence you, yourself have in the U.S. Supreme Court?

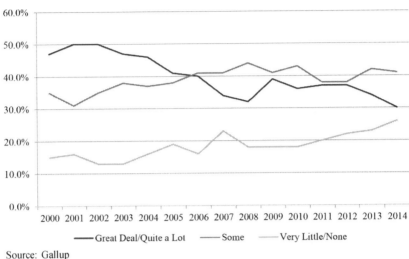

Source: Gallup

Figure 6.1. Public Confidence in the U.S. Supreme Court, 2000–2014.

appellate judge to harbor resentment toward the party which claimed that the appellate judge was incapable of being fair," writes one appellate advocate. "After all, judges are only human. And therefore, a recusal request that unsuccessfully challenges the perception of a judge's impartiality can serve as a self-fulfilling prophesy."[12] Attorneys might also worry that they could put their long-term relationships with the justices at risk by making ill-considered recusal bids.[13] Were the justices to clarify their criteria for granting recusal motions, so that attorneys better understood when they were appropriate, these concerns could be reduced and the number of filings might increase.

A third argument in favor of reform is that it is inherently good for the justices to behave ethically, even if strictly following the recusal guidelines has no other measurable benefits. Maintaining the integrity of the judicial system is an end in itself. As the Alliance for Justice wrote in its report advocating for reform, "A means for accountability and transparency in Supreme Court recusal decisions is necessary to ensure an independent and impartial Court."[14] Supporters of this view are likely to reject the more pragmatic approach to recusals that the justices have taken, even if it means that the justices are less capable of fulfilling their institutional responsibility to decide cases and controversies. According to the Alliance for Justice, "while a 4-4 split may not be a desirable outcome, a 5-4 split in which the allegedly biased justice casts the deciding vote is arguably worse. 5-4 splits are always controversial, but never more so than when the deciding vote is cast by a potentially biased justice, calling into question the legitimacy of the decision itself."[15] If the Supreme Court is to be an institution of law and justice, then it is important to maintain the integrity of its decision-making processes.

The final justification turns the tables on the opponents of reform and asks why Supreme Court justices should *not* be more transparent about their recusal practices, particularly in an age when most government officials— and all other federal judges—are held to higher ethical standards.[16] What possible justification could there be for treating the Supreme Court any differently? At times, the Supreme Court conducts itself as though it were a "quasi-royal body" whose members are undeserving of the close scrutiny that members of other institutions consider routine.[17] For the Supreme Court to function as a democratically accountable institution, it must be willing to make public the reasons for its decisions. Otherwise, there is no way of knowing whether the justices are truly acting in the country's best interests.

These arguments are powerful and might indeed justify some type of reform of the recusal process. I describe several proposals in the rest of the chapter, along with their costs and benefits. Yet, as I discuss below, I am ultimately unpersuaded that the proposed alternatives are a significant improvement over the current system, even though I concede that many of them do have merit. Nor am I convinced that the proposals are likely to achieve the goals that reformers would like to accomplish. On the contrary, there is a good chance that they will be counterproductive, operating primarily as a nuisance to the justices and a drain on the Court's administrative efficiency. In the absence of clear benefits to these alternatives, it is better to maintain the current system than to pursue untested and potentially unconstitutional reforms.

An Overview of Reform Proposals

Recent proposals for reforming the recusal process tend to be procedural in nature, seeking to hold the justices accountable to the existing recusal standards instead of defining new categories of proscribed misconduct. The reason for this emphasis is that Congress has already approved a comprehensive set of substantive recusal guidelines.[18] Although the Judicial Conference's Code of Conduct does not apply to Supreme Court justices, Congress made the portions of the Code that concern disqualification applicable to them with the 1974 revisions to the federal recusal statute.[19] It is not clear, then, that more substantive rules are needed. Yet federal law does not describe how justices are supposed to review recusal motions, it imposes no reporting requirements on the justices, nor does it provide any oversight of their recusal decisions. Reform proposals therefore focus on filling these gaps in the statutory framework, developing procedures that will encourage the justices to follow the recusal guidelines more closely.

Examples of two recent reform bills introduced to Congress are in Figures 6.2 and 6.3 (on pages 124–126). The first proposal, from Representative Chris Murphy (D-Conn.) and co-sponsored by Representative Anthony Weiner (D-N.Y.), would have instituted comprehensive ethics reform, applying the Code of Conduct to Supreme Court justices and permitting the Judicial Conference to develop procedures for investigating violations of the Code, including recusal misconduct.[20] The Murphy Bill also would have required the justices to "disclose in the public record" their reasons for self-disqualifications and for denying recusal motions. What is noteworthy about this proposal is the amount of authority that it would have given the Judicial Conference to craft new procedural rules. Even supporters of ethics reform have described the bill as "unusually open-ended."[21] Variations of this proposal would have let Congress develop the procedures or required the justices to do it themselves.[22]

The second bill, sponsored by Senator Patrick Leahy (D-Vt.), is narrower in scope and would have permitted retired justices to act as substitutes when recusals occur, with the approval of a majority of the active justices.[23] The goal of this proposal was to reduce the justices' reliance on the duty to sit by eliminating the possibility that a recusal would cause the Court to divide evenly. As Senator Leahy explained, "[i]n recent history, Justices have refused to recuse themselves and one of their justifications has been that the Supreme Court is unlike lower courts because no other judge can serve in their place when Justices recuse."[24] Leahy's bill was designed to ease this concern. "The bill I am introducing today will ensure that the Supreme Court can continue to serve its essential function."[25] Because retired justices already sit on lower courts by designation, it would not be unprecedented for them to take on this additional role.

Putting aside for a moment the potential policy benefits of these proposals, a question that accompanies all such attempts at reform is whether they are constitutional. It is by no means clear that Congress has the authority to regulate the justices' recusal practices, and in fact the constitutional status of even the 1974 reforms is in doubt. Chief Justice Roberts, in his 2011

Year-End Report, noted that the justices have never decided that Congress can regulate their recusal practices,[26] and academic commentary on the subject is mixed.[27] On the one hand, supporters of reform say that two sections of the federal Constitution justify congressional regulation. Article III grants Congress the authority to create lower federal courts and, by implication, to define the federal judicial structure.[28] The necessary and proper clause of Article I, section 8, also permits Congress "to make all Laws which shall be necessary and proper for carrying into Execution the . . . Powers vested by this Constitution in the Government of the United States." Supporters of reform would say that recusal legislation, as well as other types of ethics reform, are unremarkable extensions of the power to regulate the Supreme Court and the rest of the federal judiciary, which Congress has done since at least the passage of the 1789 Judiciary Act. Few question, for example, that Congress can change the number of justices, the length of the Court's term, and even the scope of its appellate jurisdiction.[29]

For critics, however, recusal regulations step too far in the direction of interfering with judicial independence and the prerogative of the Supreme Court to exercise the judicial power.[30] While Article III of the federal Constitution does not define the precise contours of the judicial power, opponents of reform would say that, minimally, the judicial power permits the justices to determine the final resolution of disputes. As Virelli notes, "there is widespread agreement that this power must at least include the ability to independently and completely decide individual cases that fall within the jurisdiction of the federal courts."[31] Recusal reforms threaten to interfere with this responsibility by requiring the removal of justices in certain circumstances, even if it means that the justices cannot resolve the cases before them. A further obstacle to the constitutionality of recusal reform is that, for much of its history, Congress did not assume that it had this authority. Although Congress has legislated on the recusal practices of the lower federal courts since the earliest days of the republic, they have mostly excluded the Supreme Court from these measures. Legislation targeting the justices' recusal practices emerged only in the past half century, and as noted above, the Supreme Court has not acknowledged its constitutionality. Opponents of reform would say that the refusal of the founding generation to regulate the justices on the subject of ethics implies that they did not believe that they had the power.[32]

These arguments against the constitutionality of recusal reform are strong but not necessarily persuasive to its supporters. At most, reformers might concede that the authority of Congress to regulate judicial ethics is

Figure 6.2. Murphy Bill

H.R. 862

112th Congress

In The House of Representatives

March 1, 2011

Mr. Murphy of Connecticut (for himself and Mr. Weiner) introduced the following bill; which was referred to the Committee on the Judiciary

A Bill

To apply to the justices of the Supreme Court the Code of Conduct for United States Judges, to establish certain procedures with respect to the recusal of justices, and for other purposes.

Be it enacted by the Senate and House of Representatives of the United States of America in Congress assembled,

SECTION 1. SHORT TITLE.

This Act may be cited as the "Supreme Court Transparency and Disclosure Act of 2011."

SEC. 2. CODE OF CONDUCT.

(a) Applicability.—The Code of Conduct for United States Judges adopted by the Judicial Conference of the United States shall apply to the justices of the United States Supreme Court to the same extent as such Code applies to circuit and district judges.

(b) Enforcement.—The Judicial Conference shall establish procedures, modeled after the procedures set forth in chapter 16 of title 28, United States Code, under which—

(1) complaints alleging that a justice of the Supreme Court has violated the Code of Conduct referred to in subsection (a) may be filed with or identified by the Conference;

(2) such complaints are reviewed and investigated by the Conference; and

(3) further action, where appropriate, is taken by the Conference, with respect to such complaints.

(c) Submission to Congress; Effective Date—

(1) SUBMISSION TO CONGRESS.—The Judicial Conference shall, not later than the 180th day after the date of the enactment of this Act, submit to Congress the procedures established under subsection (b).

(2) EFFECTIVE DATE.—Such procedures shall take effect upon the expiration of the 270-day period beginning on the date of the enactment of this Act.

SEC. 3. RECUSAL OF JUSTICES.

(a) Disclosures by Justices—

(1) SELF DISQUALIFICATION.—In any case in which a justice of the Supreme Court disqualifies himself or herself in a proceeding under section 455 of title 28, United States Code, the justice shall disclose in the public record of the proceeding the reasons for the disqualification.

(2) DENIAL OF DISQUALIFICATION MOTION.—If a justice of the Supreme Court denies a motion brought by a party to a proceeding before the Court that the justice should be disqualified in the proceeding under section 455 of such title, the justice shall disclose in the public record of the proceeding the reasons for the denial of the motion.

(b) Process for Determining Recusal.—The Judicial Conference of the United States shall establish a process under which, if a disqualification motion has been denied as described in subsection (a)(2) and the party making the motion seeks further review of the motion, other justices or judges of a court of the United States (as defined in section 451 of title 28, United States Code), among whom retired justices and senior judges eligible for assignment under section 294 of title 28, United States Code, may be included, shall decide whether the justice with respect to whom the motion is made should be so disqualified.

(c) Submission to Congress; Effective Date—

(1) SUBMISSION TO CONGRESS.—The Judicial Conference shall, not later than the 180th day after the date of the enactment of this Act, submit to Congress the process established under subsection (b).

(2) EFFECTIVE DATE.—Such process shall take effect upon the expiration of the 270-day period beginning on the date of the enactment of this Act.

Figure 6.3. Leahy Bill

S. 3871

111th Congress

In The Senate of the United States

September 29, 2010

Mr. Leahy introduced the following bill; which was read twice and referred to the Committee on the Judiciary

A Bill

To amend chapter 13 of title 28, United States Code, to authorize the designation and assignment of retired justices of the Supreme Court to particular cases in which an active justice is recused.

Be it enacted by the Senate and House of Representatives of the United States of America in Congress assembled,

SECTION 1. DESIGNATION AND ASSIGNMENT OF RETIRED SUPREME COURT JUSTICES.

Section 294 of title 28, United States Code, is amended—

(1) in subsection (a), by inserting "(1)" after "(a)";

(2) by adding at the end the following:

"(2) Any retired Chief Justice of the United States or any retired Associate Justice of the Supreme Court may be designated and assigned to serve as a justice on the Supreme Court of the United States in a particular case if—

"(A) any active justice is recused from that case; and

"(B) a majority of active justices vote to designate and assign that retired Chief Justice or Associate Justice."; and

(3) in subsection (d), by striking "No such designation or assignment shall be made to the Supreme Court." and inserting "Except as provided under subsection (a)(2), no designation or assignment under this section shall be made to the Supreme Court."

murky and perhaps concurrent with that of the Court.[33] Yet they would point out that Congress has already interfered with the exercise of the judicial power in other ways. For example, Congress has at times set the number of justices at six, despite the fact that doing so has made it possible for the justices to divide evenly.[34] Congress can also use the Exceptions Clause to strip the Court of its appellate jurisdiction, denying the Court the ability to exercise the judicial power in certain areas.[35] Additionally, reformers would put less emphasis on the fact that previous Congresses have chosen not to regulate the justices' recusal practices. As Chief Justice Roberts himself has stated, "Legislative novelty is not necessarily fatal; there is a first time for everything."[36]

From a practical standpoint, however, what matters is not whether recusal legislation is theoretically constitutional but whether the justices are likely to uphold its constitutionality when the question is before them, and the justices have offered strong hints that they do not favor it. Chief Justice Roberts's remarks on the subject in his 2011 *Year-End Report* are not particularly supportive of reform,[37] and Justice Breyer testified before Congress that he also opposes it.[38] In light of the justices' resistance, it is probably wiser for supporters to emphasize procedural reforms that will encourage the justices to be more attentive to the existing rules.

Oversight Procedures

The first type of procedural reform would increase accountability by making recusal decisions reviewable by another panel composed either of lower court judges, the justices themselves, or some other decision makers. A version of this proposal is in the Murphy Bill, which would have authorized the Judicial Conference to determine what such a review panel would look like. The rationale behind this approach is that the justices cannot be objective about their own recusal decisions. As one commentator stated, "The challenged Justice is simultaneously both the best and worst suited person to make the determination. On the one hand, the Justice in question should know the intimate factual details well, but on the other hand, the Justice's ability to act objectively is necessarily compromised because no one should be the judge in her own case."[39]

There are different ways that the Judicial Conference could implement such a proposal. One alternative would be to establish an external review body staffed with judges from the U.S. District Courts, the U.S. Courts of Appeals, or other federal judgeships created for this purpose. Another alternative would be for the entire Supreme Court to evaluate the recusal decisions of its members. Of these approaches, the first one promises to be more effective at holding the justices accountable, and it seems to be the approach favored by the Murphy Bill,[40] but it is also likely to encounter greater constitutional obstacles. Even supporters of reform have indicated that external review panels might be unconstitutional.[41]

The problem is that Article III clearly states that there shall be "one Supreme Court." The Constitution authorizes Congress to create "inferior courts," but it is silent on the question of whether Congress can create other judicial institutions that have supervisory authority over the Court. Critics of reform maintain that it would subvert the judicial structure to permit lower federal court judges to evaluate the recusal decisions of Supreme Court justices, particularly if the new procedures permit lower court judges to reverse and remand the Court's final decisions on the merits because of ethics violations.[42] Equally problematic would be permitting the Judicial Conference to prescribe the rules for evaluating recusal decisions.[43] Indeed, one of the reasons that the justices decline to apply the Code of Conduct to themselves is that they deny the authority of the Judicial Conference to make rules that bind Supreme Court justices.[44] Critics of reform would say that if Congress wishes to conduct an external review of the justices' recusal practices, the appropriate procedures are their investigatory and impeachment powers.[45]

Less constitutionally problematic are proposals requiring the justices to review their colleagues' recusal decisions. Unlike proposals for external review, this proposal would not infringe upon the "one Supreme Court" principle because it would require the justices to monitor their own conduct. However, it is not clear how effective such a proposal would be. The justices have long-standing practices against reviewing the ethical decisions of their colleagues,[46] so it is possible that they would only conduct very deferential, *pro forma* review in order to maintain collegiality.[47]

Judicial Substitutions

A second type of procedural reform would permit other judges to substitute for Supreme Court justices who recused themselves. Senator Leahy's proposal falls into this category of reform by authorizing retired justices to act as substitutes, while other proposals would permit chief judges from the U.S. Courts of Appeals to sit by designation.[48] The objective of these proposals is to make recusals seem less costly to justices by reducing the possibility of dividing evenly. If justices know that other judges are available to sit, they might feel less obligated to participate and therefore adhere more closely to the ethical guidelines. The proposal would also take the pressure off of the justices to participate despite illness.[49]

This approach would emulate procedures that are already in place in the lower federal courts.[50] The proposal is also unlikely to encounter the same constitutional problems that review panels would face because no external body would have supervisory authority over the Supreme Court. Any of the replacement judges would be Article III judges appointed by the president and confirmed by the Senate. With regard to retired Supreme Court justices in particular, there would seem to be little reason to doubt the proposal's constitutionality.[51] Retired Supreme Court justices already take assignments on lower federal courts, so there is precedent for them to continue to serve in this capacity.[52] For lower federal court judges, the situation would be different because senators would not have confirmed them for this purpose, but there are potential workarounds for this problem.[53] For example, it might be possible to specify that only future appointees to the lower courts would be eligible to act as substitutes so that the confirmation process could proceed with full knowledge that judges would perform this function.

It is not clear, however, that such proposals would encourage the justices to follow the recusal statute any more closely than they do now. On the contrary, the proposals might discourage recusals because the justices would have greater uncertainty about how substitute judges would resolve disputes in their absence.[54] For example, over the previous decade, members of the Supreme Court's 5-4 conservative majority would probably have been dubious at the prospect of being replaced by Justices Stevens, Souter, and even O'Connor because the replacement justices all would have had more liberal voting records. A disqualification risked ceding a vote to the liberal minority, which could have changed the result in a close case. No doubt Senator Leahy, a Democrat, supported the proposal for precisely this reason. Expanding the pool of potential substitutes to include lower court judges would reduce the risk of an ideologically incompatible replacement, but the uncertainty would remain, and it would almost certainly make the confirmation hearings for lower court judges more contentious.

Reporting Requirements

A third alternative would require the justices to report in writing the reasons for their recusal decisions, as specified in the Murphy Bill. An extension of this proposal might also require the justices to be more forthcoming about when they considered recusing themselves from cases but did not, and to put into the public record any financial conflicts of interest that their disclosure reports do not clearly specify.[55] Of the different alternatives, this one has the most widespread support,[56] and it raises the fewest constitutional objections, as even critics of the proposal concede.[57] Congress would, in effect, be asking the justices to do no more than what they already do for their decisions on the merits.

The proposal does have many potential benefits, the greatest of which is that it would increase the Court's transparency, which could help the justices to maintain public confidence in the institution. A written record would make the recusal process seem more principled and less ad hoc and mysterious than it is now. The proposal would also facilitate the creation of a body of precedents that could help lawyers and litigants know when to file recusal motions, and the justices themselves might find it easier to resolve ethical dilemmas. "If nothing else," writes one commentator, "a judge considering disqualification will get a clearer sense of how often his colleagues have made the choice to step aside . . . making it psychologically easier for a judge to take the same course of action."[58]

The proposal is not without costs, however. What the Court gains in transparency, it loses in flexibility, which currently permits the justices to participate in cases as needed. Unless a version of the Leahy Bill accompanied the proposal, providing for substitute justices when recusals occurred, the justices might find that their precedents obligated them to withdraw from cases even when the institutional need to participate was greater than the ethical concerns. Critics of reform have also suggested that there could be privacy costs associated with a mandatory reporting requirement, especially when conflicts of interest arise because of personal matters or medical conditions that the justices would prefer not to reveal.[59]

Critics also say that too much transparency could damage legitimacy by putting judicial ethics constantly on the public agenda, even when alleged ethical violations are groundless. The public might be surprised to learn how interconnected the justices are with both Washington politics and the lawyers who argue before them. As one critic of reform notes, "many of the elite attorneys who appear in the Supreme Court have clerked for the very Justices before whom they are arguing."[60] Justice Scalia wrote in his *Cheney* memorandum that it was not uncommon for justices to maintain friendships with presidents and other powerful figures in Washington.[61] Indeed, these connections likely helped many of them to get their appointments in the first place. If the justices had to document every occasion in which a case touched upon one of these relationships, it might raise undue suspicions about *ex parte* communications.

For my part, I am not sure that it would be such a bad thing for the public to become more knowledgeable about how connected the justices are to Washington politics. For the Court to be democratically accountable, the public should be aware of these relationships as well as the full scope of the justices' potential conflicts, even if it causes the public to be unduly skeptical of the justices and their motives. I am doubtful, however, that in practice a reporting requirement will substantially increase our knowledge of the justices' recusal behavior. Justices will have incentives to keep their reports brief, and those who wish to disguise misconduct will only need to develop persuasive rhetorical justifications for remaining on cases. As one critic of reform notes, "requirements that Justices publish their reasons for failing to recuse themselves could, in the absence of defined, binding criteria for recusal decisions, do little to promote the integrity or public perception of the Court because there will be no baseline against which to measure the quality of the Justice's explanations."[62] The justices might even develop formulaic language for explaining recusal decisions that would convey little information of substance.

In the end, a reporting requirement might only just prove to be a nuisance to the justices that will distract them from their real business of deciding cases and controversies.[63] Such measures might be justified if there were proof of corruption on the Court, but my research has found little evidence of it, and I am doubtful that greater transparency will reveal more. This is not to say that we would not see more frequent accusations of misconduct if reforms were implemented. Committed partisans will always be capable of finding grounds for complaint in an enhanced public record. But I suspect that, instead of enhancing judicial ethics, the increased public scrutiny will only make the recusal process even more politicized than it is now.

Conclusion

Proposals for reforming the recusal process do have merit. They promise to break through the justices' long-standing tradition of silence, establishing disqualification procedures on the Supreme Court that are more transparent and accountable. If Congress were to enact comprehensive reform legislation, the public could be more confident that the Court was actually following the ethical rules instead of having to take the justices' word for it. Litigants would have greater certainty that the justices were reviewing their claims impartially, and lawyers would know better when to file disqualification motions.

However, reforms also have the potential to be costly to the justices in ways that could undermine their capacity to serve the public. At the very least, reforms would impose additional administrative costs on the justices that would distract them from their business of deciding cases and controversies. By reducing judicial discretion over disqualification, reforms could impair the ability of the justices to resolve disputes at times when their judgments are needed. There is also the possibility that reforms will reduce public confidence in the Supreme Court by increasing public scrutiny of the justices' recusal practices and creating new opportunities for the opponents of the Court's policies to file frivolous disqualification claims.

The arguments on both sides of this debate are strong, but what ultimately makes me skeptical about the need for reform is the absence of a compelling public policy justification. My research has found no evidence of an ethics crisis on the Supreme Court. There is no reason to believe that the justices have become more corrupt in recent years, nor is there cause for thinking that recusal misconduct has historically been a problem. While there have been a handful of questionable judgment calls in which justices arguably should have sat out of cases,[64] it is not typical for the justices' recusal behavior to raise these questions, and when controversies do arise, the arguments in favor of disqualification are rarely clear-cut.

Instead of an ethics crisis, what I have found is that in the past several decades, public discourse about judicial ethics has increased and become more politicized. As I demonstrated in Chapter 4, since the *Cheney* controversy, political commentators have proved more willing to use judicial ethics to game the Court, playing the ethics card in an attempt to remove justices whose policies they dislike. Conservatives know that they cannot vote Kagan out of office, so they impeach her integrity. Liberals know how Thomas is likely to vote in the *Sebelius* case, so they attempt to neutralize his vote. All of this talk about recusals has generated a sense of crisis that has at times made it seem like reforms are needed, but the evidence simply does not support many of the concerns that commentators raise. The real problem is not with judicial ethics, but with politics.

A more fruitful area for pursuing reform might be in the state courts, particularly those that have competitive elections. Cases such as *Caperton v. Massey* highlight the potential of campaign contributions to compromise judicial integrity,[65] and research demonstrates that these contributions can genuinely threaten legitimacy.[66] More research is needed to determine the full scope of the problem, or if indeed there really is one. It could be that cases like *Caperton* are outliers and that corruption is no more widespread among elected judges than it is among Supreme Court justices. However, the preliminary evidence indicates that the role of money in campaigns is worth investigating further and might justify further regulations to ensure that elected judges are recusing themselves from cases that involve their major campaign donors.

There is no evidence of a comparable problem on the Supreme Court. At most, one can say that Supreme Court justices are political actors who seek to advance their sincere policy preferences and who participate in cases that advance these preferences. However, the reality is that the Supreme Court is a policy-making institution with the power to shape the direction of legal policy consistently with the justices' values. The proposed reforms are unlikely to make the justices less political, nor will they erase all doubts about whether the justices are behaving ethically. "Ultimately," said Judge Kozinski of the Ninth Circuit, "there is no choice but to trust the judges."[67] So far the evidence suggests that the justices have, for the most part, behaved in ways that merit our trust. While there will always be exceptional cases in which justices skirt the ethical boundaries, there does not appear to be need for comprehensive reform at this time.

Notes

Preface

1. Robert J. Hume, "Deciding Not to Decide: The Politics of Recusals on the U.S. Supreme Court," 48 Law & Society Rev. 621–55 (2014).

Chapter 1

1. *National Federation of Independent Business v. Sebelius,* 132 S.Ct. 2566 (2012).

2. *See* Joan Biskupic, "Calls for Recusal Intensify in Health Care Case; Kagan, Thomas Questioned," USA Today, November 21, 2011, at 6A; and Robert Barnes, "A Health Law Warm-Up Fight for High Court," Washington Post, Nov. 28, 2011, at A1.

3. *See, for example,* Eric J. Segall, "An Ominous Silence on the Supreme Court; Justice Elena Kagan Should Explain Why She's Not Heeding the Calls to Recuse Herself from the Soon-To-Be-Heard Obama Healthcare Case," Los Angeles Times, Feb. 12, 2012, at A26 ("Was Kagan a 'counselor or advisor' on the constitutionality of the health-care act for the administration? . . . [E]ven though Kagan may not have been directly involved in the administration's litigation strategy defending the act while she was the head of the solicitor general's office, her deputy, Neal Katyal, was. It exalts form over substance to suggest that Katyal, had he been named to the Supreme Court, would have to recuse himself but his boss, who knew of and supported his participation, does not"); and Lamar Smith, "What Did Kagan Do?," Washington Post, Dec. 2, 2011, at A21 ("Despite claims from Obama administration officials that Kagan was not involved in the health-care discussions, e-mails released last month indicate that there may be more to the story. . . . This exchange of emails raises the question of whether she tried to hide her involvement by conducting conversations over the phone to limit any paper trail").

4. *Bush v. Gore,* 531 U.S. 98 (2000). A *Los Angeles Times* poll taken shortly after the decision found that 48% of Americans supported the recusal of Justices Scalia and Thomas but 43% opposed. See "Poll #450: Historical Aftermath of the 2000 Presidential Election," Los Angeles Times, Dec. 14–16, 2000, retrieved from the iPOLL Databank,

The Roper Center for Public Opinion Research, University of Connecticut, http://www. ropercenter.uconn.edu.

5. Ginni Thomas, "Clip: Ginni Thomas Remarks at Steamboat Institute," C-SPAN VIDEO LIBRARY (2010), http://www.c-spanvideo.org/clip/412028.

6. John G. Roberts, Jr., 2011 YEAR-END REPORT ON THE FEDERAL JUDICIARY, U.S. Supreme Court Public Information Office, http://www.supremecourt.gov/publicinfo/ year-end/2011year-endreport.pdf.

7. *Id.*, at 10.

8. *See, for example,* Jeffrey W. Stempel, "Rehnquist, Recusal, and Reform," 53 BROOKLYN L. REV. 589 (1987); Caprice L. Roberts, "The Fox Guarding the Henhouse?: Recusal and the Procedural Void in the Court of Last Resort," 57 RUTGERS L. REV. 107 (2004); Debra Lynn Bassett, "Recusal and the Supreme Court," 56 HASTINGS L. J. 657 (2005); Amanda Frost, "Keeping Up Appearances: A Process-Oriented Approach to Judicial Recusal," 53 KAN. L. REV. 531 (2005); Richard E. Flamm, "History of and Problems with the Federal Judicial Disqualification Framework," 58 DRAKE L. REV. 751 (2010); Dmitry Bam, "Making Appearances Matter: Recusal and the Appearance of Bias," 2011 B.Y.U. L. REV. 943 (2011); Kristen L. Henke, "If It's Not Broke, Don't Fix It: Ignoring Criticisms of Supreme Court Recusals," 57 ST. LOUIS L. J. 521 (2013); James Sample, "Supreme Court Recusal from *Marbury* to the Modern Day," 26 GEO. J. LEGAL ETHICS 95 (2013).

9. *See* Ryan Black & Lee Epstein, "Recusals and the 'Problem' of an Equally Divided Supreme Court," 7 J. APP. PRAC. & PROCESS 75, at 75–76 (2005) (commenting that "it seems as though no feature of the Court has escaped our attention—with one notable exception: recusal").

10. *See, for example, Morgan Stanley Capital Group Inc. v. Pub. Util. Dist. No. 1,* 554 U.S. 527 (2008) ("Roberts, C.J., and Breyer, J., took no part in the consideration or decision of the cases"); and *Credit Suisse Sec. (USA) LLC v. Billing,* 551 U.S. 264 (2007) ("Kennedy, J., took no part in the consideration or decision of the case").

11. Warren Weaver, Jr., "High Court and Disqualification," NEW YORK TIMES, Mar. 3, 1975, at 22.

12. *See* JEFFREY A. SEGAL & HAROLD J. SPAETH, THE SUPREME COURT AND THE ATTITUDINAL MODEL REVISITED (2002).

13. Tom S. Clark, "Measuring Ideological Polarization on the United States Supreme Court," 62 POL. RES. Q. 146–57 (2009); David Paul Kuhn, "The Incredible Polarization and Politicization of the Supreme Court," THE ATLANTIC, June 29, 2012, http://www.theatlantic.com/politics/archive/2012/06/ the-incredible-polarization-and-politicizationof-the-supreme-court/259155/.

14. Joan Maisel Leiman, "The Rule of Four," 57 COLUM. L. REV. 975 (1957); H. W. PERRY, DECIDING TO DECIDE: AGENDA SETTING IN THE UNITED STATES SUPREME COURT (1991); DAVID M. O'BRIEN, STORM CENTER: THE SUPREME COURT IN AMERICAN POLITICS (8th ed. 2008).

15. *See* Steven Lubet, "Disqualification of Supreme Court Justices: The *Certiorari* Conundrum," 80 MINN. L. REV. 657, 663 (1996) ("To illustrate, assume a 0.1 probability that any Justice will vote to grant *certiorari* in any case, and that three already

have decided to grant a *certiorari* petition. If six Justices are yet to vote, the probability of granting *certiorari* is .47. With only five remaining Justices, however, the probability of review drops to .41, a difference of .06. This relationship remains constant, although the ratios change, for all probabilities less than 1.0"); and Bassett, *supra* note 8, at 686–87.

16. Press Release, Supreme Court, *Statement of Recusal Policy* (Nov. 1, 1993), Ethics & Public Policy Center, http://www.eppc.org/docLib/20110106_RecusalPolicy23.pdf.

17. 28 U.S.C. § 455 (a).

18. 28 U.S.C. § 455 (b).

19. *See* Bradley C. Canon & Charles A. Johnson, Judicial Policies: Implementation and Impact (1999) ("A court can undermine its legitimacy by making seemingly unfair or unrealistic decisions. Conversely, a court that is perceived as having a strong record of impartiality . . . may win acceptance of an unpopular decision"); and James L. Gibson & Gregory A. Caldeira, "Has Legal Realism Damaged the Institutional Legitimacy of the U.S. Supreme Court?," 45 L. & Soc'y Rev. 195, at 214 (2011) (finding that "what distinguishes judges in the minds of the American people is that judges exercise discretion in a principled fashion").

20. For lower court judges, recusal decisions are reviewable by higher courts, but Supreme Court justices do not review their own recusal decisions. *See* Roberts, *supra* note 6, at 9.

21. At least one appellate advocate has cautioned against filing recusal motions for this reason. *See* Howard J. Bashman, "On Appeal: An Appellate Advocate's Perspective," 7 J. App. Prac. & Process 59, 68 (2005) ("Because an appellate judge whose recusal is sought will often be not only the first but also the final arbiter of whether sufficient grounds exist for recusal, appellate lawyers ought to advise their clients that requests for recusal should not be filed unless the grounds for recusal are compelling").

22. Two notable exceptions are *Laird v. Tatum*, 409 U.S. 824 (1972) (Rehnquist, J., denying the motion to recuse); and *Cheney v. U.S. District Court*, 541 U.S. 913 (2004) (Scalia, J., denying the motion to recuse).

23. Louis J. Virelli, "Congress, the Constitution, and Supreme Court Recusal," 69 Wash. & Lee L. Rev. 1535–606, at 1547 (2012).

24. *See* Segal & Spaeth, *supra* note 12; Lee Epstein & Jack Knight, The Choices Justices Make (1998); Forrest Maltzman, James F. Spriggs, & Paul J. Wahlbeck, Crafting Law on the Supreme Court (2000).

25. Segal & Spaeth, *supra* note 12; Harold J. Spaeth, "An Analysis of Judicial Attitudes in the Labor Relations Decisions of the Warren Court," 25 J. Pol. 290 (1963); Glendon Schubert, The Judicial Mind: The Attitudes and Ideologies of Supreme Court Justices, 1946–63 (1965).

26. Paul J. Wahlbeck, "Strategy and Constraints on Supreme Court Opinion Assignment," 154 U. Pa. L. Rev. 1729–55 (2006); Rosen, Jeffrey, "The Dissenter, Justice John Paul Stevens," New York Times, Sept. 23, 2007.

27. Maltzman et al., *supra*, note 24; Paul J. Wahlbeck, James F. Spriggs, & Forrest Maltzman, "Marshalling the Court: Bargaining and Accommodation on the United States Supreme Court," 42 Am. J. Pol. Sci. 294–315 (1998).

28. Gregory A. Caldeira, John R. Wright, & Christopher J. W. Zorn, "Sophisti-cated Voting and Gate-Keeping in the Supreme Court," 15 J.L. Econ. & Org. 549–72 (1999); Perry, *supra* note 14.

29. Ryan C. Black, Timothy R. Johnson, & Justin Wedeking, Oral Argu-ments and Coalition Formation on the U.S. Supreme Court (2012).

30. One of the fullest elaborations of the duty to sit by a Supreme Court justice is found in *Laird v. Tatum*, 409 U.S. 824 (1972) (Rehnquist, J., denying the motion to recuse). Although Congress statutorily limited the "duty to sit" in 28 U.S.C. § 455 (1974), it is still important to the justices, as the comments below attest.

31. Ruth Bader Ginsburg, "An Open Discussion with Justice Ruth Bader Gins-burg," 36 Conn. L. Rev. 1033, 1039 (2004).

32. Roberts, *supra* note 6, at 9.

33. The two newspapers were chosen because the *New York Times* has a tradition-ally liberal editorial page while the *Wall Street Journal's* is traditionally conservative, and because data for both newspapers are available for the entire period. Data were obtained using LexisNexis for the period 1980–2012 and ProQuest Historical Newspapers for years prior to 1980. For Lexis, I searched using " 'supreme court' and (recuse or recusal or disqualify or disqualifies) AND (SECTION(opinion) OR SECTION(editorial))." The ProQuest search was " 'supreme court' AND (recuse or recusal or disqualify or disqualification)" in the content areas "Editorial" and "Letter to the editor." Data were screened to exclude entries that did not focus on recusals or the U.S. Supreme Court.

34. Letter to the Editor, "The Brandeis Selection and Its Possible Bearing Upon Pending Trust Prosecutions," New York Times, Jan. 30, 1916, at 16.

35. *Ibid.*

36. *Wickard v. Filburn*, 317 U.S. 111 (1942).

37. *See Gastelum-Quinones v. Kennedy*, 374 U.S. 469 (1963); *Kennedy v. Mendoza-Martinez*, 372 U.S. 144 (1963). Justice Scalia discusses both anecdotes at length in *Cheney v. U.S. District Court*, 541 U.S. 913, 914–16 (2004) (Scalia, J., denying the motion to recuse).

38. Editorial, "Supreme Court Quorum," New York Times, June 21, 1943, at 16 ("Last year and again this year the Supreme Court was unable to act in cases of high importance for want of a quorum").

39. *U.S. v. Aluminum Company of America*, 320 U.S. 708, at 708–709 (1943).

40. "Supreme Court Quorum," *supra*, note 38, at 16.

41. "High Court Defers Anti-Trust Cases; Lack of a Quorum Delays Action on Alcoa and North American Indefinitely," New York Times, Oct. 9, 1943, at 39.

42. *U.S. v. Aluminum Company of America*, 148 F.2d 416 (2nd Cir., 1945). *See also* Robert Taylor, "Way Opened to Hear Alcoa Monopoly Suit; House Bill Would End Legal Deadlock," Pittsburgh Press, Apr. 2, 1944, at 13.

43. Andrew L. Kaufman, "Haynsworth Debate," Letter to the Editor, New York Times, Oct. 1, 1969, at 46.

44. Ernest Angell, Letter to the Editor, New York Times, Nov. 16, 1969, at E13.

45. Fred P. Graham, "Determined Not to 'Bend Over Backward': Rehnquist," NEW YORK TIMES, Oct. 15, 1972, at E8; Frances Hardie, "Rehnquist Should Step Down," Letter to the Editor, NEW YORK TIMES, May 9, 1973, at 46.

46. *Laird v. Tatum*, 408 U.S. 1, 2 (1972).

47. *Laird v. Tatum*, 409 U.S. 824, 839 (1972) (Rehnquist, J., denying the motion to recuse).

48. Lustgarten, Laurence, "Self-Disqualification of Justices," Letter to the Editor, NEW YORK TIMES, Sept. 21, 1972, at 46.

49. *See* CODE OF CONDUCT FOR UNITED STATES JUDGES, http://www.uscourts. gov/judges-judgeships/code-conduct-united-states-judges.

50. 28 U.S.C. § 455.

51. *See, for example,* David S. Broder, "Those Memos Will Tell," WASHINGTON POST, Aug. 6, 1986, at A15; and John P. MacKenzie, "The Editorial Notebook; Mr. Rehnquist's Opinion," NEW YORK TIMES, Aug. 25, 1986, at A24.

52. *See, for example,* Editorial, "A Cloud on the Breyer Nomination," NEW YORK TIMES, July 26, 1994, at A18.

53. Edward M. Kennedy, "Alito's Credibility Problem," WASHINGTON POST, Jan. 7, 2006, at A17; Editorial, "Judge Alito, in His Own Words," NEW YORK TIMES, Jan. 12, 2006, at A30.

54. *Hamdan v. Rumsfeld*, 548 U.S. 557 (2006).

55. *See, for example,* Ronald D. Rotunda, "Does John Roberts Have an Ethics Problem?," WASHINGTON POST, Sept. 6, 2005, at A25 ("The case, *Hamdan v. Rumsfeld*, which concerns a key issue in the administration's war on terrorism, may be headed for the Supreme Court, and at the time of the appeals court ruling, Roberts was being considered for a vacancy on the high court, though it did not yet exist").

56. *Cheney v. United States Dist. Court*, 541 U.S. 913, 915 (Mar. 18, 2004) (Scalia, J., denying the motion to recuse).

57. *See, for example,* Scheer, Robert, "Commentary: Old MacDonald Had a Judge," LOS ANGELES TIMES, Feb. 17, 2004, at B11; Editorial, "If It Walks Like a Duck . . . ," CHICAGO TRIBUNE, Feb. 13, 2004, at C26; Editorial, "Justice Scalia and Mr. Cheney," NEW YORK TIMES, Feb. 28, 2004, at A14; Bernard Ries, "Outlook: You Can't Duck This Conflict, Mr. Justice," WASHINGTON POST, Feb. 29, 2004, at B4; Editorial, "Recuse to Lose," WALL STREET JOURNAL, Mar. 9, 2004, at A16.

58. Tammany Kramer, Letter to the Editor, "An Institution Damaged," WASHINGTON POST, Feb. 19, 2004, at A22.

59. *Cheney*, at 916.

60. *Id.*, at 929. As far as the plane ride was concerned, Justice Scalia stated that he had purchased a round-trip ticket from a commercial airline for the ride home, so he ended up receiving no financial benefit for riding to the duck hunt on Vice President Cheney's jet.

61. The six newspapers were the *New York Times, Wall Street Journal, Washington Post, Los Angeles Times, Chicago Tribune,* and *St. Louis Post-Dispatch.* These papers were

chosen because three have traditionally liberal editorial pages (*NYT, Wash. Post, St. Louis Post-Disp.*), and three have traditionally conservative pages (*WSJ, LA Times, Chic. Trib.*). Data were obtained using LexisNexis, using search terms described in *supra*, note 33.

62. Lee Epstein & Jack Knight, THE CHOICES JUSTICES MAKE (1998); John M. Scheb II & William Lyons, "The Myth of Legality and Popular Support for the Supreme Court," 81 SOCIAL SCIENCE QUARTERLY 928 (2000); Vanessa A. Baird & Amy Gangl, "Shattering the Myth of Legality: The Impact of the Media's Framing of Supreme Court Procedures on Perceptions of Fairness," 27 POL. PSYCHOL. 597 (2006); and Dion Farganis, "Do Reasons Matter? The Impact of Opinion Content on Supreme Court Legitimacy," 65 POL. RES. Q. 206 (2012).

63. *See* James L. Gibson & Gregory A. Caldeira, "Has Legal Realism Damaged the Institutional Legitimacy of the U.S. Supreme Court?," 45 L. & SOC'Y REV. 195, at 214 (2011) (finding that "what distinguishes judges in the minds of the American people is that judges exercise discretion in a principled fashion").

64. Farganis, *supra* note 62, at 213 ("Broadly speaking, the results suggest that the Court's perceived legitimacy level is highest when the justices used legalistic arguments and lowest when they rely on extraconstitutional justifications").

65. Eric J. Segall, "An Ominous Silence on the Supreme Court," LOS ANGELES TIMES, Feb. 12, 2012, at A26.

66. A 1958 story by Anthony Lewis on the justices' recusal practices reads like a contemporary account. "The Supreme Court itself has no formal rules as to when a justice should recuse himself," he wrote. "Nor do the individual justices ordinarily announce their reasons for staying out." *See* Anthony Lewis, "Tie in High Court a Major Problem," NEW YORK TIMES, Jan. 13, 1958, at 22; *see also* Weaver, *supra* note 11, at 22 ("Ostensibly, a Justice bases his refusal to reveal his reasons for disqualification on personal privacy, a belief that he need not make public the fact that he holds stock in a corporation or that he had some past relationship with a party in a dispute. But more often, this reluctance to explain an official act that can have important public consequences appears to be based on a sort of protective arrangement among the Justices of the high court, more an act of deference to his colleagues by the recuser than any attempt to shield personal facts").

67. Weaver, *id.*, at 22 ("For if each Justice who stepped aside in a case issued a brief statement of his reason, the Supreme Court would inescapably begin to compile an informal ethics code of its own. Within a year or two, it would become clear what sort of propriety [*sic*] guidelines some of the Justices, if not all of them, imposed on themselves. And such a body of precedent, even though personal and unofficial, would almost certainly put increased pressure on Justices who seldom if ever excuse themselves from participating in a decision"). *See also* Linda Greenhouse, "Questions for a Reticent High Court," NEW YORK TIMES, Nov. 22, 1989, at A22 ("By making it impossible to ascertain what standards they are applying, the Justices' silence about recusals short-

circuits public discussion, making it less likely that these ambiguities can be resolved through informed debate").

68. For more on legitimacy theory, *see* Robert A. Dahl, "Decision-Making in a Democracy: The Supreme Court as a National Policy-Maker," 6 J. PUB. L. 279 (1957); Michael J. Petrick, "The Supreme Court and Authority Acceptance," 21 W. POL. Q. 5 (1968); Walter F. Murphy & Joseph Tanenhaus, "Public Opinion and the United States Supreme Court," 2 LAW & SOC'Y REV. 357 (1968); WALTER F. MURPHY, JOSEPH TANENHAUS, & DANIEL KASTNER, PUBLIC EVALUATIONS OF CONSTITUTIONAL COURTS: ALTERNATIVE EXPLANATIONS (1973); Gregory Casey, "The Supreme Court and Myth: An Empirical Investigation," 8 LAW & SOC'Y REV. 385 (1974); Gregory A. Caldeira & James L. Gibson, "The Etiology of Public Support for the Supreme Court," 36 AM. J. POL. SCI. 635 (1992); James L. Gibson, Gregory A. Caldeira, & Vanessa A. Baird, "On the Legitimacy of National High Courts," 92 AM. POL. SCI. REV. 343 (1998); and JAMES L. GIBSON & GREGORY A. CALDEIRA, CITIZENS, COURTS, AND CONFIRMATIONS: POSITIVITY THEORY AND THE JUDGMENTS OF THE AMERICAN PEOPLE (2009).

69. 28 U.S.C. § 455 (a).

70. *Cheney v. United States Dist. Court*, 541 U.S. 913 (Mar. 18, 2004) (Scalia, J, denying the motion to recuse).

Chapter 2

1. *See* Lori Ann Foertsch, "Scalia's Duck Hunt Leads to Ruffled Feathers: How the U.S. Supreme Court and Other Federal Judiciaries Should Change Their Recusal Approach," 43 HOUS. L. REV. 457, 493 (2006) ("The Court should require Justices to provide a written explanation of their recusal decision in a particular case. This written explanation should occur both when a Justice recuses and does not recuse him or herself from a case. Further, the other Justices should sign off or comment on the reasoning used in the Justice's recusal decision"); Timothy J. Goodson, "Duck, Duck, Goose: Hunting for Better Recusal Practices in the United States Supreme Court in Light of *Cheney v. United States District Court*," 84 N.C.L. REV. 181, 216 ("Requiring Justices to give reasons for their recusal when they recuse themselves *sua sponte* lays a foundation of cases in which recusal is appropriate, making the recusal decision clearer for later cases presenting the same circumstances"); and Frost, *supra* Chapter 1, note 8, at 589 ("judges should give reasons for deciding to remove themselves").

2. Transcript, "Supreme Court 2012 Budget," Testimony of Justices Anthony Kennedy and Stephen Breyer before the House Appropriations Subcommittee on Financial Services and General Government" (Apr. 14, 2011).

3. *Ibid.*

4. *Ibid.*

5. *Ibid.*

6. *Ibid.*

7. *Ibid.*

8. HAROLD J. SPAETH, THE SUPREME COURT DATABASE (Version 2011, Release 3), http://scdb.wustl.edu/documentation.php?s=2. Data are based on the justice-centered data. Justices were counted as recusing themselves when their votes were unlisted ("."), indicating that they were on the bench but played no role in the resolution of the case. As detailed below in Chapter 3, data were adjusted to exclude entries when justices did not participate because of illness or because they were appointed after the oral arguments.

9. For example, 28 U.S.C. § 144 permits parties to disqualify judges by filing affidavits alleging bias, but it applies only to federal district court judges. Appellate judges are governed by 28 U.S.C. § 47, which prohibits them from presiding over cases in which they served as trial judges, but § 47 is redundant to provisions in § 455, which also require recusal in these circumstances. A fourth recusal provision, 28 U.S.C. § 2106, permits the Supreme Court to disqualify a district court judge by remanding the case to another judge, "as may be just under the circumstances." *See* CHARLES GARDNER GEYH, JUDICIAL DISQUALIFICATION: AN ANALYSIS OF FEDERAL LAW (2010).

10. Some might object that § 455 (a) ("impartiality might reasonably be questioned") is not a clear standard, but Judge M. Margaret McKeown of the Ninth Circuit observes that "Judges apply reasonableness standards all the time. . . . Thus, the consideration of whether a particular judicial act would undermine the appearance of propriety is the application of a routine judicial task." *See* M. Margaret McKeown, "On Appeal: Don't Shoot the Canons: Maintaining the Appearance of Propriety Standard," 7 J. APP. PRAC. & PROCESS 45, 49–50 (2005).

11. *See United States v. Edwards*, 334 F.2d 360, 362 (5th Cir., 1964) ("It is a judge's duty to refuse to sit when he is disqualified, but it is equally his duty to sit when there is no valid reason for recusation"); and *Laird v. Tatum*, 409 U.S. 824, 837 (1972) (Rehnquist, J., denying the motion to recuse) ("Those federal courts of appeals that have considered the matter have unanimously concluded that a federal judge has a duty to *sit* where *not disqualified* which is equally as strong as the duty to *not sit* where *disqualified*").

12. M. Margaret McKeown, "To Judge or Not to Judge: Transparency and Recusal in the Federal System," 30 REV. LITIG. 653, 654 (2011).

13. *See* Roberts, *supra* Chapter 1, note 6, at 9.

14. THE FEDERALIST No. 78, at 465 (Clinton Rossiter, ed., 1961).

15. *See, for example,* Petrick, "The Supreme Court and Authority Acceptance," *supra* Chapter 1, note 68; Murphy & Tanenhaus, "Public Opinion and the United States Supreme Court," *supra* Chapter 1, note 68; MURPHY ET AL., PUBLIC EVALUATIONS OF CONSTITUTIONAL COURTS, *supra* Chapter 1, note 68; and Casey, "The Supreme Court and Myth," *supra* Chapter 1, note 68.

16. *See* GIBSON & CALDEIRA (2009), *supra* Chapter 1, note 68, at 8.

17. 28 U.S.C. § 455 (b)(4).

18. *See, for example, AT&T Corp. v. Iowa Utilities Board*, 525 U.S. 366 (1999).

19. *See* Adam Liptak, "Justice to Examine Rights of Corporations," NEW YORK TIMES, Sept. 29, 2010, at A20; and Mark Sherman, "Pfizer Stock Sold, Roberts to Hear Company's Cases," ASSOCIATED PRESS FINANCIAL WIRE, Sept. 29, 2010.

20. *See American Isuzu Motors, Inc. v. Ntsebeza*, 553 U.S. 1028, 1028–29 (2008) ("Because the Court lacks a quorum . . . and since a majority of the qualified Justices are of the opinion that the case cannot be heard and determined at the next Term of the Court, the judgment is affirmed. . . . The Chief Justice, Justice Kennedy, Justice Breyer, and Justice Alito took no part in the consideration or decision of this petition"). Justice Kennedy did not own stock, but his son was the managing director of one of the companies. *See* David Stout, "Justices Won't Hear Apartheid Suit," NEW YORK TIMES, May 12, 2008.

21. *See* GEYH, JUDICIAL DISQUALIFICATION, *supra* note 9, at 5.

22. The Act, which applied only to district court judges, also required disqualification when a judge "has been of counsel for either party." Act of May 8, 1792, ch. 36, § 11, 1 Stat. 178–79 (1792).

23. It was Chief Justice Marshall who, as Secretary of State in the John Adams administration, failed to deliver to William Marbury the commission that became the subject of *Marbury v. Madison*, 5 U.S. 137 (1803).

24. *Martin v. Hunter's Lessee*, 14 U.S. 304 (1816).

25. Bassett, *supra* Chapter 1, note 8, at 665.

26. Jeff Bleich & Kelly Klaus, "Deciding Whether to Decide: Should There Be Standards for Recusals?," 61 OR. ST. B. BULL. 9, at 12.

27. *Caperton v. Massey*, 556 U.S. 868 (2009). *See also Tumey v. Ohio*, 273 U.S. 510 (1927).

28. *Id.*, at 872.

29. *Caperton v. Massey*, 223 W. Va. 624 (2008).

30. The focus of *Caperton* was the Fourteenth Amendment's Due Process Clause, which restricts state governments. However, the justices have similar standards for interpreting the Due Process Clause of the Fifth Amendment, which applies to the federal government, so presumably the principles of *Caperton* also apply to federal judges.

31. *Caperton v. Massey*, 556 U.S. 868, 872 (2009) (internal quotation marks removed).

32. *See Tumey v. Ohio*, 273 U.S. 510 (1927); *Ward v. Monroeville*, 409 U.S. 57 (1972); *Aetna Life Ins. Co. v. Lavoie*, 475 U.S. 813 (1986). The justices also ruled that when judges are presiding over criminal contempt cases arising from the defendant's hostility toward the same judge, there might be a due process issue. *See In re Murchison*, 349 U.S. 133 (1955); and *Mayberry v. Pennsylvania*, 400 U.S. 455 (1971).

33. *Caperton v. Massey*, 556 U.S. 868, 891 (2009) (Robert, C. J., dissenting). The dissent did not dispute the principle that the Due Process Clause requires disqualification when judges have financial interests in the outcome. "This principle is relatively

straightforward, and largely tracks the longstanding common-law rule regarding judicial recusal." *Ibid.* However, the dissent did object to expanding the reach of the Due Process Clause to include circumstances in which there is a "probability of bias." The dissent worried that the new rule "will inevitably lead to an increase in allegations that judges are biased, however groundless those charges may be." *Ibid.*

34. *Caperton v. Massey*, 556 U.S. 868, 891 (2009) (Robert, C. J., dissenting) (internal quotation marks removed).

35. *Ibid.*

36. *Id.*, at 887.

37. 28 U.S.C. § 455 (b)(2–3).

38. *See* Lewis, *supra* Chapter 1, note 66.

39. Weaver, *supra* Chapter 1, note 11, at 22.

40. *Williams v. Pennsylvania*, 579 U.S. __ (2016).

41. *Id.*, at 14.

42. *United States v. Nixon*, 418 U.S. 683 (1974).

43. Warren Weaver, Jr., "High Court and Disqualification," New York Times, Mar. 3, 1975, at 22.

44. 28 U.S.C. § 455 (b)(3).

45. *Liteky v. United States*, 510 U.S. 540, 555 (1994), clarified that recusals were not required for opinions that judges formed in the course of current or prior judicial proceedings, except when judges "display a deep-seated favoritism or antagonism that would make fair judgment impossible."

46. *Elk Grove v. Newdow*, 542 U.S. 1 (2004).

47. As Justice Ginsburg famously put it in her confirmation hearings, she would provide "no hints, no forecasts, no previews." *See* "Nomination of Ruth Bader Ginsburg to be an Associate Justice of the Supreme Court of the United States" (1993), http://www.loc.gov/law/find/nominations/ginsburg/hearing.pdf.

48. Lewis, *supra* Chapter 1, note 66, at 22.

49. *Frontiero v. Richardson*, 411 U.S. 677 (1973). *See* "*Frontiero v. Richardson*, Transcript of Oral Argument," The Oyez Project at IIT Chicago-Kent College of Law, http://www.oyez.org/cases/1970-1979/1972/1972_71_1694 (last visited June 22, 2013) (in which Ginsburg argued, "To provide the guidance so badly needed and because recognition is long overdue, amicus urges the Court to declare sex a suspect criterion").

50. *United States v. Virginia*, 518 U.S. 515, 524 (1996).

51. On the other hand, Justice Ginsburg's decision to give a speech in 2004 that was sponsored by the NOW Legal Defense and Education Fund prompted calls for her to recuse herself from abortion cases. *See, for example,* Editorial, "Another Justice Takes a Misstep," Chicago Tribune, Mar. 18, 2004, at 28.

52. Clarence Thomas, My Grandfather's Son: A Memoir, at 74 (2007) ("Affirmative action [though it wasn't yet called that] had become a fact of life at American college and universities, and before long I realized that those blacks who benefited from it were being judged by a double standard").

53. *Fisher v. University of Texas*, 579 U.S. __ (2016).

54. *See* Ginni Thomas, "Remarks at Steamboat Institute," *supra* Chapter 1, note 5.

55. For more about the organization, *see* LIBERTYCENTRAL.ORG, at http://www.libertycentral.org/.

56. *See, for example,* Eric J. Segall, "Supreme Court Recusal, the Affordable Care Act, and the Rule of Law," 160 U. PA. L. REV. PENNUMBRA 337, at 340 ("[A]bsent a direct financial stake, it is fair to assume that judges and Justices will decide cases without regard to spousal pressure. A different rule would be difficult to implement and would greatly limit what careers spouses of judges could pursue").

57. *Perry v. Brown*, 671 F.3d 1052 (9th Cir., 2012).

58. Jackie Calmes, "Activism of Thomas's Wife Could Raise Judicial Issues," NEW YORK TIMES, Oct. 8, 2010, at A1.

59. *Ibid.*

60. Erwin N. Griswold & Ernest Gellhorn, "200 Cases in Which Justices Recused Themselves," WASHINGTON POST, Oct. 18, 1988, at A25.

61. *See Statement of Recusal Policy, supra* Chapter 1, note 16.

62. *Microsoft v. United States*, 530 U.S. 1301, 1302 (2000).

63. *United States v. Edwards*, 334 F.2d 360, 362 (5th Cir., 1964).

64. *Laird v. Tatum*, 409 U.S. 824 (1972) (Rehnquist, J., denying the motion to recuse).

65. *Id.*, at 837.

66. *Ibid.*

67. *Id.*, at 838.

68. *Ibid.*

69. *See Statement of Recusal Policy, supra* Chapter 1, note 16, at 2 ("In this Court, where the absence of one Justice cannot be made up by another, needless recusal deprives litigants of the nine Justices to which they are entitled, produces the possibility of an even division on the merits of the case, and has a distorting effect upon the *certiorari* process, requiring the petitioner to obtain (under our current practice) four votes out of eight instead of four out of nine").

70. *See* Roberts, *supra* Chapter 1, note 6, at 9 ("Although a Justice's process for considering recusal is similar to that of the lower court judges, the Justice must consider an important factor that is not present in the lower courts. Lower court judges can freely substitute for one another. . . . A Justice accordingly cannot withdraw from a case as a matter of convenience or simply to avoid controversy. Rather, each Justice has an obligation to the Court to be sure of the need to recuse before deciding to withdraw from a case").

71. *Microsoft v. United States*, 530 U.S. 1301, at 1303 (2000) (statement of Rehnquist, C. J.) ("Finally, it is important to note the negative impact that the unnecessary disqualification of even one Justice may have upon our Court. Here—unlike the situation in a District Court or a Court of Appeals—there is no way to replace a recused Justice. Not only is the Court deprived of the participation of one of its nine members,

but the even number of those remaining creates a risk of affirmance of a lower court decision by an equally divided court").

72. *See* Ginsburg, *supra* Chapter 1, note 31, at 1039 ("Because there's no substitute for a Supreme Court justice, it is important that we not lightly recuse ourselves").

73. Transcript, "Supreme Court 2012 Budget," *supra* note 2.

74. Bassett, *supra* Chapter 1, note 8, at 684–85 ("In most instances, by the time a case reaches the Supreme Court, at least two, sometimes three, other courts have evaluated the litigants' challenges. The genuine need for a third (or fourth) judicial determination is rare. This is particularly true in light of the fact that the Supreme Court has repeatedly stated that its purpose is not merely to correct errors committed by the lower courts").

75. Stempel, *supra* Chapter 1, *note* 8, at 652–53.

76. Black & Epstein, "Recusals and the 'Problem' of an Equally Divided Supreme Court," *supra* Chapter 1, note 9; *see also* Ryan C. Black & Amanda C. Bryan, "Explaining the (Non)Occurrence of Equal Divisions on the U.S. Supreme Court," AMERICAN POLITICS RESEARCH (Published online before print), Apr. 29, 2014.

77. *Id.*, at 86 ("If the probability of any particular vote division was equal, then we would expect ties in 2/9 or 22.22 percent of all cases. But that was not the case").

78. *Id.*, at 96. Another possible explanation for these trends is grounded in selection: "It simply could be that justices are more likely to recuse themselves in cases they think will *not* result in a split vote." *Id.*, at 95.

79. Black & Bryan, "Explaining the (Non)Occurrence of Equal Divisions on the U.S. Supreme Court," *supra* note 78, at 1.

80. *United States v. Will*, 449 U.S. 200 (1980).

81. *Id.*, at 217.

82. Stempel, *supra* Chapter 1, *note* 8, at 650–51.

83. SEGAL & SPAETH, THE SUPREME COURT AND THE ATTITUDINAL MODEL REVISITED, *supra* Chapter 1, note 12; Andrew D. Martin & Kevin M. Quinn, "Dynamic Ideal Point Estimation via Markov Chain Monte Carlo for the U.S. Supreme Court, 1953–1999," 10 POL. ANALYSIS 134 (2002).

84. SEGAL & SPAETH, *supra* Chapter 1, note 12.

85. Judges at other tiers of the federal judiciary, including the U.S. Courts of Appeals, are less free to act on their sincere policy preferences. *See* FRANK CROSS, DECISION MAKING IN THE U.S. COURTS OF APPEALS (2007).

86. The justices themselves have observed that they come to the Court with attitudes about legal policy. As Rehnquist discussed in *Laird*, 409 U.S. at 835, "Since most Justices come to this bench no earlier than their middle years, it would be unusual if they had not by that time formulated at least some tentative notions which would influence them in their interpretation of the sweeping clauses of the Constitution. . . . Proof that a Justice's mind at the time he joined the Court was a complete tabula rasa in the area of constitutional adjudication would be evidence of lack of qualification, not lack of bias."

87. Only one Supreme Court justice, Samuel Chase, has been impeached, but the impeachment occurred in 1805, and Chase was acquitted by the Senate. Impeachment

and removal have been somewhat more common for lower federal court judges. *See* Richard K. Neumann, Jr., "The Revival of Impeachment as a Partisan Political Weapon," 34 HASTINGS CONST. L. Q. 161 (2007).

88. Transcript, "Supreme Court 2012 Budget," *supra*, note 2.

89. Specifically, Breyer said, "If I recuse myself on the Supreme Court, there is no one else and that could switch the result." *See* Lloyd Grove, "Supremes on Defense," THE DAILY BEAST, June 29, 2011, http://www.thedailybeast.com/articles/2011/06/29/supreme-court-justices-defend-thomas-bush-v-gore-at-aspen-ideas-festival.html.

90. *See Statement of Recusal Policy*, *supra* Chapter 1, note 16, at 2 ("Given the size and number of today's national law firms, and the frequent appearance before us of many of them in a single case, recusal might become a common occurrence, and opportunities would be multiplied for 'strategizing' recusals, that is, selecting law firms with an eye to producing the recusal of particular Justices. . . . Absent some special factor, therefore, we will not recuse ourselves by reason of a relative's participation as a lawyer in earlier stages of the case").

91. FRANK R. CROSS, THE FAILED PROMISE OF ORIGINALISM, at 165 (2013).

92. Raymond S. Nickerson, "Confirmation Bias: A Ubiquitous Phenomenon in Many Guises," 1 REV. GEN. PSYCH. 175, 180 (1998); *also quoted in* CROSS, THE FAILED PROMISE OF ORIGINALISM, *supra* note 93, at 166.

93. Ziva Kunda, "The Case for Motivated Reasoning," 108 PSYCH. BULL. 480, at 495 (1990).

Chapter 3

1. *See* CANON & JOHNSON, JUDICIAL POLICIES: IMPLEMENTATION AND IMPACT, *supra* Chapter 1, note 19, at 156 ("The success of political institutions and even of governments themselves depends in large part on whether citizens believe that the institutions are behaving legitimately"). On the importance of impartiality to legitimacy, Canon and Johnson explain, "A court can undermine its legitimacy by making seemingly unfair or unrealistic decisions. Conversely, a court that is perceived as having a strong record of impartiality . . . may win acceptance of an unpopular decision." *Id.*, at 158. *See also* STEPHEN WASBY, THE SUPREME COURT IN THE FEDERAL JUDICIAL SYSTEM (1978).

2. *See* Roberts, 2011 YEAR-END REPORT, *supra* Chapter 1, note 6.

3. *Microsoft v. United States*, 530 U.S. 1301, at 1302 (2000) (statement of Rehnquist, C. J.).

4. *See* James L. Gibson, " 'New Style' Judicial Campaigns and the Legitimacy of State High Courts," 71 J. POL. 1285, at 1288 (2009). *See also* James L. Gibson, "Challenges to the Impartiality of State Supreme Courts: Legitimacy Theory and 'New-Style' Judicial Campaigns," 102 AM. POL. SCI. REV. 59 (2008); and JAMES L. GIBSON, ELECTING JUDGES: THE SURPRISING EFFECTS OF CAMPAIGNING ON JUDICIAL LEGITIMACY (2012).

5. *See, for example, Martin v. Hunter's Lessee*, 14 U.S. 304 (1816) (in which Chief Justice Marshall recused himself because of a financial conflict of interest).

6. Bassett, *supra* Chapter 1, note 8.

7. Justice Scalia has remarked that one of the "generally accepted concrete rules of statutory construction" is that "when the text of a statute is clear, that is the end of the matter." ANTONIN SCALIA, A MATTER OF INTERPRETATION: FEDERAL COURTS AND THE LAW, at 16 (1997).

8. *National Federation of Independent Business v. Sebelius*, 132 S.Ct. 2566 (2012).

9. Justice Kagan recused herself from four of the seventy-five cases decided in the October 2011 term, and twenty-nine of the ninety-six cases the year before. *See* the "Stat Pack Archive," SCOTUSBLOG, http://www.scotusblog.com/reference/stat-pack/.

10. Segall, "An Ominous Silence on the Supreme Court," *supra* Chapter 1, note 3; Smith, "What Did Kagan Do?," *supra* Chapter 1, note 3.

11. In an email to Harvard Law Professor Laurence Tribe, who was then a senior counsel at the Justice Department, Kagan remarked, "I hear they have the votes, Larry!! Simply amazing." Smith, "What Did Kagan Do?," *supra* Chapter 1, note 3.

12. Biskupic, "Calls for Recusal Intensify in Health Care Case," *supra* Chapter 1, note 2; Barnes, "A Health Law Warm-Up Fight for High Court," *supra* Chapter 1, note 2.

13. Kuhn, "The Incredible Polarization and Politicization of the Supreme Court," *supra* Chapter 1, note 13 ("Many of the Court's rulings that have the greatest influence on American life are increasingly decided by the narrowest possible margin").

14. *Elk Grove v. Newdow*, 542 U.S. 1 (2004).

15. Pamela Gould, "Religious Freedom Praised; Justice Scalia Decries Change in U.S. Norms," THE FREE LANCE-STAR, Jan. 13, 2003, at A1.

16. 28 U.S.C. § 455 (b)(3).

17. *Cheney v. U.S. District Court*, 541 U.S. 913, 921 (2004) (Scalia, J., denying the motion to recuse).

18. One could argue that § 455 (b)(4) was implicated because the Vice President permitted Scalia to use Air Force Two on his flight down to the hunting trip. However, as Scalia explained in his memorandum declining to recuse himself, "though our flight down on the Vice President's plane was indeed free, since we were not returning with him we purchased (because they were least expensive) round-trip tickets that cost precisely what we would have paid if we had gone both down and back on commercial flights. In other words, none of us saved a cent by flying on the Vice President's plane." *Cheney v. U.S. District Court*, 541 U.S. 913, 921 (2004) (Scalia, J., denying the motion to recuse).

19. *Id.*, at 927.

20. A Lexis search reveals only two cases in which Supreme Court justices responded directly to motions to recuse themselves: *Laird v. Tatum*, 409 U.S. 824 (1972) (Rehnquist, J., denying the motion to recuse); and *Cheney v. United States Dist. Court*, 541 U.S. 913 (2004) (Scalia, J., denying the motion to recuse). In *Microsoft v. United States*, 530 U.S. 1301 (2000), Chief Justice Rehnquist's statement declining to recuse himself was issued *sua sponte*.

21. Weaver, "High Court Disqualification," *supra* Chapter 1, note 11.

22. Lewis, "Tie in High Court a Major Problem," *supra* Chapter 1, note 66.

23. Justices who served as the Solicitor General between 1946 and 2010 were Stanley Reed (1935–1938), Robert Jackson (1938–1940), Thurgood Marshall (1938–1940), John Roberts (acting, 1990), and Elena Kagan (2009–2010).

24. *See* Joseph Tanenhaus, Marvin Schick, Matthew Muraskin, & David Rosen, "The Supreme Court's *Certiorari* Jurisdiction: Cue Theory," in G. Schubert, ed., Judicial Decision-Making (1963); Perry, Deciding to Decide, *supra* Chapter 1, note 14; and Ryan Black & Ryan J. Owens, "Agenda Setting in the Supreme Court: The Collision of Policy and Jurisprudence," 71 J. Pol. 1062 (2009).

25. Stefanie A. Lindquist & David E. Klein, "The Influence of Jurisprudential Considerations on Supreme Court Decisionmaking: A Study of Conflict Cases," 40 L. & Soc. Rev. 135 (2006).

26. Ginsburg, "An Open Discussion with Justice Ruth Bader Ginsburg," *supra* Chapter 1, note 31; Roberts, 2011 Year-End Report, *supra* Chapter 1, note 6.

27. Perry, Deciding to Decide, *supra* Chapter 1, note 14; Pamela C. Corley, Amy Steigerwalt, & Artemus Ward, The Puzzle of Unanimity: Consensus on the United States Supreme Court (2013).

28. Virginia A. Hettinger, Stefanie A. Lindquist, & Wendy L. Martinek, "Comparing Attitudinal and Strategic Accounts of Dissenting Behavior on the U.S. Courts of Appeals," 48 Am. J. Pol. Sci. 123–37 (2004); Virginia A. Hettinger, Stefanie A. Lindquist, & Wendy L. Martinek, Judging on a Collegial Court: Influences on Federal Appellate Decision-Making (2006).

29. Paul H. Edelman, David E. Klein, & Stefanie A. Lindquist, "Measuring Deviations from Expected Voting Patterns on Collegial Courts," 5 J. Empirical Legal Stud. 819–52, at 836 (2008).

30. Corley et al., *supra* note 27, at 91.

31. *But see* Richard L. Hasen, "End of the Dialogue? Political Polarization, the Supreme Court, and Congress," 86 S. Cal. L. Rev. 205 (2013) (finding that polarization and gridlock has reduced Congress's capacity to override the Supreme Court's statutory decisions).

32. Corley et al., *supra* note 27, at 75.

33. Andrew D. Martin, Kevin M. Quinn, & Lee Epstein, "The Median Justice on the U.S. Supreme Court," 83 N.C. L. Rev. 1275 (2005).

34. Chris W. Bonneau, Thomas H. Hammond, Forrest Maltzman, & Paul J. Wahlbeck, "Agenda Control, the Median Justice, and the Majority Opinion on the U.S. Supreme Court," 51 Am. J. Pol. Sci. 890 (2007); Tom S. Clark & Benjamin Lauderdale, "Locating Supreme Court Opinions in Doctrine Space," 54 Am. J. Pol. Sci. 871 (2010); and Cliff Carrubba, Barry Friedman, Andrew D. Martin, & Georg Vanberg, "Who Controls the Content of Supreme Court Opinions?," 56 Am. J. Pol. Sci. 400 (2012).

35. Benjamin E. Lauderdale & Tom S. Clark, "The Supreme Court's Many Median Justices," 106 Am. Pol. Sci. Rev. 847 (2012).

36. Peter K. Enns & Patrick C. Wohlfarth, "The Swing Justice," 75 J. Pol. 1089 (2013).

37. Although the justices can make educated guesses about who the members of majority coalitions will be before the oral arguments, research suggests that the justices make use of the information obtained in the arguments to make more precise predictions. *See* Black et al., *supra* Chapter 1, note 29.

38. Enns & Wohlfarth, *supra* note 36.

39. *See* Carrubba et al., *supra* note 34.

40. Spaeth, The Supreme Court Database, *supra* Chapter 2, note 8.

41. I also selected the version of the dataset in which cases were organized by Supreme Court citation (which, for users of the earlier database, means Analu = 0).

42. Black & Epstein, "Recusals and the 'Problem' of an Equally Divided Supreme Court," *supra* Chapter 1, note 9.

43. It was necessary to recode 368 entries for justices who were confirmed after the oral arguments, including Charles Whittaker, Anthony Kennedy, and Samuel Alito.

44. In total, 363 entries were recoded for absences attributable to illness. The justices with the highest rate of withdrawal were Felix Frankfurter (3.4%), Lewis Powell (2.5%), and William Douglas (2.5%).

45. The Business Petitioner/Respondent variable was coded "1" when the Petitioner or Respondent variables in the Supreme Court Database were 101 (advertising business or agency), 102 (agent, fiduciary, trustee, or executor), 103 (airplane manufacturer or manufacturer of parts of airplanes), 104 (airline), 105 (distributor, importer, or exporter of alcoholic beverages), 113 (bank, savings and loan, credit union, investment company), 114 (bankrupt person or business, including trustee in bankruptcy or business in reorganization), 119 (broker, stock exchange, investment or securities firm), 120 (construction industry), 122 (business, corporation), 123 (buyer, purchaser), 124 (cable TV), 128 (chemical company), 132 (coal company or coal mine operator), 133 (computer business or manufacturer, hardware or software), 135 (creditor, including institution appearing as such; e.g., a finance company), 139 (real estate developer), 141 (distributor), 143 (drug manufacturer), 147 (electric equipment manufacturer), 148 (electric or hydroelectric power utility, power cooperative, or gas and electric company), 151 (employer, if employer's relations with employees are governed by the nature of the employer's business rather than labor law), 157 (fisherman or fishing company), 158 (food, meat packing, or processing company, stockyard), 160 (franchiser), 171 (insurance company or surety), 173 (investor), 181 (medical supply or manufacturing company), 184 (manufacturer), 185 (management, executive officer, or director of business entity), 187 (mining company or miner, excluding coal, oil, or pipeline company), 189 (auto manufacturer), 195 (owner, landlord, or claimant to ownership, fee interest, or possession of land as well as chattels), 196 (shareholders to whom a tender offer is made), 198 (oil company or natural gas producer), 205 (telephone, telecommunications, or telegraph company), 209 (pipeline company), 220 (publisher, publishing company), 231 (railroad), 233 (seller or vendor), 234 (shipper, including importer and exporter),

235 (shopping center, mall), 237 (stockholder, shareholder, or bondholder), 238 (retail business or outlet), 243 (forest products, lumber, or logging company), 245 (trucking company or motor carrier), 252 (wholesale trade).

46. In addition to including justices Reed, Jackson, T. Marshall, and Kagan, I also coded the SOLICITOR GENERAL as "1" for J. Roberts, who served briefly as Acting Solicitor General, temporarily replacing Kenneth Starr.

47. Justices with prior federal appellate experience are Minton, Harlan, Whittaker, Stewart, T. Marshall, Burger, Blackmun, Stevens, Scalia, Kennedy, Souter, Thomas, Ginsburg, Breyer, J. Roberts, Alito, and Sotomayor. *See* Lee Epstein, Andrew D. Martin, Kevin M. Quinn, & Jeffrey A. Segal, "Circuit Effects: How the Norm of Federal Judicial Experience Biases the Supreme Court," 157 U. PA. L. REV. 101 (2009).

48. The CONFLICT variable was coded 1 when the CERTREASON variable was a value of 2 ("federal court conflict"), 3 ("federal court conflict and to resolve important or significant question"), 4 ("putative conflict"), 5 ("conflict between federal court and state court"), 6 ("state court conflict"), 7 ("federal court confusion or uncertainty"), 8 ("state court confusion or uncertainty"), and 9 ("federal court and state court confusion or uncertainty").

49. Lee Epstein & Jeffrey A. Segal, "Measuring Issue Salience," 44 AM. J. POL. SCI. 66 (2000).

50. It is true that Epstein and Segal's measure records the salience of cases after they have already been handed down, but alternative measures, such as Clark et al.'s measure of early salience, do not cover the entire study period. *See* Tom S. Clark, Jeffrey R. Lax, & Douglas Rice, "Measuring the Political Salience of Supreme Court Cases," 3 *J. L. & Courts* 37–65 (2015). The Epstein & Segal measure is also defensible because the underlying attribute that it measures, issue salience, should be evident to the justices at an early point in the proceedings, even if they cannot be certain about which cases will actually be published on the front page of the *New York Times*.

51. I coded STATUTORY 1 when LAWTYPE assumed a value of 2 ("Federal Statute"), 6 ("Infrequently litigated statutes [title and section of U.S. Code]"), 7 ("Infrequently litigated statute [volume and page of session law]"), and 8 ("State or local law or regulation").

52. Martin & Quinn, "Dynamic Ideal Point Estimation via Markov Chain Monte Carlo for the U.S. Supreme Court," *supra* Chapter 2, note 83.

53. The direction of the lower court decision is based on the LCDISPOSITIONDIRECTION variable in the Supreme Court Database, coded +1 for conservative decisions and −1 for liberal decisions.

54. Because I used justice-centered data, with multiple entries for each case, I clustered by CASEID, using the same variable from the Supreme Court Database. The models include dummy variables for each of the chief justices who served during the study period (VINSON, WARREN, REHNQUIST, ROBERTS), with BURGER excluded as the baseline category. I also introduced dummy variables for each justice and issue area.

55. The marginal effects in Figures 3.2 and 3.3 were generated using the *margins* command in Stata 12.0.

56. Ai and Norton urge the use of caution when interpreting interaction coefficients in nonlinear models because "the interaction effect may have different signs for different values of covariates." Chunrong Ai & Edward C. Norton, "Interaction Terms in Logit and Probit Models," 80 ECON. LETTERS 123, at 124 (2003). However, my interpretation of the interaction term is consistent with the predicted probabilities reported in Figure 3.2.

57. CORLEY ET AL., *supra* note 27.

58. It is possible that one would find a relationship with a more nuanced measure of the ideology of lower court decisions, but it is also possible that justices simply have incentives to participate in cases when they would like to affirm what the court below has done.

59. Figure 3.4 was generated using the *plot_margins.ado* command, a special graphing function for polynomials developed by Hsiang for Stata 12.0. Solomon Hsiang, "Plot Polynomial of Any Degree in Stata (With Controls)," http://www.fight-entropy.com/2013/01/plot-polynomial-of-any-degree-in-stata.html (2013).

60. Justice Burger was used as the baseline category in the model.

61. *Laird v. Tatum*, 409 U.S. 824, 839 (1972) (Rehnquist, J., denying the motion to recuse).

62. *FCC v. Fox Television Stations*, 556 U.S. 502 (2008); *see* Mark Sherman, "Alito Owned Stock, Voted in Case with Disney's ABC," ASSOCIATED PRESS, May 31, 2011.

63. The nine justices (and the total reported assets) were Alito (337), Breyer (673), Ginsburg (140), Kagan (92), Kennedy (49), Roberts (509), Scalia (216), Sotomayor (45), Stevens (65) and Thomas (136).

64. It is more frequent for a named party to appear before the Court at the *certiorari* stage. The present analysis focuses only on cases that were fully briefed and argued.

65. Justice Breyer owned stock in Duke Energy until two years before the company appeared before the Supreme Court in *Environmental Defense v. Duke Energy Corp.*, 549 U.S. 561 (2007); and he owned Wal-Mart stock until 2009, two years before *Wal-Mart Stores v. Dukes*, 564 U.S. __ (2011).

66. *Janus Capital Group v. First Derivative Traders*, 564 U.S. __ (2011); *Gabelli v. SEC*, 568 U.S. __ (2013).

67. At least one federal judge has commented that it would "result in chaos" if the securities held by a mutual fund could trigger a recusal. According to Judge Richard G. Andrews of the United States District Court in Delaware, "as a practical matter, I would be excluded from having mutual fund holdings." *See Pi-Net International v. Citizens Financial Group*, Civil Action No. 12-355-RGA (D-Del., 2015).

68. "Confirmation Hearing on the Nomination of Samuel A. Alito, Jr., to Be an Associate Justice of the Supreme Court of the United States," Washington, D.C.: U.S. Government Printing Office, 2006, at 493.

69. Jesse J. Holland, "Alito Refutes Conflict-of-Interest Concerns," ASSOCIATED PRESS, Nov. 11, 2005.

70. *BP American Production Co. v. Burton*, 549 U.S. 84 (2006).

71. *Exxon Shipping Co. v. Baker*, 554 U.S. 471 (2008).

72. *Microsoft Corp. v. AT&T Corp.*, 550 U.S. 437 (2007); *Microsoft Corp. v. I4I Limited Partnership*, 564 U.S. __ (2011).

73. *See* Frost, "Keeping Up Appearances," *supra* Chapter 1, note 8, at 589 (suggesting that "judges should give reasons for deciding to remove themselves"); and Goodson, "Duck, Duck, Goose," *supra* Chapter 2, note 1, at 220 ("Requiring Justices to write opinions respecting their recusal decisions . . . gives the public a meaningful procedure on which to base their confidence in the judicial process").

Chapter 4

1. The Judicial Conference's Code of Conduct for United States Judges is explicit on this point, stating that federal judges are "to act in a manner that promotes public confidence in the integrity and impartiality of the judiciary."

2. *See National Federation of Independent Business v. Sebelius*, 132 S.Ct. 2566 (2012).

3. Editorial, "Kagan and ObamaCare," Wall Street Journal, July 13, 2010, at A18.

4. *See Cheney v. United States District Court*, 542 U.S. 367 (2004). Scalia issued a memorandum defending his decision to participate at 541 U.S. 913 (Mar. 18, 2004).

5. Editorial, "Mr. Cheney's Day in Court," New York Times, Apr. 27, 2004, at A24.

6. Erwin Chemerinsky & Steven Lubet, "In One Key Area, (the Chief) Justice Is Indeed Blind," Los Angeles Times, Mar. 19, 2004, at B15.

7. Editorial, "Recuse to Lose," *supra* Chapter 1, note 57, at A16.

8. *American Isuzu Motors, Inc. v. Ntsebeza*, 553 U.S. 1028 (2008).

9. Editorial, "Court Without a Quorum," New York Times, May 18, 2008, at Weekend 11.

10. Editorial, "New Trip Trouble for Scalia," Los Angeles Times, Feb. 28, 2004, at B22.

11. Editorial, "Justice in a Blind," St. Louis Post-Dispatch, Mar. 21, 2004, at B2.

12. Henke, *supra* Chapter 1, note 8, at 540–41.

13. *Id.*, at 540.

14. *See* "Poll #450: Historical Aftermath of the 2000 Presidential Election," *supra* Chapter 1, note 4.

15. Data are from the iPOLL Databank, The Roper Center for Public Opinion Research, University of Connecticut. The telephone survey was conducted on December 14–16, 2000, using a national sample of 865 respondents.

16. Data were obtained by using LexisNexis with search terms described in *supra* Chapter 1, note 33.

17. Conservative editorial pages were the *Wall Street Journal, Chicago Tribune,* and *Los Angeles Times.* Liberal pages were the *New York Times, Washington Post,* and *St.*

Louis Post-Dispatch. When a single editorial wrote about the recusal of multiple justices, it was counted again, once for each justice mentioned.

18. Editorial, "Beyond the Duck Blind," NEW YORK TIMES, Mar. 15, 2004, at A20; *see also* Editorial, "Justice Scalia and Mr. Cheney," *supra* Chapter 1, note 57; Editorial, "Justice in a Bind," NEW YORK TIMES, Mar. 20, 2004, at A12; and Editorial, "Mr. Cheney's Day in Court," *supra* note 5, at A24.

19. Editorial, "Scalia's Smackdown," WALL STREET JOURNAL, Mar. 19, 2004, at A14; *see also* Editorial, "Recuse to Lose," *supra* Chapter 1, note 57, at A16.

20. Data were coded by the author, using the same editorials collected for Figure 4.2. Editorials were content analyzed to determine whether they supported or opposed the disqualification of particular justices. I also looked for whether editorial writers mentioned any of four potential justifications for supporting or opposing recusals: (a) public confidence would be affected, either positively or negatively; (b) judicial integrity would be affected, again either positively or negatively; (c) the Court risked dividing evenly; and (d) the Court risked lacking a quorum. Occasionally editorial writers commented about multiple justices in the same editorial. For example, an editorial writer might have advocated for the recusal of Justice Thomas to promote judicial integrity but opposed the recusal of Justice Kagan for another reason. In these circumstances, I counted the editorial twice, once for each justice mentioned, with each entry including only the reasons advanced for the recusal of that particular justice.

21. *See* CANON & JOHNSON, JUDICIAL POLICIES: IMPLEMENTATION AND IMPACT, *supra* Chapter 1, note 19; Caldeira & Gibson, "The Etiology of Public Support for the Supreme Court," *supra* Chapter 1, note 68; and GIBSON & CALDEIRA (2009), *supra* Chapter 1, note 68.

22. SEGAL & SPAETH, *supra* Chapter 1, note 12.

23. *See* CROSS, DECISION MAKING IN THE U.S. COURTS OF APPEALS, *supra* Chapter 2, note 85.

24. SEGAL & SPAETH, *supra* Chapter 1, note 12.

25. MALTZMAN ET AL., *supra* Chapter 1, note 24.

26. Caldeira, Wright, & Zorn, "Sophisticated Voting and Gate-Keeping in the Supreme Court," *supra* Chapter 1, note 28; PERRY, *supra* Chapter 1, note 14.

27. Editorial, "What Case Was That Again?," WALL STREET JOURNAL, July 21, 2010, at A16.

28. Robert Scheer, "Commentary: The Dangers of a 'What the Heck' Vote," LOS ANGELES TIMES, Sept. 28, 2004, at B13.

29. To be sure, recusal misconduct can affect the substance of judicial policy making in other ways as well. Another serious concern is that the justices might vote in ways that advance their financial interests, as explored in the previous chapter. The focus of this analysis is on the potential for recusal misconduct to produce ideological bias, even though I recognize that other forms of bias might also matter and are worth investigating further.

30. Martin, Quinn, & Epstein, "The Median Justice on the U.S. Supreme Court," *supra* Chapter 3, note 33.

31. For more on polarization, *see* Clark, "Measuring Ideological Polarization on the United States Supreme Court," *supra* Chapter 1, note 13; and Kuhn, "The Incredible Polarization of the Supreme Court," *supra* Chapter 1, note 13.

32. Bonneau, Hammond, Maltzman, & Wahlbeck, "Agenda Control, the Median Justice, and the Majority Opinion on the U.S. Supreme Court," *supra* Chapter 3, note 34; Clark & Lauderdale, "Locating Supreme Court Opinions in Doctrine Space," *supra* Chapter 3, note 34; and Carrubba, Friedman, Martin, & Vanberg, "Who Controls the Content of Supreme Court Opinions?," *supra* Chapter 3, note 34.

33. Indeed, justices have been known to concur separately with their own majority opinions for this reason. *See, for example, Bush v. Vera*, 517 U.S. 952, at 990 (1996) (O'Connor, J., concurring).

34. Maltzman et al., *supra* Chapter 1, note 24.

35. Spaeth, The Supreme Court Database, *supra* Chapter 2, note 8.

36. Martin & Quinn, "Dynamic Ideal Point Estimation via Markov Chain Monte Carlo for the U.S. Supreme Court," *supra* Chapter 2, note 83.

37. As in the previous chapter, cases were excluded when justices withdrew because of illness or because they were confirmed after the oral arguments. *See* Black & Epstein, "Recusals and the 'Problem' of an Equally Divided Supreme Court," *supra* Chapter 1, note 9.

38. When multiple liberal or conservative recusals occurred in the same case, the coding of the independent variables remained 1. I considered using a count variable, but multiple recusals are rare.

39. A third category of recusals occurs when median justices recuse themselves, but earlier versions of the model that featured a Median Justice Recusal variable found no systematic influence.

40. Martin, Quinn, & Epstein, "The Median Justice on the U.S. Supreme Court," *supra* Chapter 3, note 33.

41. Bonneau, Hammond, Maltzman, & Wahlbeck, "Agenda Control, the Median Justice, and the Majority Opinion on the U.S. Supreme Court," *supra* Chapter 3, note 34; Clark & Lauderdale, "Locating Supreme Court Opinions in Doctrine Space," *supra* Chapter 3, note 34; and Carrubba, Friedman, Martin, & Vanberg, "Who Controls the Content of Supreme Court Opinions?," *supra* Chapter 3, note 34.

42. Martin & Quinn, "Dynamic Ideal Point Estimation via Markov Chain Monte Carlo for the U.S. Supreme Court," *supra* Chapter 2, note 83.

43. Specifically, the Lower Court Direction variable was coded 1 when the lcDispositionDirection variable in the Supreme Court Database was coded as 1 (indicating a conservative result), and 0 otherwise.

44. D. Marie Provine, Case Selection in the United States Supreme Court (1980); Kevin T. McQuire, "Explaining Executive Success in the U.S. Supreme Court,"

51 Pol. Res. Q. 505 (1998); and Lee Epstein, William M. Landes, & Richard A. Posner, "Inferring the Winning Party in the Supreme Court from the Pattern of Questioning at Oral Argument," 39 J. Legal Stud. 433 (2010).

45. Results were generated using the *mfx* command in Stata 10.0.

46. In both salient cases and civil liberties cases, the Liberal Recusal variable was nearly significant at the $p < 0.05$ levels.

47. The mean Martin-Quinn score was 0.803 for the Vinson Court, –0.150 for the Warren Court, 0.485 for the Burger Court, 0.682 for the Rehnquist Court, and 0.935 for the Roberts Court. Positive values are associated with more conservative ideologies. *See* Martin & Quinn, *supra* Chapter 2, note 83.

48. For example, in the health care dispute, it might ultimately matter less that Chief Justice Roberts voted to uphold the individual mandate than that he wrote an opinion restricting the scope of congressional power under the commerce clause. The Court's opinion, more than the disposition, will be what determines how Congress can regulate in the future. *See National Federation of Independent Business v. Sebelius,* 132 S.Ct. 2566 (2012).

49. Once again, the marginal effects were generated using the *mfx* command in Stata 10.0.

50. Because Martin-Quinn scores vary by year, the ideology scores reflect judicial ideology at different points in time. Justice Stewart's score was 0.323 in 1977, White's was 0.324 in 1976, O'Connor's was 0.326 in 2001, Breyer's was –0.033 in 2009, Ginsburg's was –0.025 in 2009, and Stevens's was –0.024 in 1977. For more about the scores, *see* Martin & Quinn, *supra* Chapter 2, note 83.

51. Justice Clark's Martin-Quinn score was 0.260 in 1956, Blackmun's was 0.270 in 1977, White's was 0.526 in 1991, and Stewart's was 0.553 in 1978.

52. Douglas Rice, "The Impact of Supreme Court Activity on the Judicial Agenda," 48 Law & Soc'y Rev. 63 (2014).

53. Pamela C. Corley & Justin Wedeking, "The (Dis)Advantage of Certainty: The Importance of Certainty in Language," 48 Law & Soc'y Rev. 35 (2014).

54. *See* Mark J. Richards & Herbert M. Kritzer, "Jurisprudential Regimes in Supreme Court Decision Making," 96 Am. Pol. Sci. Rev. 305–20 (2002) (finding that key precedents structure subsequent decision making on the Supreme Court); and Herbert M. Kritzer & Mark J. Richards, "Jurisprudential Regimes and Supreme Court Decisionmaking: The Lemon Regime and Establishment Clause Cases," 37 Law & Soc'y Rev. 827 (2003) (applying the theory of jurisprudential regimes to Establishment Clause cases); *but see* Jeffrey R. Lax & Kelly T. Rader, "Legal Constraints on Supreme Court Decision Making: Do Jurisprudential Regimes Exist?," 72 J. Pol. 273, 282 (2010) (finding "only weak evidence that major Supreme Court precedents affect the way the justices themselves vote in subsequent cases"); and Thomas G. Hansford & James F. Spriggs II, The Politics of Precedent on the Supreme Court (2006) (finding that precedent both constrains the justices and provides them opportunities to shape the law).

55. SEGAL & SPAETH, *supra* Chapter 1, note 12.

56. *See* Gibson & Caldeira, "Has Legal Realism Damaged the Institutional Legitimacy of the U.S. Supreme Court?," *supra* Chapter 1, note 19 (finding that public confidence in the Supreme Court is not damaged when respondents understand that justices make decisions based on their own biases and preferences).

57. *See* LEE EPSTEIN & JEFFREY A. SEGAL, ADVICE AND CONSENT: THE POLITICS OF JUDICIAL APPOINTMENTS (2005) (finding that, despite some exceptions, Supreme Court justices vote consistently with the expectations of their appointing presidents).

58. Within the legal community, there is much more serious concern about judicial ethics and its impact on public confidence in courts. *See, for example,* Stempel, "Rehnquist, Recusal, and Reform," *supra* Chapter 1, note 8; Bassett, "Recusal and the Supreme Court," *supra* Chapter 1, note 8; Caprice Roberts, "The Fox Guarding the Henhouse?," *supra* Chapter 1, note 8; Frost, "Keeping Up Appearances," *supra* Chapter 1, note 8; Flamm, "History of and Problems with the Federal Judicial Disqualification Framework," *supra* Chapter 1, note 8; and Virelli, "Congress, the Constitution, and Supreme Court Recusal," *supra* Chapter 1, note 23.

Chapter 5

1. *See* Editorial, "Recuse to Lose," *supra* Chapter 1, note 57, at A16; and Editorial, "Court Without a Quorum," *supra* Chapter 4, note 9, at Weekend 11.

2. *See* Roberts, *supra* Chapter 1, note 6; Ginsburg, *supra* Chapter 1, note 31; Transcript, "Supreme Court 2012 Budget," *supra* Chapter 2, note 2.

3. *Laird v. Tatum,* 409 U.S. 824 (1972) (Rehnquist, J., denying the motion to recuse); *United States v. Edwards,* 334 F.2d 360, 362 (5th Cir., 1964).

4. Rule 10 of the Rules of the U.S. Supreme Court states that Justices are more likely to grant *certiorari* when "a United States court of appeals has entered a decision in conflict with the decision of another United States court of appeals on the same important matter." Social scientists have found that, in fact, the presence of a conflict is a good predictor of a grant of *certiorari*. *See* Tanenhaus, Schick, Muraskin, & Rosen, "The Supreme Court's *Certiorari* Jurisdiction: Cue Theory," *supra* Chapter 3, note 24; S. Sidney Ulmer, "The Supreme Court's *Certiorari* Decisions: Conflict as a Predictive Value," 78 AM. POL. SCI. REV. 901–11 (1984); PERRY, DECIDING TO DECIDE, *supra* Chapter 1, note 14; Saul Brenner, "Granting *Certiorari* by the United States Supreme Court: An Overview of the Social Science Studies," 92 LAW LIB. J. 193–201 (2000).

5. SPAETH, THE SUPREME COURT DATABASE, *supra* Chapter 2, note 8. Cases in which justices recused themselves were identified using the same procedures employed in Chapter 3.

6. Black & Epstein, "Recusals and the 'Problem' of an Equally Divided Supreme Court," *supra* Chapter 1, note 9; *see also* Black & Bryan, "Explaining the (Non)Occurrence of Equal Divisions on the U.S. Supreme Court," *supra* Chapter 2, note 76.

7. Data are the same employed in Table 5.1 and are based on an augmented version of the Supreme Court Database. *See* SPAETH, THE SUPREME COURT DATABASE, *supra* Chapter 2, note 8.

8. In fact, Supreme Court justices decide many of their cases unanimously. *See* Adam Liptak, "Justices Agree to Agree, at Least for the Moment," NEW YORK TIMES, May 28, 2013, at A11; CORLEY, STEIGERWALT, & WARD, THE PUZZLE OF UNANIMITY, *supra* Chapter 3, note 27.

9. For the measurement of the LIBERAL RECUSAL and CONSERVATIVE RECUSAL variables, *see* Chapter 4.

10. I found no evidence that a liberal recusal had a comparable effect during the Warren Court.

11. *Zubik v. Burwell*, 578 U.S. __ (2016).

12. *Friedrichs v. California Teachers Association*, 578 U.S. __ (2016).

13. *See, for example,* Adam Liptak, "Supreme Court Seems Poised to Deal Unions a Major Setback," NEW YORK TIMES, Jan. 12, 2016, at A1.

14. Once again, I used case-centered data. *See* SPAETH, THE SUPREME COURT DATABASE, *supra* Chapter 2, note 8.

15. To identify when the Court divided evenly, I used two variables in the Supreme Court Database, MAJVOTES (recording the number of majority votes) and MINVOTES (recording the number of minority votes).

16. These variables are the same employed in Table 5.3.

17. Martin & Quinn, "Dynamic Ideal Point Estimation via Markov Chain Monte Carlo for the U.S. Supreme Court," *supra* Chapter 2, note 83.

18. All variables are measured the same as in previous chapters. As in Chapter 3, coefficients for the issue area variables are not reported.

19. It was infeasible to include two other measures of case divisiveness that I used in Chapter 3 (CONFLICT and DISSENT BELOW) because they are based on reports of this activity in the majority opinions. Cases that divide evenly produce no majority opinions, so there is no variation.

20. Marginal effects were generated using the *mfx* command in Stata 10.0. The baseline probability of dividing evenly is 7.5%.

21. Contrary to expectations, Table 5.4 reports no significant correlation between IDEOLOGICAL DIVERSITY and dividing evenly. This result replicates findings by Black and Bryan, who used the interquartile range to measure ideological heterogeneity instead of the standard deviation. *See* Black & Bryan, "Explaining the (Non)Occurrence of Equal Divisions on the U.S. Supreme Court," *supra* Chapter 2, note 76.

22. Martin, Quinn, & Epstein, "The Median Justice on the U.S. Supreme Court," *supra* Chapter 3, note 33.

23. Black & Epstein, "Recusals and the 'Problem' of an Equally Divided Supreme Court," *supra* Chapter 1, note 9.

24. *See* Editorial, "Kagan and ObamaCare," *supra* Chapter 4, note 3; Editorial, "Mr. Cheney's Day in Court," *supra* Chapter 4, note 5; Chemerinsky & Lubet, "In One Key Area, (the Chief) Justice Is Indeed Blind," *supra* Chapter 4, note 6.

25. As Gibson put it, "legitimacy is for losers," which is to say that the real test of legitimacy is whether citizens will agree with—or at least acquiesce to—court decisions that they oppose. *See* James L. Gibson, "Legitimacy Is for Losers: The Role of Institutional Legitimacy and the Symbols of Judicial Authority in Inducing Acquiescence to Disagreeable Court Rulings," Presented at the 62nd *Nebraska Symposium on Motivation—"Motivating Cooperation and Compliance with Authority: The Role(s) of Institutional Trust and Confidence"* (Keynote Speaker), Apr. 24–25, 2014; *see also* GIBSON, ELECTING JUDGES, at 5–6 ("Legitimacy becomes crucial in the context of dissatisfaction; legitimacy requires an 'object precondition.' Problems of compliance do not typically arise when court decisions align with the preferences of the institution's constituents; when they do not align, legitimacy or institutional loyalty provides the rationale for accepting or acquiescing to the ruling of a court").

26. DAVID EASTON, A SYSTEMS ANALYSIS OF POLITICAL LIFE (1965).

27. GIBSON & CALDEIRA (2009), *supra* Chapter 1, note 68.

28. GIBSON, ELECTING JUDGES, at 5.

29. *Ibid.*

30. For example, Justice Breyer has observed that "public acceptance is not automatic and cannot be taken for granted. The Court itself must help maintain the public's trust in the Court, the public's confidence in the Constitution, and the public's commitment to the rule of law." STEPHEN BREYER, MAKING OUR DEMOCRACY WORK: A JUDGE'S VIEW (2010), at xiii.

31. GIBSON & CALDEIRA (2009), *supra* Chapter 1, note 68; Gibson & Caldeira, "Has Legal Realism Damaged the Institutional Legitimacy of the U.S. Supreme Court?," *supra* Chapter 1, note 19.

32. Gibson & Caldeira, "Has Legal Realism Damaged the Institutional Legitimacy of the U.S. Supreme Court?," *supra* Chapter 1, note 19, at 209 ("Support for the Court is not damaged by acceptance of the basic tenets of legal realism, but support depends upon seeing judges as different from ordinary politicians, in part because, unlike politicians, they are principled in their decisionmaking").

33. Caldeira & Gibson, "The Etiology of Public Support for the Supreme Court," *supra* Chapter 1, note 68; James L. Gibson & Gregory A. Caldeira, "Blacks and the United States Supreme Court: Models of Diffuse Support," 54 J. POL. 1120–45; and Vanessa A. Baird, "Building Institutional Legitimacy: The Role of Procedural Justice," 54 POL. RES. Q. 333–54.

34. 531 U.S. 98 (2000).

35. James L. Gibson, Gregory A. Caldeira, & Lester Kenyatta Spence, "The Supreme Court and the US Presidential Election of 2000: Wounds, Self-Inflicted or Otherwise?," 33 BRIT. J. POL. SCI., 535–56 (2003), at 555.

36. Anke Grosskopf & Jeffrey J. Mondak, "Do Attitudes Toward Specific Supreme Court Decisions Matter? The Impact of Webster and *Texas v. Johnson* on Public Confidence in the Supreme Court," 51 POL. RES. Q. 633–54 (1998).

37. *But see* Brandon L. Bartels & Christopher D. Johnston, "On the Ideological Foundations of Supreme Court Legitimacy in the American Public," 57 AM. J. POL.

Sci. 184–99 (2012) (finding that "ideological disagreement exhibits a potent, deleterious impact on legitimacy").

38. Survey data are from three nationally representative surveys taken from the Roper Center archive. Gallup Organization, "Gallup/CNN/USA Today Poll # 2003-33: Iraq/Stock Market/Hillary Clinton/Sammy Sosa's Illegal Bat/Martha Stewart" (June 9–10, 2003); Gallup Organization, "Gallup News Service Poll # 2004–18: 2004 Presidential Election/Price of Gasoline/European Union" (May 21–23, 2004); and Gallup Organization, "Gallup/CNN/USA Today Poll # 2004-11A: George W. Bush/Taxes/Social Security/Same-Sex Marriage/Religion" (Nov. 18–21, 2004). All surveys were retrieved from the iPOLL Databank, The Roper Center for Public Opinion Research, University of Connecticut, http://www.ropercenter.uconn.edu.

39. If any single event caused the decline of confidence in November 2004, it was most likely the presidential election, which preceded the survey. Among Democratic respondents, confidence in the Supreme Court dropped from 47% to 32% between May and November 2004, probably because of the reelection of George W. Bush and the prospect of an even more conservative Supreme Court. Republican support was unchanged during this period.

40. James L. Gibson, Gregory A. Caldeira, and Lester Kenyatta Spence, "Measuring Attitudes Toward the United States Supreme Court," 47 Am. J. Pol. Sci. 354–67, at 358 (2003).

41. It should be noted, however, that similar measures have been used in other studies of legitimacy. See Grosskopf & Mondak, "Do Attitudes Toward Specific Supreme Court Decisions Matter?," supra note 36; and Sara C. Benesh, "Understanding Public Confidence in American Courts," 68 J. Pol. 697–707 (2006).

42. Caldeira & Gibson, "The Etiology of Public Support for the Supreme Court," supra Chapter 1, note 68; Gibson & Caldeira, "Blacks and the United States Supreme Court: Models of Diffuse Support," supra note 33; and Baird, "Building Institutional Legitimacy: The Role of Procedural Justice," supra note 33.

43. Farganis, "Do Reasons Matter?," supra Chapter 1, note 62.

44. Financial conflicts have been a subject of controversy at some of the justices' confirmation hearings. See, for example, Editorial, "A Cloud on the Breyer Nomination," supra Chapter 1, note 52; Kennedy, "Alito's Credibility Problem," supra Chapter 1, note 53; and Editorial, "Judge Alito, in His Own Words," supra Chapter 1, note 53.

45. See James L. Gibson, " 'New Style' Judicial Campaigns and the Legitimacy of State High Courts," 71 J. Pol. 1285, at 1288 (2009). See also James L. Gibson, "Challenges to the Impartiality of State Supreme Courts: Legitimacy Theory and 'New-Style' Judicial Campaigns," 102 Am. Pol. Sci. Rev. 59 (2008); and James L. Gibson, Electing Judges: The Surprising Effects of Campaigning on Judicial Legitimacy (2012).

46. 223 W. Va. 624 (2008).

47. The survey was developed using Qualtrics, and results are based on a nonprobability sample of 1,002 respondents recruited with Amazon's Mechanical Turk. Only U.S. residents over the age of 18 were eligible to participate. Overall, the sample was

55.5% male and 45.5% female. Respondents were 78.6% white, 8.8% Asian, 6.1% black, 4.6% Hispanic, and 1.9% "other." The median birth year was 1985 (i.e., thirty-one years old); the median household income was $40,000 to $50,000; and the median education level was "College graduate." The sample was 19.3% Republican, 43.6% Democratic, and 32.8% Independent. All fifty states were represented, with the most from California (9.6%), followed by New York (7.6%), Florida (7.5%), Pennsylvania (5.8%), and Texas (5.5%).

48. These and other measures of public attitudes about the Court were collected only after the respondents were first asked to record their attitudes about the possibility of the justices dividing evenly.

49. *See, e.g.*, Caldeira & Gibson, "The Etiology of Public Support for the Supreme Court," *supra* Chapter 1, note 68; and Gibson, Caldeira, & Spence, "Measuring Attitudes Toward the United States Supreme Court," *supra* note 40.

50. To minimize survey instrument effects, the ordering of these questions was randomized.

51. The S.C. LEGITIMACY index ranged from a value of 3 to a value of 15, with higher values associated with higher levels of legitimacy. Because the questions in Figures 5.6 and 5.7 were scaled differently, the responses were inverted before being combined with the responses to the third question in Figure 5.8.

52. IDEOLOGY ranged from a value of −10 to +10, with positive values associated with more conservative respondents. For PARTY IDENTIFICATION, higher values are associated with Republican respondents, with the categories Strong Democrat (20.7%); Not Very Strong Democrat (23.0%); Lean Democrat (15.6%); Neither (14.6%); Lean Republican (7.0%); Not Strong Republican (12.4%); and Strong Republican (6.9%). The categories for HOUSEHOLD INCOME were "Less than $15,000" (9.3%); "$15,000 to $20,000" (6.2%); "$20,000 to $25,000" (7.5%); "$25,000 to $30,000" (6.9%); "$30,000 to $40,000" (12.6%); "$40,000 to $50,000" (10.4%); "$50,000 to $75,000" (20.9%); "$75,000 to $100,000" (12.8%); "$100,000 to $150,000" (10.2%); "$150,000 to $200,000" (2.3%); and "$200,000 or more" (1.1%). The categories for EDUCATION LEVEL were "High school education or less" (12.0%); "Some college/Technical school" (31.5%); "College graduate" (41.6%); and "Postgraduate work or degree" (14.9%).

53. The reported coefficients also cluster standard errors by state.

54. *See, for example*, PERRY, DECIDING TO DECIDE, *supra* Chapter 1, note 14, at 144–45, in which one of the justices he interviewed said, "We don't negotiate, we accommodate. And this is a perfectly appropriate and good procedure because this is a court of nine people and it is our responsibility to have an opinion of the Court—a unanimous opinion if possible when the Court can come up with one."

55. Adam Liptak, "Justices Divided Over 8-Member Court," NEW YORK TIMES, May 31, 2016, at A10.

56. MALTZMAN ET AL., *supra* Chapter 1, note 24.

57. *Ibid. See also* Wahlbeck et al., "Marshalling the Court: Bargaining and Accommodation on the United States Supreme Court," *supra* Chapter 1, note 27.

58. Paul J. Wahlbeck, James F. Spriggs II, & Forrest Maltzman, THE BURGER COURT OPINION WRITING DATABASE, http://supremecourtopinions.wustl.edu/, Aug. 6, 2009.

59. MALTZMAN ET AL., *supra* Chapter 1, note 24; Wahlbeck et al., *supra* Chapter 1, note 27.

60. Previous studies, e.g., Wahlbeck et al., *supra* Chapter 1, note 27, have calculated the size of the majority coalition by looking at the initial conference votes, but the final vote on the merits is a defensible proxy.

61. Martin & Quinn, "Dynamic Ideal Point Estimation via Markov Chain Monte Carlo for the U.S. Supreme Court," *supra* Chapter 2, note 83.

62. The model also includes dummy variables for each justice, the coefficients for which are not reported. The measure of case salience uses Clark et al.'s measure of early salience. *See* Clark, Law, & Rice, "Measuring the Political Salience of Supreme Court Cases," *supra* Chapter 3, note 50.

63. Replacing these three variables with a single measure also did not yield statistically significant results.

64. Neither of the other determinants of bargaining activity had the hypothesized effect. In fact, COALITION DIVERSITY is signed in the opposite direction from what was hypothesized. The reason for this effect is not immediately clear, although it is worth noting that Maltzman, Spriggs, and Wahlbeck measured the heterogeneity of a coalition by using issue-specific ideology scores. *See* Wahlbeck et al., *supra* Chapter 1, note 27, at 304.

65. The recusal of a liberal justice or the median justice does not have a comparable effect. Liberal recusals cause a *decline* of about 0.3 circulations when there is a minimum winning coalition, while the recusal of the median justice increases circulations by 0.2 circulations, but neither effect is statistically significant.

66. *See* Martin, Quinn, & Epstein, "The Median Justice on the U.S. Supreme Court," *supra* Chapter 3, note 33, at 1302.

67. PERRY, DECIDING TO DECIDE, *supra* Chapter 1, note 14.

68. Lubet, "Disqualification of Supreme Court Justices," *supra* Chapter 1, note 15; Bassett, "Recusal and the Supreme Court," *supra* Chapter 1, note 8; and Supreme Court, *Statement of Recusal Policy*, *supra* Chapter 1, note 16.

69. Lee Epstein, Jeffrey A. Segal, & Harold J. Spaeth, THE DIGITAL ARCHIVE OF THE PAPERS OF JUSTICE HARRY A. BLACKMUN (2007), http://epstein.usc.edu/research/BlackmunArchive.html.

70. The Court's practice is to discuss at conference only those cases that are placed on the Discuss List. Any justices can add a case to the list, but petitions that are not listed are automatically denied *certiorari*. *See* O'BRIEN, STORM CENTER, *supra* Chapter 1, note 14, at 201–2.

71. Ryan C. Black & Ryan J. Owens, "Analyzing the Reliability of Supreme Court Justices' Agenda-Setting Records," 30 JUST. SYS. J. 254–64, at 262 (2009) ("Our results suggest that scholars wishing to analyze the agenda-setting process using Justice Blackmun's papers may do so with the knowledge that these data are both accurate and reliable").

72. *Dow Jones & Company, Inc., v. Simon, Stanley, et al.*, 488 U.S. 946 (1988) (*cert. denied*).

73. *Nebraska Press Association v. Stuart*, 427 U.S. 539 (1976).

74. Compare *Radio & Television News Assn. v. United States District Court*, 781 F.2d 1443 (9th Cir., 1986), with *CBS Inc. v. Young*, 522 F.2d 234 (6th Cir., 1975).

75. *Nebraska,* at 617 (Stevens, J., concurring in the judgment).

76. *Keane v. United States*, 490 U.S. 1084 (1989) (*cert. denied*).

77. *McNally v. United States*, 483 U.S. 350 (1987).

78. *United States v. Keane*, 852 F.2d 199 (7th Cir., 1988) (*cert. denied*).

79. *McNally,* at 362 (Stevens, J., dissenting).

80. *Wallace v. Arizona*, 494 U.S. 1047 (1990) (*cert. denied*).

81. Specifically, they wrote, "Adhering to our views that the death penalty is in all circumstances cruel and unusual punishment prohibited by the Eighth and Fourteenth Amendments, *Gregg v. Georgia*, 428 U.S. 153, 227, 231 (1976), we would grant *certiorari* and vacate the death sentence in this case."

82. *Minnesota Mining & Mfg. Co. v. Freeman*, 494 U.S. 1070 (1990) (*cert. denied*).

83. *Lewis v. Adamson*, 497 U.S. 1031 (1990) (*cert. denied*).

84. *Adamson v. Ricketts*, 865 F.2d 1011 (9th Cir., 1990).

85. *Walton v. Arizona*, 497 U.S. 639 (1990); *Lewis v. Jeffers*, 497 U.S. 764 (1990); *Alabama v. Smith*, 490 U.S. 794 (1989).

86. *Lewis v. Jeffers*, 497 U.S. 764 (1990).

87. *Willner v. Barr*, 502 U.S. 1020 (1991) (*cert. denied*).

88. "Join-3" votes occur when justices indicate that they will join three other votes in favor of granting *certiorari*, but would deny the petition otherwise. *See* PERRY, DECIDING TO DECIDE, *supra* Chapter 1, note 14.

89. *Smith v. United States*, 502 U.S. 1017 (1991) (*cert. denied*).

90. Organized by term, the total number of cases the Supreme Court disposed of was 4,349 in 1986, 4,387 in 1987, 4,830 in 1988, 4,932 in 1989, 4,514 in 1990, 5,828 in 1991, 6,366 in 1992, and 6,682 in 1993. Data are from the Federal Judicial Center, http://www.fjc.gov/history/caseload.nsf/page/caseloads_Sup_Ct_totals.

Chapter 6

1. Transcript, "Supreme Court 2012 Budget," *supra* Chapter 2, note 2 (in which Justice Breyer directly referenced the importance of the "duty to sit").

2. Jeffrey W. Stempel, "Chief William's Ghost: The Problematic Persistence of the Duty to Sit Doctrine," 57 BUFF. L. REV. 813–958, at 871 (2009) ("Although the duty to sit concept as a barrier to disqualification has been rejected by federal law since 1974 and the ABA since 1972, a few federal courts appear not to have realized the impact of the legislative changes and continue to endorse the problematic duty to sit counseling against recusal unless the case for disqualification is beyond serious question").

3. Judge Alex Kozinski of the Ninth Circuit has denied that stock ownership is likely to bias judges: "I can't imagine that I could possibly be tempted to change my vote in a case because I own stock in one of the parties. I don't claim a special virtue

in this, if virtue means resisting temptation. What I'm saying is, I wouldn't be tempted. If money were important to me, I'd be in private practice and, in a month or a week—maybe in an hour—I would make much more than my one hundred shares of AT&T could possibly change in value based on my vote in a case. The idea that I would give up my honest judgment in a case for a few dollars is beyond silly—it's ludicrous and insulting." *See* Alex Kozinski, "The Real Issues of Judicial Ethics," 32 HOFSTRA L. REV. 1095, at 1105 (2004).

4. EPSTEIN & SEGAL, ADVICE AND CONSENT, *supra* Chapter 4, note 57, at 143 ("Judges and justices have always been political beings. Since the earliest days of the Republic, the vast majority of federal jurists have been affiliated with a partisan group, and, in fact, have shared the party affiliation of the president who nominated them. On top of that, many, perhaps even a majority, attracted the attention of key players in the appointments process precisely because they had been active in party politics").

5. As Jeffrey Toobin of the *New Yorker* stated in an interview on the Diane Rehm show, "I think it's a symptom of the Washington obsession with turning substantive disagreements into supposed ethical transgressions. When you have liberals trying to get Thomas off the health care case, you have a very small number of conservatives trying to get Justice Kagan off the case. And I think both are silly. I think both should be on the case. I think there is no ethical problem with either of them participating." Transcript, "The Diane Rehm Show: Conflict of Interest on the Supreme Court," NPR (Aug. 25, 2011), http://thedianerehmshow.org/shows/2011-08-25/conflict-interest-supreme-court/transcript.

6. *See, for example,* Ginsburg, *supra* Chapter 1, note 31; Transcript, "Supreme Court 2012 Budget," *supra* Chapter 2, note 2.

7. *Cheney v. U.S. District Court*, 541 U.S. 913 (2004) (Scalia, J., denying the motion to recuse).

8. Roberts, *supra* Chapter 1, note 6, at 9.

9. It should be noted once again that these measures of public confidence may not capture institutional loyalty but the public's dissatisfaction with the Court's outputs at the moment. *See* Gibson, Caldeira, & Spence, "Measuring Attitudes Toward the United States Supreme Court," *supra* Chapter 5, note 40. Yet it remains striking that the trend has been consistently downward, especially because at least some research does suggest that short-term policy dissatisfaction can contribute to a decline in diffuse support. *See* Bartels & Johnston, "On the Ideological Foundations of Supreme Court Legitimacy in the American Public," *supra* Chapter 5, note 37. Certainly it would not be irrational for supporters of reform to find the direction of the trend worrying.

10. It is unknown what is responsible for the decline in confidence levels. Henke suggests that the trends might reflect dissatisfaction with the Court's *Citizens United* decision and that it has been sustained by "broad national discontent." *See* Henke, *supra* Chapter 1, note 8, at 544 ("The Supreme Court's approval rating has been declining since its *Citizens United* decision in January 2010, and the ratings have been unable to rebound amidst profound cynicism about our capitalist democracy and acutely polarized

politics") (*internal quotation marks removed*). A problem with this explanation is that Figure 6.1 shows that the decline in public confidence levels actually pre-dated *Citizens United*, although the trends have accelerated since then.

11. Notably, however, Justice Scalia suggested in his *Cheney* memorandum that reforms might actually decrease legitimacy if increased regulation creates a presumption that the justices are corruptible. *See Cheney v. U.S. District Court*, 541 U.S. 913, at 928 (2004) (Scalia, J., denying the motion to recuse) ("The people must have confidence in the integrity of the Justices, and that cannot exist in a system that assumes them to be corruptible by the slightest friendship or favor, and in an atmosphere where the press will be eager to find foot-faults").

12. Bashman, "On Appeal: An Appellate Advocate's Perspective," *supra* Chapter 1, note 21, at 68.

13. Flamm, "History of and Problems with the Federal Judicial Disqualification Framework," *supra* Chapter 1, note 8, at 761 ("Although a litigant is unlikely to appear before a particular judge again, and therefore may feel that she has little to lose in seeking that judge's removal, an attorney who frequently handles litigation in federal court is likely to be less than eager to make or endorse a recusal motion for one client if she perceives that doing so may prejudice her ability to effectively litigate before that judge in future cases").

14. Alliance for Justice, A SUPREME COURT JUSTICE'S RECUSAL DECISIONS SHOULD BE TRANSPARENT AND REVIEWABLE (2011), at 7, http://www.afj.org/wp-content/uploads/2013/11/recusal-afj-memo.pdf.

15. *Id.*, at 6.

16. *See* Kathleen Clark, "Do We Have Enough Ethics in Government Yet?: An Answer From Fiduciary Theory," 1996 U. ILL. L. REV. 57 (1996), at 58 ("All government employees, from the highest level officials to the lowest level workers, face an increasingly complicated set of detailed ethics regulations").

17. The justices have received similar criticism for refusing to disclose their medical records. *See* Susan Okie, "Illness and Secrecy on the Supreme Court," 351 NEW ENG. J. MED. 2675 (2004), at 2677 (quoting legal historian David J. Garrow of Emory University, "The culture of Washington has allowed the justices to define themselves as this quasi-royal body who are not subject to most of the norms and questions that apply to the other two branches of government"); *see also* Foertsch, "Scalia's Duck Hunt Leads to Ruffled Feathers," *supra* Chapter 2, note 1, at 487.

18. As Justice Breyer testified before Congress, "I personally have seven volumes of ethics rules, the same that every district judge has." *See* Transcript, "Supreme Court 2012 Budget," *supra* Chapter 2, note 2.

19. 28 U.S.C. § 455 (1974).

20. Supreme Court Transparency and Disclosure Act of 2011, H.R. 862, 112th Cong. (2011).

21. Amanda Frost, "Judicial Ethics and Supreme Court Exceptionalism," 26 GEO. J. LEGAL ETHICS 443, 456 (2013).

22. This latter approach was endorsed by 138 law professors in a letter to the House & Senate Judiciary Committees. *See* Changing Ethical and Recusal Rules for Supreme Court Justices (Mar. 17, 2011), http://www.afj.org/wp-content/uploads/2013/09/judicial_ethics_sign_on_letter.pdf.

23. S. 3871, 111th Cong. (2010).

24. Press Release, "Leahy Proposes Bill to Allow Retired Justices to Sit on Court by Designation" (Sept. 29, 2010), http://www.leahy.senate.gov/press/leahy-proposes-bill-to-allow-retired-justices-to-sit-on-court-by-designation.

25. *Ibid.*

26. Roberts, *supra* Chapter 1, note 6, at 7 ("As in the case of financial reporting and gift requirements, the limits of Congress's power to require recusal have never been tested. The Justices follow the same general principles respecting recusal as other federal judges, but the application of those principles can differ due to the unique circumstances of the Supreme Court").

27. *Compare*, for example, Louis J. Virelli, "The (Un)Constitutionality of Supreme Court Recusal Standards," 2011 *Wis. L. Rev.* 1181, 1185 (2011) (arguing that "any legislative interference with Supreme Court recusal decisions is an unconstitutional intrusion into the judicial power vested in the Court by Article III of the Constitution"); *with* Frost, "Judicial Ethics and Supreme Court Exceptionalism," *supra* note 21, at 447 (maintaining that, "Ethics statutes, which promote the effective and legitimate exercise of the 'judicial power,' fall well within Congress's broad legislative authority over the Court's administration and operation").

28. Frost, *supra* note 21, at 457–458, citing James E. Pfander, One Supreme Court: Supremacy, Inferiority, and the Judicial Department of the United States 2 (2009) (arguing that Article III "creates a framework for the federal judiciary and leaves Congress in charge of many of the details"); *see also* Caprice Roberts, "The Fox Guarding the Henhouse?," *supra* Chapter 1, note 8, at 166 ("Article III of the Constitution provides Congress considerable control over the Supreme Court's structure and its jurisdiction").

29. Frost, *supra* note 21, at 459 ("Congress continues to control by legislation most of the areas over which it initially assumed authority in 1789. For example, federal laws currently in place authorize the Justices to hire librarians, marshals, clerks, law clerks, and secretaries to assist them in their work. The size of the Court, quorum requirements, dates of the Court's sessions, and oath of office all continues to be set by statute. A federal statute even purports to control the outcome of a case should the Court foresee the absence of a quorum for two Terms in a row.")

30. U.S. Const. art. III, § 1, cl. 1 ("The judicial power of the United States, shall be vested in one Supreme Court, and in such inferior courts as the Congress may from time to time ordain and establish").

31. Virelli, "Congress, the Constitution, and Supreme Court Recusal," *supra* Chapter 1, note 23, at 1573.

32. *Id.*, at 1564 ("With regard to the Supreme Court in particular, the early Congresses chose not to intervene in the Justices' exercise of their recusal power even

after they chose to do so for the lower federal courts. This practice indicates that, at the time the Constitution was drafted, Supreme Court recusal was a matter for the Court through its exercise of the judicial power granted to it by Article III").

33. Caprice Roberts, "The Fox Guarding the Henhouse?," *supra* Chapter 1, note 8, at 166 ("Depending on the scope of any solutions, the power to correct the process is likely an area of concurrent authority. Thus, the power to remedy the mechanism may lie in Justice Robert Houghwout Jackson's 'zone of twilight' where both Congress and the Supreme Court have overlapping authority and the line of demarcation is unclear").

34. Frost, *supra* note 21, at 462 ("Congress initially staffed the Court with only six Justices, then expanded and contracted its membership over the next eighty years before finally settling on its present size of nine in 1869. These changes in the Court's membership raise some of the same issues that a recusal of one of the nine would create today. Yet no one claims that Congress transgressed constitutional limits on its authority over the Court by altering the Court's size permanently, further supporting Congress's authority to mandate recusal for actual or perceived conflicts of interest").

35. U.S. CONST. art. III, § 2 ("In all the other cases before mentioned, the Supreme Court shall have appellate jurisdiction, both as to law and fact, with such exceptions, and under such regulations as the Congress shall make"). It should be noted, however, that it is rare for Congress to use the Exceptions Clause in this way, nor is it without political costs. The Supreme Court has pushed back against jurisdiction-stripping measures in cases such as *Boumediene v. Bush*, 553 U.S. 723 (2008).

36. *National Federation of Independent Business v. Sebelius*, 132 S.Ct. 2566, at 2586 (2012).

37. Frost, *supra* note 21, at 446 (describing Roberts's comments as "a shot across Congress's bow").

38. Transcript, "Supreme Court 2012 Budget," *supra* Chapter 2, note 2 (in which Justice Breyer stated, "The answer to your question, should the justices be bound by the same rules of ethics, I think is yes. All right. The second, different question is, does that mean you should legislate? Then I think the answer is no").

39. Caprice Roberts, "The Fox Guarding the Henhouse?," *supra* Chapter 1, note 8, at 168–69.

40. The Murphy Bill states in Section 3(b) that if a party seeks further review of a recusal motion, "other justices or judges of a court of the United States" will review the motion. The judges might include "retired justices and senior judges eligible for assignment."

41. *See, for example,* Frost, *supra* note 21, at 470 ("If the inferior courts must remain subordinate to the Supreme Court, then arguably Congress cannot assign the lower federal court judges a supervisory role over the Justices' ethics").

42. Russell Wheeler, "Regulating Supreme Court Justices' Ethics—'Cures Worse Than the Disease?,'" BROOKINGS INSTITUTION, http://www.brookings.edu/research/opinions/2011/03/21-justices-ethics-wheeler (Mar. 21, 2011) ("A denial of a recusal motion is a judicial act, subject to appeal, except as to Supreme Court justices. Given that it's a 'supreme' court, there's no high court to which litigants may appeal a justice's

decision. Creating one would take the judiciary into uncharted territory, creating a cure that could be worse than the occasional problems created by the status quo's lack of transparency. And let's be clear: despite the terminology, the proposals would create such a court—and in so doing, probably run afoul of the constitutional mandate that there be 'one Supreme Court' ").

43. Frost, *supra* note 21, at 470 ("The Judicial Conference is chaired by the Chief Justice, but its membership consists of judges on the circuit and district courts. If one adopts the strictest reading of the supreme/inferior dichotomy by concluding that it requires the lower courts be subordinate to the Supreme Court, and that it bars judges on those courts from policing the Justices' ethical conduct, then the Murphy Bill's delegation of authority to the Judicial Conference raised constitutional questions").

44. Chief Justice Roberts stated as much in his 2011 *Year-End Report*, *supra* Chapter 1, note 6, at 3–4 ("The Code of Conduct, by its express terms, applies only to lower federal court judges. That reflects a fundamental difference between the Supreme Court and the other federal courts. Article III of the Constitution creates only one court, the Supreme Court of the United States, but it empowers Congress to establish additional lower federal courts that the Framers knew the country would need. Congress instituted the Judicial Conference for the benefit of the courts it had created. Because the Judicial Conference is an instrument for the management of the lower federal courts, its committees have no mandate to prescribe rules or standards for any other body").

45. Virelli, "Congress, the Constitution, and Supreme Court Recusal," *supra* Chapter 1, note 23, at 1587–89 and 1597–99.

46. In the *Cheney* case, for example, the justices refused to rule on the recusal motion, referring it to Justice Scalia. *See Cheney v. United States District Court*, 540 U.S. 1217 ("In accordance with its historic practice, the Court refers the motion to recuse in this case to Justice Scalia").

47. Henke, *supra* Chapter 1, note 8, at 532–33.

48. *See* Caprice Roberts, "The Fox Guarding the Henhouse?," *supra* Chapter 1, note 8, at 176–77 ("The pool of judges who would fill the slot should be the Chief Judges of all of the circuits of the United States courts of appeals. These judges would be among the highest caliber of judges who are already serving on a federal appellate bench. They represent the next best option of judges from which a sufficient pool of replacements could be chosen").

49. *Id.*, at 176.

50. *See* McKeown, "To Judge or Not to Judge," *supra* Chapter 2, note 12.

51. Rebekah Saidman-Krauss, "A Second-Sitting: Assessing the Constitutionality and Desirability of Allowing Retired Supreme Court Justices to Fill Recusal-Based Vacancies on the Bench," 116 PENN ST. L. REV. 253–83, at 283 (2011) (noting that, at least with regard to retired Supreme Court justices, "because Leahy's legislation merely enables the assignment of previously-appointed officers, it does not violate the Appointments Clause").

52. 28 U.S.C. § 294 (a) ("Any retired Chief Justice of the United States or Associate Justice of the Supreme Court may be designated and assigned by the Chief Justice

of the United States to perform such judicial duties in any circuit, including those of a circuit justice, as he is willing to undertake").

53. Caprice Roberts, "The Fox Guarding the Henhouse?," *supra* Chapter 1, note 8, at 177–78 ("Although the Senate has already confirmed sitting federal appellate judges, the scope of such confirmations did not encompass the assumption of a new role—the role of possibly sitting as a substitute Justice on the Supreme Court. Thus, the Appointments Clause of the Constitution would require that the President appoint judges for this new role and secure the Senate's advice and consent").

54. Lisa T. McElroy & Michael C. Dorf, "Coming Off the Bench: Legal and Policy Implications of Proposals to Allow Retired Justices to Sit by Designation on the Supreme Court," 61 DUKE L.J. 81–122, at 99–100 (2011) ("As the law now stands, in making her recusal decision, that Justice must consider whether the potential conflict would affect her ability to decide the case neutrally and whether the conflict might create the appearance of impropriety. But were Congress to authorize the substitution of a retired Justice to fill the vacancy, she might well consider one additional factor: which retired Justice might take her place in deciding the case were she to recuse herself").

55. A model for automating the collection and reporting of such conflicts is already operational in the lower federal courts. *See* McKeown, "To Judge or Not to Judge," *supra* Chapter 2, note 12, at 664 ("Under this mandatory policy, each judge must develop a list of financial interests that could trigger recusal. Special conflicts-screening software compares a judge's recusal list with information filed in each case. The system flags potential conflicts, which enables the judge to decline an assignment or, if the case has been assigned, to recuse if necessary").

56. *See, for example,* Frost, "Keeping Up Appearances," *supra* Chapter 1, note 8, at 589 (arguing that "judges should give reasons for deciding to remove themselves (or, if the motion is transferred to a new judge, that judge should articulate the basis for his decision). The explanations need not be long or detailed, particularly in straightforward cases. These decisions will fill the void left by silent recusals"); also Foertsch, "Scalia's Duck Hunt Leads to Ruffled Feathers," *supra* Chapter 2, note 1, at 493 ("The Court should require Justices to provide a written explanation of their recusal decision in a particular case"); and Goodson, "Duck, Duck, Goose," *supra* Chapter 2, note 1, at 216 ("Perhaps the best approach is to require a written opinion either when Justices recuse themselves or whenever a party moves for recusal").

57. Virelli, "Congress, the Constitution, and Supreme Court Recusal," *supra* Chapter 1, note 23, at 1592 (noting that such procedural reforms "are less susceptible to constitutional arguments invoking the separation of powers than substantive recusal requirements").

58. Foertsch, "Scalia's Duck Hunt Leads to Ruffled Feathers," *supra* Chapter 2, note 1, at 589–90.

59. Henke, *supra* Chapter 1, note 8, at 536–37 (arguing that a reporting requirement is "intrusive because the reasons on which the Justice's recusal decision is based could be highly personal or of a sensitive nature, and the Justice's privacy, or another person's

privacy, might need to be protected. The Justices' right to maintain a modicum of privacy outweighs the benefits of satisfying the public's curiosity and establishing precedent").

60. *Id.*, at 537–38.

61. *Cheney v. U.S. District Court*, 541 U.S. 913, at 926 (2004) (Scalia, J., denying the motion to recuse) (noting that "the well-known and constant practice of Justices' enjoying friendship and social intercourse with Members of Congress and officers of the Executive Branch has not been abandoned, and ought not to be").

62. Virelli, "Congress, the Constitution, and Supreme Court Recusal," *supra* Chapter 1, note 23, at 1593.

63. On this point, I share the conclusion of Henke, *supra* Chapter 1, note 8, at 536 (who states that "requiring Justices to provide the public beyond the vast amount that is already publicly available is a nuisance").

64. The most persuasive argument in favor of a recusal could be made with regard to *Laird v. Tatum,* 409 U.S. 824 (1972) (Rehnquist, J., denying the motion to recuse). However, it should be noted that this case preceded the enactment of the 1974 reforms to the federal recusal statute. Justice Scalia's memorandum in *Cheney* was also controversial, but the arguments in favor of his recusal are less decisive. *Cheney v. United States Dist. Court*, 541 U.S. 913 (2004) (Scalia, J., denying the motion to recuse).

65. *Caperton v. Massey*, 556 U.S. 868 (2009).

66. Gibson, "Challenges to the Impartiality of State Supreme Courts," *supra* Chapter 5, note 15; Gibson, " 'New Style' Judicial Campaigns and the Legitimacy of State High Courts," *supra* Chapter 5, note 15.

67. Kozinski, "The Real Issues of Judicial Ethics," *supra* note 3, at 1106.

Works Cited

Ai, Chunrong, and Edward C. Norton. 2003. "Interaction Terms in Logit and Probit Models." *Economics Letters* 80: 123–29.

Alliance for Justice. 2011. *A Supreme Court Justice's Recusal Decisions Should Be Transparent and Reviewable.* http://www.afj.org/wp-content/uploads/2013/11/recusal-afj-memo.pdf.

Angell, Ernest. 1969. Letter to the Editor. *New York Times,* November 16. E13.

Baird, Vanessa A. 2001. "Building Institutional Legitimacy: The Role of Procedural Justice." *Political Research Quarterly* 54: 333–54.

Baird, Vanessa A., and Amy Gangl. 2006. "Shattering the Myth of Legality: The Impact of the Media's Framing of Supreme Court Procedures on Perceptions of Fairness." *Political Psychology* 27: 597–613.

Bam, Dmitry. 2011. "Making Appearances Matter: Recusal and the Appearance of Bias." *Brigham Young University Law Review* 2011: 943–1002.

Barnes, Robert. 2011. "A Health Law Warm-Up Fight for High Court." *Washington Post,* November 28. A1.

Bartels, Brandon L., and Christopher D. Johnston. 2013. "On the Ideological Foundations of Supreme Court Legitimacy in the American Public." *American Journal of Political Science* 57: 184–99.

Bashman, Howard J. 2005. "On Appeal: An Appellate Advocate's Perspective." *Journal of Appellate Practice and Process* 7: 59–74.

Bassett, Debra Lynn. 2005. "Recusal and the Supreme Court." *Hastings Law Journal* 56: 657–98.

Baum, Lawrence. 2006. *Judges and Their Audiences: A Perspective on Judicial Behavior.* Princeton, NJ: Princeton University Press.

———. 1997. *The Puzzle of Judicial Behavior.* Ann Arbor, MI: University of Michigan Press.

Benesh, Sara C. 2006. "Understanding Public Confidence in American Courts." *Journal of Politics* 68: 697–707.

Biskupic, Joan. 2011. "Calls for Recusal Intensify in Health Care Case; Kagan, Thomas Questioned." *USA Today,* November 21. 6A.

Black, Ryan C., and Amanda C. Bryan. 2014. "Explaining the (Non)Occurrence of Equal Divisions on the U.S. Supreme Court." *American Politics Research* 42: 1077–95.

Black, Ryan, and Lee Epstein. 2005. "Recusals and the 'Problem' of an Equally Divided Supreme Court." *Journal of Appellate Practice and Process* 7: 75–99.

Black, Ryan C., Timothy R. Johnson, and Justin Wedeking. 2012. *Oral Arguments and Coalition Formation on the U.S. Supreme Court.* Ann Arbor, MI: University of Michigan Press.

Black, Ryan, and Ryan J. Owens. 2009. "Agenda Setting in the Supreme Court: The Collision of Policy and Jurisprudence." *Journal of Politics* 71: 1062–75.

———. 2009. "Analyzing the Reliability of Supreme Court Justices' Agenda-Setting Records." *Justice System Journal* 30: 254–64.

Bleich, Jeff, and Kelly Klaus. "Deciding Whether to Decide: Should There Be Standards for Recusals?" *Oregon State Bar Bulletin* 61: 9–20.

Bonneau, Chris W., Thomas H. Hammond, Forrest Maltzman, and Paul J. Wahlbeck. 2007. "Agenda Control, the Median Justice, and the Majority Opinion on the U.S. Supreme Court." *American Journal of Political Science* 51: 890–905.

Brenner, Saul. 2000. "Granting *Certiorari* by the United States Supreme Court: An Overview of the Social Science Studies." *Law Library Journal* 92: 193–201.

Breyer, Stephen. 2011. *Making Our Democracy Work: A Judge's View.* New York, NY: Alfred A. Knopf.

Broder, David S. 1986. "Those Memos Will Tell." *Washington Post*, August 6. A15.

Caldeira, Gregory A., and James L. Gibson. 1992. "The Etiology of Public Support for the Supreme Court." *American Journal of Political Science* 36: 635–64.

Caldeira, Gregory A., John R. Wright, and Christopher J. W. Zorn. 1999. "Sophisticated Voting and Gate-Keeping in the Supreme Court." *Journal of Law, Economics, & Organization* 15: 549–72.

Calmes, Jackie. 2010. "Activism of Thomas's Wife Could Raise Judicial Issues." *New York Times*, October 8.

Canon, Bradley C., and Charles A. Johnson. 1999. *Judicial Policies: Implementation and Impact.* 2nd ed. Washington, DC: CQ Press.

Carrubba, Cliff, Barry Friedman, Andrew D. Martin, and Georg Vanberg. 2012. "Who Controls the Content of Supreme Court Opinions?" *American Journal of Political Science* 56: 400–12.

Casey, Gregory. 1974. "The Supreme Court and Myth: An Empirical Investigation." *Law & Society Review* 8: 385–420.

Chemerinsky, Erwin, and Steven Lubet. 2004. "In One Key Area, (the Chief) Justice Is Indeed Blind." *Los Angeles Times*, March 19. B15.

Clark, Kathleen. 1996. "Do We Have Enough Ethics in Government Yet?: An Answer From Fiduciary Theory." *University of Illinois Law Review* 1996, no. 57: 57–102.

Clark, Tom S. 2009. "Measuring Ideological Polarization on the United States Supreme Court." *Political Research Quarterly* 62: 146–57.

Clark, Tom S., and Benjamin Lauderdale. 2010. "Locating Supreme Court Opinions in Doctrine Space." *American Journal of Political Science* 54: 871–90.

Clark, Tom S., Jeffrey R. Lax, and Douglas Rice. 2015. "Measuring the Political Salience of Supreme Court Cases." *Journal of Law and Courts* 3: 37–65.

Corley, Pamela C., Amy Steigerwalt, and Artemus Ward. 2013. *The Puzzle of Unanimity: Consensus on the United States Supreme Court.* Palo Alto, CA: Stanford University Press.

Corley, Pamela C., and Justin Wedeking. 2014. "The (Dis)Advantage of Certainty: The Importance of Certainty in Language." *Law and Society Review* 48: 35–61.

Crawford, Jan. 2012. "Roberts Switched Views to Uphold Health Care Law." CBSNews.com. http://www.cbsnews.com/8301-3460_162-57464549/roberts-switched-views-to-uphold-health-care-law/.

Cross, Frank. 2007. *Decision Making in the U.S. Courts of Appeals.* Palo Alto, CA: Stanford University Press.

Dahl, Robert A. 1957. "Decision-Making in a Democracy: The Supreme Court as a National Policy-Maker." *Journal of Public Law* 6: 279.

Easton, David. 1965. *A Systems Analysis of Political Life.* New York, NY: John Wiley & Sons.

Edelman, Paul H., David E. Klein, and Stefanie A. Lindquist. 2008. "Measuring Deviations from Expected Voting Patterns on Collegial Courts." *Journal of Empirical Legal Studies* 5: 819–52.

Editorial. 1994. "A Cloud on the Breyer Nomination." *New York Times,* July 26. A18.

Editorial. 2004. "Another Justice Takes a Misstep." *Chicago Tribune,* March 18. 28.

Editorial. 2004. "Beyond the Duck Blind." *New York Times,* March 15. A20.

Editorial. 2008. "Court Without a Quorum." *New York Times,* May 18. Weekend 11.

Editorial. 2004. "If It Walks Like a Duck. . . ." *Chicago Tribune,* February 13. C26.

Editorial. 2006. "Judge Alito, in His Own Words." *New York Times,* January 12. A30.

Editorial. 2004. "Justice in a Bind." *New York Times,* March 20. A12.

Editorial. 2004. "Justice in a Blind." *St. Louis Post-Dispatch,* March 21. B2.

Editorial. 2004. "Justice Scalia and Mr. Cheney." *New York Times,* February 28. A14.

Editorial. 2010. "Kagan and ObamaCare." *Wall Street Journal,* July 13. A18.

Editorial. 2004. "Mr. Cheney's Day in Court." *New York Times,* April 27. A24.

Editorial. 2011. "New Trip Trouble for Scalia." *Los Angeles Times,* February 28. B22.

Editorial. 2004. "Recuse to Lose." *Wall Street Journal,* March 9. A16.

Editorial. 2004. "Scalia's Smackdown." *Wall Street Journal,* March 19. A14.

Editorial. 1943. "Supreme Court Quorum." *New York Times,* June 21. 16.

Editorial. 2011. "The Supreme Court's Recusal Problem." *New York Times,* December 1, 2011. A38.

Editorial. 2010. "What Case Was That Again?" *Wall Street Journal,* July 21. A16.

Enns, Peter K., and Patrick C. Wohlfarth. 2013. "The Swing Justice." *Journal of Politics* 75: 1089–107.

Epstein, Lee, and Jack Knight. 1998. *The Choices Justices Make.* Washington, DC: CQ Press.

Epstein, Lee, William M. Landes, and Richard A. Posner. 2010. "Inferring the Winning Party in the Supreme Court from the Pattern of Questioning at Oral Argument." *Journal of Legal Studies* 39: 433–67.

Epstein, Lee, Andrew D. Martin, Kevin M. Quinn, and Jeffrey A. Segal. 2009. "Circuit Effects: How the Norm of Federal Judicial Experience Biases the Supreme Court." *University of Pennsylvania Law Review* 157: 101–46.

Epstein, Lee, and Jeffrey A. Segal. 2005. *Advice and Consent: The Politics of Judicial Appointments.* New York, NY: Oxford University Press.

———. 2000. "Measuring Issue Salience." *American Journal of Political Science* 44: 66–83.

Epstein, Lee, Jeffrey A. Segal, and Harold J. Spaeth. 2007. *The Digital Archive of the Papers of Justice Harry A. Blackmun.* http://epstein.usc.edu/research/BlackmunArchive.html.

Farganis, Dion. 2012. "Do Reasons Matter? The Impact of Opinion Content on Supreme Court Legitimacy." *Political Research Quarterly* 65: 206–16.

Flamm, Richard E. 2010. "History of and Problems with the Federal Judicial Disqualification Framework." *Drake Law Review* 58: 751–63.

Foertsch, Lori Ann. 2005. "Scalia's Duck Hunt Leads to Ruffled Feathers: How the U.S. Supreme Court and Other Federal Judiciaries Should Change Their Recusal Approach." *Houston Law Review* 43: 457–94.

Frost, Amanda. 2013. "Judicial Ethics and Supreme Court Exceptionalism." *Georgetown Journal of Legal Ethics* 26: 443–79.

———. 2005. "Keeping Up Appearances: A Process-Oriented Approach to Judicial Recusal." *Kansas Law Review* 53: 531–93.

Gallup Organization. "Gallup/CNN/USA Today Poll # 2003-33: Iraq/Stock Market/Hillary Clinton/Sammy Sosa's Illegal Bat/Martha Stewart." June 9–10, 2003. Retrieved from the iPOLL Databank, The Roper Center for Public Opinion Research, University of Connecticut. http://www.ropercenter.uconn.edu.

———. "Gallup News Service Poll # 2004-18: 2004. Presidential Election/Price of Gasoline/European Union." May 21–23, 2004. Retrieved from the iPOLL Databank, The Roper Center for Public Opinion Research, University of Connecticut. http://www.ropercenter.uconn.edu.

———. "Gallup/CNN/USA Today Poll # 2004-11A: George W. Bush/Taxes/Social Security/Same-Sex Marriage/Religion." November 18–21, 2004. Retrieved from the iPOLL Databank, The Roper Center for Public Opinion Research, University of Connecticut. http://www.ropercenter.uconn.edu.

Geyh, Charles Gardner. 2010. *Judicial Disqualification: An Analysis of Federal Law.* Washington, DC: Federal Judicial Center.

Gibson, James L. 2008. "Challenges to the Impartiality of State Supreme Courts: Legitimacy Theory and 'New-Style' Judicial Campaigns." *American Political Science Review* 102: 59–75.

———. 2012. *Electing Judges: The Surprising Effects of Campaigning on Judicial Legitimacy.* Chicago, IL: Chicago University Press.

Gibson, James L. 2014. "Legitimacy Is for Losers: The Role of Institutional Legitimacy and the Symbols of Judicial Authority in Inducing Acquiescence to Disagreeable Court Rulings." Presented at the 62nd *Nebraska Symposium on Motivation*—Motivating Cooperation and Compliance with Authority: The Role(s) of Institutional Trust and Confidence (Keynote Speaker). April 24–25.

———. 2009. "'New Style' Judicial Campaigns and the Legitimacy of State High Courts." *Journal of Politics* 71: 1285–304.

Gibson, James L., and Gregory A. Caldeira. 1992. "Blacks and the United States Supreme Court: Models of Diffuse Support." *Journal of Politics* 54: 1120–145.

———. 2009. *Citizens, Courts, and Confirmations: Positivity Theory and the Judgments of the American People.* Princeton, NJ: Princeton University Press.

———. 2011. "Has Legal Realism Damaged the Institutional Legitimacy of the U.S. Supreme Court?" *Law & Society Review* 45: 195–219.

Gibson, James L., Gregory A. Caldeira, and Vanessa A. Baird. 1998. "On the Legitimacy of National High Courts." *American Political Science Review* 92: 343–56.

Gibson, James L., Gregory A. Caldeira, and Lester Kenyatta Spence. 2003a. "The Supreme Court and the US Presidential Election of 2000: Wounds, Self-Inflicted or Otherwise?" *British Journal of Political Science* 33: 535–56.

Gibson, James L., Gregory A. Caldeira, and Lester Kenyatta Spence. 2003b. "Measuring Attitudes Toward the United States Supreme Court." *American Journal of Political Science* 47: 354–67.

Ginsburg, Ruth Bader. 2004. "An Open Discussion with Justice Ruth Bader Ginsburg," *Connecticut Law Review* 36: 1033.

Goodson, Timothy J. 2005. "Duck, Duck, Goose: Hunting for Better Recusal Practices in the United States Supreme Court in Light of *Cheney v. United States District Court.*" *North Carolina Law Review* 84: 181–220.

Gould, Pamela. 2003. "Religious Freedom Praised; Justice Scalia Decries Change in U.S. Norms." *Free Lance-Star*, January 13. A1.

Graham, Fred P. 1972. "Determined Not to 'Bend Over Backward': Rehnquist." *New York Times*, October 15. E8.

Greenhouse, Linda. 1989. "Questions for a Reticent High Court." *New York Times*, November 22. A22.

Griswold, Erwin N., and Ernest Gellhorn. 1988. "200 Cases in Which Justices Recused Themselves." *Washington Post*, October 18. A25.

Grosskopf, Anke, and Jeffrey J. Mondak. 1998. "Do Attitudes Toward Specific Supreme Court Decisions Matter? The Impact of Webster and *Texas v. Johnson* on Public Confidence in the Supreme Court." *Political Research Quarterly* 51: 633–54.

Grove, Lloyd. 2011. "Supreme on Defense." *The Daily Beast*, June 29. http://www.thedailybeast.com/articles/2011/06/29/supreme-court-justices-defend-thomas-bush-v-gore-at-aspen-ideas-festival.html.

Hansford, Thomas G., and James F. Spriggs II. 2006. *The Politics of Precedent on the U.S. Supreme Court*. Princeton, NJ: Princeton University Press.

Hardie, Frances. 1973. "Rehnquist Should Step Down." Letter to the Editor. *New York Times*, May 9. 46.

Hasen, Richard L. 2013. "End of the Dialogue? Political Polarization, the Supreme Court, and Congress." *Southern California Law Review* 86: 205–62.

Henke, Kristen L. 2013. "If It's Not Broke, Don't Fix It: Ignoring Criticisms of Supreme Court Recusals." *Saint Louis University Law Journal* 57: 521–46.

Hettinger, Virginia A., Stefanie A. Lindquist, and Wendy L. Martinek. 2004. "Comparing Attitudinal and Strategic Account of Dissenting Behavior on the U.S. Courts of Appeals." *American Journal of Political Science* 48: 123–37.

———. 2006. *Judging on a Collegial Court: Influences on Federal Appellate Decision-Making*. Charlottesville, VA: University of Virginia Press.

"High Court Defers Anti-Trust Cases; Lack of a Quorum Delays Action on Alcoa and North American Indefinitely." 1943. *New York Times*, October 9. 39.

Holland, Jesse J. "Alito Refutes Conflict-of-Interest Concerns." *Associated Press*, November 11.

Hsiang, Solomon. 2013. "Plot Polynomial of Any Degree in Stata (With Controls)." http://www.fight-entropy.com/2013/01/plot-polynomial-of-any-degree-in-stata.html.

Kaufman, Andrew L. 1969. "Haynsworth Debate." Letter to the Editor. *New York Times*, October 1. 46.

Kennedy, Edward M. 2006. "Alito's Credibility Problem." *Washington Post*, January 7. A17.

Knight, Jack, and Lee Epstein. 1996. "The Norm of *Stare Decisis*." *American Journal of Political Science* 40: 1018–35.

Kozinski, Alex. 2004. "The Real Issues of Judicial Ethics." *Hofstra Law Review* 32: 1095–1106.

Kramer, Tammany. 2004. "An Institution Damaged." Letter to the Editor. *Washington Post*, February 19. A22.

Kritzer, Herbert M., and Mark J. Richards. 2003. "Jurisprudential Regimes and Supreme Court Decisionmaking: The Lemon Regime and Establishment Clause Cases." *Law & Society Review* 37: 827–40.

Kuhn, David Paul. 2012. "The Incredible Polarization and Politicization of the Supreme Court." *The Atlantic*. June 29. http://www.theatlantic.com/politics/archive/2012/06/the-incredible-polarization-and-politicization-of-the-supreme-court/259155/.

Kunda, Ziva. 1990. "The Case for Motivated Reasoning." *Psychological Bulletin* 108: 480–98.

Lauderdale, Benjamin E., and Tom S. Clark. 2012. "The Supreme Court's Many Median Justices." *American Political Science Review* 106: 847–66.

Lax, Jeffrey R., and Kelly T. Rader. 2010. "Legal Constraints on Supreme Court Decision Making: Do Jurisprudential Regimes Exist?" *Journal of Politics* 72: 273–84.

Leiman, Jan Maisel. 1957. "The Rule of Four." *Columbia Law Review* 57: 975–92.

Letter to the Editor. 1916. "The Brandeis Selection and Its Possible Bearing Upon Pending Trust Prosecutions." *New York Times*, January 30. 16.

Letter to the Editor. 1972. "Self-Disqualification of Justices." *New York Times*, September 21. 46.

Lewis, Anthony. 1958. "Tie in High Court a Major Problem." *New York Times*, January 13. 22.

Lewis, Neil. 1994. "Breyer Is Challenged on Apparent Conflict on Eve of Hearing." *New York Times*, July 12. A11.

Liptak, Adam. 2013. "Justices Agree to Agree, at Least for the Moment," *New York Times*, May 28. A11.

———. "Justices Divided Over 8-Member Court." *New York Times*, May 31. A10.

———. 2010. "Justices to Examine Rights of Corporations." *New York Times*, September 29. A20.

———. "Supreme Court Seems Poised to Deal Unions a Major Setback." *New York Times*, January 12. A1.

Lindquist, Stefanie A., and David E. Klein. 2006. "The Influence of Jurisprudential Considerations on Supreme Court Decisionmaking: A Study of Conflict Cases." *Law & Society Review* 40: 135–62.

Los Angeles Times. 2000. "Poll #450: Historical Aftermath of the 2000 Presidential Election." December 14–16. Retrieved from the iPOLL Databank, The Roper Center for Public Opinion Research, University of Connecticut. http://www.ropercenter.uconn.edu.

Lubet, Steven. 1996. "Disqualification of Supreme Court Justices: The *Certiorari* Conundrum." *Minnesota Law Review* 80: 657–76.

MacKenzie, John P. 1986. "The Editorial Notebook; Mr. Rehnquist's Opinion." *New York Times*, August 25. A24.

Martin, Andrew D., and Kevin M. Quinn. 2002. "Dynamic Ideal Point Estimation via Markov Chain Monte Carlo for the U.S. Supreme Court, 1953–1999." *Political Analysis* 10: 134–53.

Martin, Andrew D., Kevin M. Quinn, and Lee Epstein. 2005. "The Median Justice on the U.S. Supreme Court." *North Carolina Law Review* 83: 1275–322.

Maltzman, Forrest, James F. Spriggs, and Paul J. Wahlbeck. 2000. *Crafting Law on the Supreme Court*. New York, NY: Cambridge University Press.

McElroy, Lisa T., and Michael C. Dorf. 2011. "Coming Off the Bench: Legal and Policy Implications of Proposals to Allow Retired Justices to Sit by Designation on the Supreme Court." *Duke Law Journal* 61: 81–122.

McGuire, Kevin T. 1998. "Explaining Executive Success in the U.S. Supreme Court." *Political Research Quarterly* 51: 505–26.

McKeown, M. Margaret. 2005. "On Appeal: Don't Shoot the Canons: Maintaining the Appearance of Propriety Standard." *Journal of Appellate Practice and Process* 7: 45–58.

———. 2011. "To Judge or Not to Judge: Transparency and Recusal in the Federal System." *Review of Litigation* 30: 653–69.

Murphy, Walter F. 1964. *Elements of Judicial Strategy.* Chicago, IL: University of Chicago Press.

Murphy, Walter F., and Joseph Tanenhaus. 1968. "Public Opinion and the United States Supreme Court." *Law & Society Review* 2: 357–82.

Murphy, Walter F., Joseph Tanenhaus, and Daniel Kastner. 1973. *Public Evaluations of Constitutional Courts: Alternative Explanations.* Beverly Hills, CA: Sage.

Neumann, Richard K., Jr. 2007. "The Revival of Impeachment as a Partisan Political Weapon." *Hastings Constitutional Law Quarterly* 34: 161–327.

Nickerson, Raymond S. 1998. "Confirmation Bias: A Ubiquitous Phenomenon in Many Guises." *Review of General Psychology* 1: 175–220.

Nomination of Ruth Bader Ginsburg. 1993. "Nomination of Ruth Bader Ginsburg to Be an Associate Justice of the Supreme Court of the United States." Senate Hearings. http://www.loc.gov/law/find/nominations/ginsburg/hearing.pdf.

O'Brien, David M. 2008. *Storm Center: The Supreme Court in American Politics.* 8th ed. New York, NY: W.W. Norton & Company.

Okie, Susan. 2004. "Illness and Secrecy on the Supreme Court." *New England Journal of Medicine* 351: 2675–78.

Perry, H. W. 1991. *Deciding to Decide: Agenda Setting in the United States Supreme Court.* Cambridge, MA: Harvard University Press.

Petrick, Michael J. 1968. "The Supreme Court and Authority Acceptance." *Western Political Quarterly* 21: 5–19.

Pfander, James E. 2009. *One Supreme Court: Supremacy, Inferiority, and the Judicial Department of the United States.* New York, NY: Oxford University Press.

Press Release. 2010. "Leahy Proposes Bill to Allow Retired Justices to Sit on Court by Designation" (September 2). http://www.leahy.senate.gov/press/leahy-proposes-bill-to-allow-retired-justices-to-sit-on-court-by-designation.

Press Release. 1993. U.S. Supreme Court. *Statement of Recusal Policy.* Available at the Ethics & Public Policy Center. http://www.eppc.org/docLib/20110106_RecusalPolicy23.pdf.

Provine, D. Marie. 1980. *Case Selection in the United States Supreme Court.* Chicago, IL: University of Chicago Press.

Rice, Douglas. 2014. "The Impact of Supreme Court Activity on the Judicial Agenda." *Law & Society Review* 48: 63–90.

Richards, Mark J., and Herbert M. Kritzer. 2002. "Jurisprudential Regimes in Supreme Court Decision Making." *American Political Science Review* 96: 305–20.

Ries, Bernard. 2004. "Outlook: You Can't Duck This Conflict, Mr. Justice." *Washington Post*, February 29. B4.

Roberts, Caprice. 2004. "The Fox Guarding the Henhouse?: Recusal and the Procedural Void in the Court of Last Resort." *Rutgers Law Review* 57: 107–82.

Roberts, John G., Jr. 2011. *Year-End Report on the Federal Judiciary.* U.S. Supreme Court Public Information Office. http://www.supremecourt.gov/publicinfo/year-end/ 2011year-endreport.pdf.

Rosen, Jeffrey. 2007. "The Dissenter, Justice John Paul Stevens." *New York Times*, September 23.

Rotunda, Ronald D. 2005. "Does John Roberts Have an Ethics Problem?" *Washington Post*, September 6. A25.

Saidman-Krauss, Rebekah. 2011. "A Second Sitting: Assessing the Constitutionality and Desirability of Allowing Retired Supreme Court Justices to Fill Recusal-Based Vacancies on the Bench." *Penn State Law Review* 116: 253–83.

Sample, James. 2013. "Supreme Court Recusal from *Marbury* to the Modern Day." *Georgetown Journal of Legal Ethics* 26: 95–151.

Scheb, John M., II, and William Lyons. 2000. "The Myth of Legality and Popular Support for the Supreme Court." *Social Science Quarterly* 81: 928–40.

Scheer, Robert. 2004. "Commentary: The Dangers of a 'What the Heck' Vote." *Los Angeles Times*, September 28. B13.

———. 2004. "Commentary: Old MacDonald Had a Judge." *Los Angeles Times*, February 17. B11.

Schubert, Glendon. 1965. *The Judicial Mind: The Attitudes and Ideologies of Supreme Court Justices, 1946–1963.* Evanston, IL: Northwestern University Press.

Segal, Jeffrey A., and Harold J. Spaeth. 2002. *The Supreme Court and the Attitudinal Model Revisited.* New York, NY: Cambridge University Press.

Segal, Jeffrey A., Chad Westerland, and Stefanie A. Lindquist. 2011. "Congress, the Supreme Court, and Judicial Review: Testing a Constitutional Separation of Powers Model." *American Journal of Political Science* 55: 89–104.

Segall, Eric J. 2011. "An Ominous Silence on the Supreme Court; Justice Elena Kagan Should Explain Why She's Not Heeding the Calls to Recuse Herself from the Soon-To-Be-Heard Obama Healthcare Case." *Los Angeles Times*, February 12. A26.

———. 2012. "Supreme Court Recusal, the Affordable Care Act, and the Rule of Law." *University of Pennsylvania Penumbra* 160: 337–41.

Sherman, Mark. 2011. "Alito Owned Stock, Voted in Case with Disney's ABC." *Associated Press*, May 31.

Sherman, Mark. 2010. "Pfizer Stock Sold, Roberts to Hear Company's Cases." *Associated Press*, September 29.

Smith, Lamar. 2011. "What Did Kagan Do?" *Washington Post*, December 2. A21.

Spaeth, Harold J. 1963. "An Analysis of Judicial Attitudes in the Labor Relations Decision of the Warren Court." *Journal of Politics* 25: 290–311.

———. 2011. *The Supreme Court Database*. Version 2011 Release 03. http://scdb. wustl.edu/documentation.php?s=2.

Stempel, Jeffrey W. 2009. "Chief William's Ghost: The Problematic Persistence of the Duty to Sit Doctrine." *Buffalo Law Review* 57: 813–958.

———. 1987. "Rehnquist, Recusal, and Reform." *Brooklyn Law Review* 53: 589–667.

Stout, David. 2008. "Justices Won't Hear Apartheid Suit." *New York Times*, May 12.

Tanenhaus, Joseph, Marvin Schick, Matthew Muraskin, and David Rosen. 1963. "The Supreme Court's *Certiorari* Jurisdiction: Cue Theory." In *Judicial Decision-Making*, edited by G. Schubert. New York, NY: Free Press.

Taylor, Robert. 1944. "Way Opened to Hear Alcoa Monopoly Suit; House Bill Would End Legal Deadlock." *Pittsburgh Press*, April 2. 13.

Taylor, Stuart, Jr. 1988. "Justice Kennedy Shuns Special Prosecutor Case." *New York Times*, February 27. 7.

Thomas, Clarence. 2007. *My Grandfather's Son: A Memoir*. New York, NY: Harper.

Thomas, Virginia. 2010. "Clip: Ginni Thomas Remarks at Steamboat Institute." *C-Span Video Library*. http://www.c-spanvideo.org/clip/412028.

Transcript. 2011. "The Diane Rehm Show: Conflict of Interest on the Supreme Court." NPR (August 25). http://thedianerehmshow.org/shows/2011-08-25/conflict-interest-supreme-court/transcript.

Transcript. 2011. "Supreme Court 2012 Budget." Testimony of Justices Anthony Kennedy Stephen Breyer before the House Appropriations Subcommittee on Financial Services and General Government. April 14.

Ulmer, S. Sidney. 1984. "The Supreme Court's *Certiorari* Decisions: Conflict as a Predictive Value." *American Political Science Review* 78: 901–11.

Virelli, Louis J. 2012. "Congress, the Constitution, and Supreme Court Recusal." *Washington & Lee Law Review* 69: 1535–606.

———. 2011. "The (Un)Constitutionality of Supreme Court Recusal Standards." *Wisconsin Law Review* 2011: 1181–284.

Wahlbeck, Paul J. 2006. "Strategy and Constraints on Supreme Court Opinion Assignment." *University of Pennsylvania Law Review* 154: 1729–55.

Wahlbeck, Paul J., James F. Spriggs II, and Forrest Maltzman. 2009. *The Burger Court Opinion Writing Database*. http://supremecourtopinions.wustl.edu/, August 6.

———. 1998. "Marshalling the Court: Bargaining and Accommodation on the United States Supreme Court." *American Journal of Political Science* 42: 294–315.

Wasby, Stephen. 1978. *The Supreme Court in the Federal Judicial System*. New York, NY: Holt, Rinehart, and Winston.

Weaver, Warren, Jr. 1975. "High Court and Disqualification." *New York Times*, March 3. 22.

———. 1974. "Problem for Court in Taking Up Tapes Case." *New York Times*, May 28. 25.

Wheeler, Russell. 2011. "Regulating Supreme Court Justices' Ethics—'Cures Worse Than the Disease?' " Brookings Institution. https://www.brookings.edu/opinions/regulating-supreme-court-justices-ethics-cures-worse-than-the-disease/.

Cases Cited

Aetna Life Ins. Co. v. Lavoie, 475 U.S. 813 (1986)

American Isuzu Motors, Inc. v. Ntsebeza, 553 U.S. 1028 (2008)

AT&T Corp. v. Iowa Utilities Board, 525 U.S. 366 (1999)

Bd. of Educ. v. Tom F. ex rel. Gilbert F., 552 U.S. 1 (2007)

Boumediene v. Bush, 553 U.S. 723 (2008)

BP American Production Co. v. Burton, 549 U.S. 84 (2006)

Bush v. Gore, 531 U.S. 98 (2000)

Bush v. Vera, 517 U.S. 952 (1996)

Caperton v. Massey, 556 U.S. 868 (2009)

Caperton v. Massey, 223 W. Va. 624 (2008)

CBS Inc. v. Young, 522 F. 2d 234 (6th Cir., 1975)

Cheney v. United States Dist. Court, 541 U.S. 913 (2004) (Scalia, J., denying the motion to recuse)

Cheney v. United States District Court, 542 U.S. 367 (2004)

Credit Suisse Sec. (USA) LLC v. Billing, 551 U.S. 264 (2007)

Dow Jones & Company, Inc., v. Simon, Stanley, et al., 488 U.S. 946 (1988) (*cert. denied*)

Elk Grove v. Newdow, 542 U.S. 1 (2004)

Environmental Defense v. Duke Energy Corp. 549 U.S. 561 (2007)

Exxon Shipping Co. v. Baker, 554 U.S. 471 (2008)

FCC v. Fox Television Stations, 556 U.S. 502 (2008)

Fisher v. University of Texas, 579 U.S. __ (2016)

Florida v. U.S. Dept. of Health and Human Services, 648 F.3d 1235 (11th Cir. 2011)

Friedrichs v. California Teachers Association, 578 U.S. __ (2016)

Frontiero v. Richardson, 411 U.S. 677 (1973)

Gabelli v. SEC, 568 U.S. __ (2013)

Gregg v. Georgia, 428 U.S. 153 (1976)

Hamdan v. Rumsfeld, 548 U.S. 557 (2006)

Howsam v. Reynolds, 537 U.S. 79 (2002)

In re Murchison, 349 U.S. 133 (1955)

Janus Capital Group v. First Derivative Traders, 564 U.S. __ (2011)

Laird v. Tatum, 408 U.S. 1 (1972)

Laird v. Tatum, 409 U.S. 824 (1972) (Rehnquist, J., denying the motion to recuse)

Lewis v. Adamson, 497 U.S. 1031 (1990)

Liberty Univ., Inc. v. Geithner, 671 F. 3d 391 (4th Cir. 2011)

Liteky v. United States, 510 U.S. 555 (1994)

Marbury v. Madison, 5 U.S. 137 (1803)

Martin v. Hunter's Lessee, 14 U.S. 304 (1816)

Mayberry v. Pennsylvania, 400 U.S. 455 (1971)

McNally v. United States, 483 U.S. 350 (1987)

Microsoft Corp. v. AT&T Corp., 550 U.S. 437 (2007)

Microsoft Corp. v. I4I Limited Partnership, 564 U.S. __ (2011)

Microsoft v. United States, 530 U.S. 1301 (2000)

Minnesota Mining & Manufacturing Company v. Freeman, 494 U.S. 1070 (1990)

Morgan Stanley Capital Group Inc. v. Pub. Util. Dist. No. 1, 554 U.S. 527 (2008)

National Federation of Independent Business v. Sebelius, 132 S.Ct. 2566 (2012)

Nebraska Press Association v. Stuart, 427 U.S. 539 (1976)

PacifiCare Health System v. Book, 538 U.S. 401 (2003)

Perry v. Brown, 671 F.3d 1052 (9th Cir., 2012)

Pi-Net International v. Citizens Financial Group, Civil Action No. 12-355-RGA (D. Del., 2015)

Radio & Television News Assn. v. United States District Court, 781 F. 2d 1443 (9th Cir., 1986)

Seven-Sky v. Holder, 661 F. 3d 1 (D.C. Cir. 2011)

Smith v. United States, 502 U.S. 1017 (1991)

Thomas More Law Ctr. v. Obama, 651 F.3d 529 (6th Cir. 2011)

Tumey v. Ohio, 273 U.S. 510 (1927)

United States v. Aluminum Company of America, 320 U.S. 708 (1943)

United States v. Aluminum Company of America, 148 F.2d 416 (2nd Cir., 1945)

United States v. Edwards, 334 F.2d 360 (5th Cir. 1964)

United States v. Nixon, 418 U.S. 683 (1974)

United States v. Virginia, 518 U.S. 515, 524 (1996)

Wal-Mart Stores v. Dukes, 564 U.S. __ (2011)

Wallace v. Arizona, 494 U.S. 1047 (1990)

Ward v. Monroeville, 409 U.S. 57 (1972)

Warner-Lambert Co., LLC v. Kent, 552 U.S. 440 (2008)

Wickard v. Filburn, 317 U.S. 111 (1942)

Willner v. Barr, 502 U.S. 1020 (1991)

Zubik v. Burwell, 578 U.S. __ (2016)

Index

Made in the USA
Middletown, DE
21 February 2019